Comic Strips & Comic Books of Radio's Golden Age

1920s–1950s

A Biography of All Radio Shows Based on Comics

by **Ron Lackmann**

**Comic Strips & Comic Books of Radio's Golden Age (1920s – 1950s):
A Biography of All Radio Shows Based on Comics**
© 2004 Ron Lackmann

All rights reserved. No part of this book may be reproduced in any form or by any means, electronic, mechanical, digital, photocopying or recording, except for the inclusion in a review, without permission in writing from the the publisher.

Published in the USA by:

**Bear Manor Media
PO Box 750
Boalsburg PA 16827**

www.bearmanormedia.com

Library of Congress Cataloging-in-Publication Data

Lackmann, Ronald W.
 Comic strips & comic books of radio's golden age (1920s-1950s) : a biography of all radio shows based on comics.
   p. cm.
 Includes bibliographical references.
 ISBN 1-59393-021-6
 1. Radio programs–United States–Catalogs. 2. Radio actors and actress–United States–Biography. 3. Comic books, strips, etc.–United States–History and criticism. I. Title: Comic strips and comic books of radio's golden age (1920s-1950s). II. Title.

PN1991.3.U6L28 2004
791.44'75'097309041–dc22
                  2004027703

Printed in the United States of America.

Design and Layout by Valerie Thompson.

Cover photo of books and comics courtesy of Maggie Thompson.

Table of Contents

Acknowledgements --- 1

Introduction --- 2

Archie Andrews --- 4

Blondie --- 15

Blue Beetle --- 22

Bringing Up Father --- 25

Buck Rogers in the 25th Century --- 31

Buster Brown --- 37

Captain Midnight --- 42

Charlie Chan --- 48

Charlie McCarthy --- 51

The Cisco Kid --- 54

Dan Dunn --- 57

Dick Tracy --- 60

Don Winslow of the Navy --- 67

Flash Gordon --- 71

GANGBUSTERS	77
GASOLINE ALLEY	78
GENE AUTRY	81
THE GREEN HORNET	85
THE GUMPS	88
HAROLD TEEN	92
HOP HARRIGAN	94
JANE ARDEN	99
JOE PALOOKA	101
JUNGLE JIM	106
KING OF THE ROYAL MOUNTED	110
LI'L ABNER	113
LITTLE ORPHAN ANNIE	116
THE LONE RANGER	120
MAJOR HOOPLE	127
MANDRAKE THE MAGICIAN	131
MARK TRAIL	135
MICKEY MOUSE ON THE AIR	139
MY FRIEND IRMA	140

THE NEBBS	145
POPEYE THE SAILOR	148
RED RYDER	153
THE ROY ROGERS SHOW	157
THE SAD SACK	159
THE SAINT	162
THE SHADOW	164
SKIPPY	169
SMILIN' JACK	172
STRAIGHT ARROW	174
SUPERMAN	176
TAILSPIN TOMMY	183
TARZAN	185
TERRY AND THE PIRATES	189
TILLIE THE TOILER	193
TOM MIX	195
BIBLIOGRAPHY	200

Acknowledgements

No book probing the past can be accurate without the help of a great many fellow researchers, biographers, reference book writers, librarians, teachers, actual participants, compilers, media companies and their employees, collectors, book editors, photo archivists, and especially good friends who share a writer's knowledge and enthusiasm for a subject. This book is no exception, and I therefore humbly dedicate this volume to everyone who helped me make it possible by contributing information that they had stored away in their memories, as well as in their office files and libraries. Many people I interviewed for this book vividly recalled numerous details of the time they spent working on, listening to, or reading about the comic strip characters that were heard on the radio. I would particularly like to single out a few people who went out of their way to send me, via post, email, or telephone, invaluable directions to take for my probing, as well as hard-to-find facts, biographical information, rare photographs, and other information that had to be included in this book if it were to be at all effective. In this regard, I would be remiss not to thank Jack French, Jay Hickerson, Rosemary Rice, Cliff Carpenter, George Ansbro, Elliott (Ted) Reid, David and Barbara Davies, Peg Lynch, Barbara Gelman, and especially Howard Mandelbaum of Photofest, whose photographs and long telephone chats about many of the personalities mentioned in this book, have been both enlightening and always entertaining. I would also like to thank all of those dear, departed performers who befriended me over the years. Their memories of the times they spent in front of the microphones during Radio's Golden Age have been stored in my mind and were and are a constant source of inspiration for all of the books I have already written and those I hope to write in the future. I think fondly of all my good friends: Miriam Wolfe, Sybil Trent, Alice Reinheart, Dwight Weist, Frank Nelson, Florence Williams, Fran Carlon, Parley Baer, and Robert Dryden.

Finally, I know this book would never have materialized, if not for the kindness and guidance of my mentor and friend, the legendary comic art collector and comic strip and comic book artist and film animator, Woodrow Gelman. Although Woody died several years ago, he is my most important influence, as far as collecting and a love of all things related to the past, and writing about nostalgic subjects is concerned. Thank you, Woody, for having been a very significant part of my life.

Introduction

The wonderful thing about Radio, as it used to be in the 1930s, 1940s and 1950s, is that whoever or whatever you were hearing over the airwaves was your very own visual creation. It was your imagination that supplied the images of what the people, places and situations you heard looked like. The "pretty" girl was your version of what "pretty" was…and the "handsome" hero was your visualization of what constituted "handsome." During the memorable years when Radio was America's favorite home entertainment medium, the airwaves were permeated with all sorts of programming. There were the daytime dramas of domestic stress, or soap operas as they were called because they were usually sponsored by soap detergent companies. There were the five-day-a-week children's adventure serials that were heard in the late afternoon when youngsters came home from school. There were prime-time mystery programs, and comedy and variety shows, game and panel programs, and even adaptations of great works of the theater and literature, as well as radio versions of well-known films, for the mind's eye to envision. Most of us who were lucky enough to have lived through those 1930s years of the Great Depression, the early 1940s World War II years, and the post-War years of the late 1940s and early 1950s, cannot think back upon those years, or indeed even have gotten through them, without *Radio* and the wonderful hours of entertainment that medium gave us. As strange as it seems saying it was "lucky" to have lived through those terrible times, listening to the radio made those times bearable and not quite as horrific as they actually were. Most of us who were alive during those years can surely remember the fun of thumbing through radio fan magazines such as *Radio Mirror* and *Radio Guide* to see what those people whose voices we heard actually looked like. We were disappointed when a much-admired, rough-and-ready private detective turned out to be a rather ordinary looking man who was either much thinner or much fatter, or balder and older, than we had imagined him to be. We were crestfallen when the actress with the intriguing voice, who we imagined to be tall, blonde and willowy, turned out to be more mature and less attractive than we thought. We were, however, delighted when the magazine photos of our favorite radio characters turned out to look just like we imagined them to look. There were two kinds of radio show characters whose actual appearances never disappointed us. We already knew what the popular movie stars and comedians of the day looked like, because we saw them on the silver screen or in newspapers and magazines photos. We also knew what many of our favorite comic strip and comic book characters who we heard on the radio looked like because we saw their images regularly in the Sunday newspaper color comics supplements (often called the "Sunday Funnies"), as well as in the daily comic strips, and comic books we read. We knew as we listened to him that Popeye the Sailor had lower arms as thick as his torso, wore a sailor suit, and smoked a corncob pipe. Little Orphan Annie had curly orange hair and large white circles for eyes and her dog, Sandy, was yellow. Terry of the *Terry and the Pirates* comic strip was young, had blond hair, and usually wore a leather aviator's jacket. His friend and mentor, Pat Ryan, was taller and a bit older than Terry and had dark, black curly hair. Terry's nemesis, the exotically menacing Dragon Lady, was a gorgeous, dark-haired, sloe-eyed glamorous-looking Eurasian woman. We could "see" them all in our mind's eye, as we listened to their adventures on the radio and sat with our ears practically glued to our radio receivers, and they thrilled us with their fifteen-minute, five-day-a-week adventures.

It is certainly surprising looking back, on what filmmaker Woody Allen called those "Radio Days," in his film of that name, just how many of our favorite comic strip and comic book characters were radio regulars. This book chronicles the numerous comic book and comic strip characters whose adventures we listened to faithfully and whose decoding rings and badges, books and pamphlets, secret messages, and other paraphernalia we sent for regularly as we mailed in our "thin dimes" and labels from breakfast cereal box tops or labels from Ovaltine jars. In this book, the names of the comic strip-inspired radio programs or radio-inspired comic strip or book, have been listed A to Z and biographies of the actors who enacted the major roles of our favorite characters follow the program/comic entry. Biographies of the cartoon artists who had the original ideas for the comic strips and comic books that were heard on radio are also included within the entries themselves.

Hopefully, this book will recapture some of the wonder and excitement that those of us experienced when we first listened to our favorite comic strip and comic book characters come alive on the radio those many, many years ago. As the announcer on *The Lone Ranger*, one of those shows heard on the radio and seen in comic strips and comic books, used to say at the opening of the radio program, "Return with us now to those thrilling days of yesteryear."

A

ARCHIE ANDREWS
(A.K.A. THE ADVENTURES OF ARCHIE ANDREWS)

The *Archie Andrews* comic book and comic strip were created by artist Bob Montana (1920-1975). Cartoonist Montana was only seven years old when he first began drawing caricatures of the customers in his father's restaurant; later, when he was an adult, he said that he knew then he was going to be a professional artist when he grew up. When Montana graduated from high school, he attended the Phoenix Art Institute in New York City, and then went to work as a freelance artist drawing magazine illustrations and comic book covers for various publishers. One of the covers he drew was for the *Batman* comic book. While he was drawing covers for MLJ Comics in December 1941 (MLJ was published by Morris Coyne, Louis Silberkleit and John Goldwater…thus the MLJ logo), the publishers asked Montana to draw a sample cartoon character and propose a storyline for a new comic book about a teenaged male called "Archie." The character was to be the major character in a brand-new MLJ comics publication they planned to introduce to the public in the spring. Montana, who was only 21 at the time, created a redheaded, freckled-faced, sixteen-year-old Huckleberry Finn-type teenager who suffered through all of the typical adolescent problems most boys experience during their teen years. The publishers were so pleased with Montana's new comic creation that they commissioned him to draw an entire comic book, as well as a subsequent comic strip which was sold in syndication to various newspapers throughout the country. In the Archie comic books, and the subsequent comic strips that are still being published, Archie is the son of Fred and Mary Andrews. He is a perennial adolescent who, as of this date, has been sixteen years old for more than sixty years. Archie, like most teenage boys, has lots of girl trouble and he divides his romantic attentions between a sophisticated and wealthy, raven-haired brunette named Veronica Lodge, and a spirited, middle class, pretty, blonde girl-next-door-named Betty Cooper. Archie is a good-hearted lad and well liked by his peers at Riverdale High School, which is located in the town of Riverdale where he lives. He is a loyal friend to his pal, Forsythe "Jughead" Jones, who is somewhat of a misfit and a bit goofy. Archie's only problems are that he is inclined to be somewhat accident-prone and is always getting entangled in one problematic, if amusing, situation or another. The only people in town who seem to hold Archie in rather low esteem are Riverdale High's cranky principal Mr. Weatherbee, Veronica's rich father Hiram Lodge, and, on occasion, Riverdale High's star athlete, Reggie Mantle, who is Archie's sometime-rival for Veronica's affections. By 1945, the Archie Andrews character had become so popular with comic book devotees that MLJ even changed the company's name to *Archie Comics*. By the mid-1940s, Archie had even surpassed America's longtime comic book teen hero *Harold Teen* in popularity. *Harold Teen* had been a comic strip favorite of the public since 1919 and was still appearing in newspapers throughout the country in the 1940s. Bob Montana continued drawing the *Archie* comic book and daily and Sunday-supplement newspaper comic strips until the day he died in 1975 at the age of 55. The talented Dan DeCarlo took over drawing the *Archie Andrews* comics shortly after Montana died. DeCarlo was born in

Veronica Lodge, Archie Andrews, Betty Cooper and "Jughead" Jones, who were created by Bob Montana, as drawn by Dan DeCarlo

New Rochelle, New York, and attended New York Art Students League after he graduated from high school. After spending five years in the Army working as an artist with the 8th Air Force during, and shortly after, World War II, DeCarlo joined the staff of Marvel Comics in the late 1940s. In the 1950s, he drew two popular titles for Marvel, *Millie the Model* and *My Friend Irma*, which was based on the hit radio situation comedy series of the late 1940s-early 1950s. DeCarlo drew all of the very funny stories for the *My Friend Irma* comic books from its first issue in 1950 until the last issue was published in 1955. In the 1950s, *Millie the Model* and *My Friend Irma*, mainly due to DeCarlo's drawings of curvaceous girls, were Marvel's most successful comic books, especially with adolescent boys. DeCarlo not only took over the drawing of the *Archie Andrews* comic, but he also drew a spin-off comic book called *Betty and Veronica* with Archie's girlfriends as its major characters, that also sold very well. As if that wasn't enough to keep DeCarlo busy, he also penned two other short-lived comics, *My Girl Pearl* and *Sherry the Showgirl*, as well as the comic book versions of the TV series characters *Sabrina the Teenaged Witch* and *Josie and the Pussycats*. Shortly before he died at the age of 82 in 2001, Dan DeCarlo received a well-deserved tribute at the annual National Comics Convention for his many years of excellent work as a cartoonist.

In 1943, Montana's *Archie Andrews* comic book was adapted for radio as a half-hour situation comedy series that was first heard on the Mutual radio network and starred Jack Grimes as Archie Andrews. In 1945, the radio series was heard as a Saturday morning program on the NBC network, following the same format as the popular comic books and comic strips, and featuring many of the same incidents that had been seen in the comics. In 1949, *Archie Andrews* became a prime-time (7:30 P.M.) program, but in 1950, the radio program returned to its Saturday morning slot where it remained until 1953, when it finally departed the airwaves. The radio series, brought to you by Swift and Company, when the series had a national sponsor, was written for radio by one of the comic book's publishers, John L. Goldwater, and the program was directed by Ken MacGregor, Floyd Holmes, and Herbert M. Moss. Each show usually began with announcers Ken Banghart, Dick Dudley, or Bob Shaerer saying, "Yes, here is the youngster millions of readers of Archie Andrews comics know so well...Archie Andrews and his gang!" When the series first went on the air on Saturday mornings, actor Charles Mullen played the part of Archie. Burt Boyer, and finally Bob Hastings, followed in the role, and it was Hastings who played the role the longest and is the Archie Andrews most fans of the radio show remember best. Hal (Harlan) Stone, Jr. and, for shorter periods of time, Cameron Andrews and Arnold Stang played Archie's pal Jughead Jones. Doris Grundy, Joy Geffin, and, for most of the show's run, Rosemary Rice, played Betty Cooper. Vivian Smolen played Veronica Lodge on the original series when it was first aired on the Mutual network, and Gloria Mann played the role for most of the years the show was a Saturday morning series on NBC. Also heard in the cast at various times were Vinton Hayworth, Arthur Kohl, and Reese Taylor as Archie's father, Fred Andrews, Alice Yourman, and then Peggy Allenby, as Archie's mother, Mary Andrews. Paul Gordon played Reggie Mantle, Arthur Maitland was Riverdale High School's principal, Mr. Weatherbee, Pat Hosley played Jughead's girlfriend, Agatha, and Bill Griffis played Veronica's father, Mr. Lodge. All of the actors who played Archie had perfect voice-changing, typical teenage boy voices and they delivered their lines with humor and believability. The storylines for the radio series remained true to the spirit of the *Archie* comic books and strip and

The *Archie Andrews* radio show cast pay tribute to the show's sponsor, Swift Premium Tender Frankfurters. From left to right, Rosemary Rice (Betty), Bob Hastings (Archie), Gloria Mann (Veronica), and Hal Stone (Jughead).

many of the episodes on the show were taken directly from the pages of the comics. The success of the radio series was in large part due to it being heard on Saturday mornings, when there was little, if any, competition. Only Nila Mack's half-hour fairy tale anthology show for children, *Let's Pretend*, which was heard on CBS, rivaled *Archie* as a Saturday morning radio listening favorite, and both *Let's Pretend* and *Archie Andrews* were always at the top of the list of "most popular shows" in the Saturday morning time slot. Typical of the humorous weekly episodes that were heard on the radio series, and made it popular with young listeners, were such titles as "Archie Andrews Takes a

Bath," "The Drugstore Mix-Up," "Nazi POW In Riverdale," "Veronica's Coming Out Party," "Archie Has a Cold," "Wallpapering," "Going to Bed Early," "Suffering From the Heat," "Archie's in Love," "Locked Out of the House," "Careful, Don't Wake Up Father," "Christmas Shopping," "The Big Dance," "Archie Gets a Drugstore Job," "Baby Sitting to Earn Money for a Tuxedo," "New Years Sitter," and "Sunburned," to name just a few.

ARCHIE ANDREWS RADIO SERIES PERFORMERS

GRIMES, JACK B. 1926 (ARCHIE ANDREWS)

One of radios' busiest child actors, Jack Grimes, appeared in several Broadway plays including *The Old Maid* (1935), *Stork Mad* (1936), *Western Waters* (1937) and *Excursions* (1937) before he was ten years old. He made his radio acting debut in 1934 when he was eight. While he was working on Broadway and on the radio, Grimes attended the Professional Children's School in New York City. During the late 1930s into the 1940s and 1950s, Grimes was heard on as many as sixty radio shows a week. Among the radio programs he was featured on were Nila Mack's *Let's Pretend*, which he continued to be heard on well into his young adult years, *The Adventures of Huckleberry Finn* (as Huckleberry), *The Affairs of Peter Salem*, *Archie Andrews* (as Archie, when it was first aired on the Mutual network), *Bright Horizon*, *Lorenzo Jones*, *Joe and Mabel*, *The Life of Riley*, *The Man I Married*, *Second Husband*, *Valiant Lady* and *Joyce Jordan, Girl Intern*. Grimes also played Jimmy Olson on *The Adventures of Superman* radio series and he played Chester Gump on the short-lived series *The Gumps*, which, like *Archie Andrews*, had been adapted for radio from popular comic strips. As a young adult actor, Grimes was heard on *Dimension X*, *Yours Truly, Johnny Dollar* and on Himan Brown's 1970s radio series, *CBS Mystery Theater*, performing in more than 49 mystery dramas on that program. When television replaced radio as America's favorite home entertainment medium, Grimes had little trouble adapting to acting on TV and had regular roles on the TV series *Tom Corbett, Space Cadet* (1950), *The Aldrich Family* (1952–53, as Homer Brown), and *On the Rocks* (1975). Grimes was also the voice of Jimmy Olson for *The New Adventures of Superman* film cartoon series for many years. On occasion, Grimes also had featured roles on such TV series as *The Web*, *Armstrong Circle Theater*, *The Detectives*, *Mayberry, R.F.D.*, *All in the Family*, *Maude* and *Police Woman*.

HASTINGS, BOB B. 1925 (ARCHIE ANDREWS)

Brooklyn-born Bob Hastings made his professional performing debut as "Little Bobby Hastings, the twelve-year-old soprano" on the *Coast to Coast on a Bus* children's variety radio show in 1937. Hastings went on to perform on several other radio variety programs such as *The National Barn Dance*, and then began to get work as a child, and then teenaged radio actor on *Let's Pretend, A Right to Happiness, The Sea Hound, The Eternal Light, The Lady Next Door, This is Nora Drake, The Aldrich Family*, and *X Minus One*, to name just a few of the programs on which he was featured. It is, however, as the title character on the *Archie Andrews* radio series, playing the perennial adolescent Archie, that he is best remembered by radio listeners. After the demise of radio drama in the late 1950s-early 1960s, Hastings went to Hollywood where he soon was appearing in *The Great Imposter* (1961), *Moon Pilot* (1962), *The Poseidon Adventure* (1972), *The All-American Boy* (1973), *No Deposit, No Return* (1976), and *Separate Ways* (1981),

Bob Hastings primps before a broadcast of radio's *Archie Andrews*.

(Credit: Photofest)

and many others. He also became one of television's most active performers and had sustaining roles on such series as *McHale's Navy* (as Lt. Elroy Carpenter), *Ellery Queen, All in the Family* (as Tommy Kelsey, the owner of Kelsey's saloon), and *Batman*, at one time or another. Hastings also had featured roles on practically every major TV series including *The Real McCoys, The Untouchables, Gunsmoke, Ben Casey, Car 54, Where Are You?, The Twilight Zone, Petticoat Junction, Green Acres, Hogan's Heroes, Adam-12, I Dream of Jeannie, Ironside, Here's Lucy, Nanny and the Professor, Emergency, The Odd Couple, The Streets of San Francisco, The Rockford Files, Quincy, Alice, Three's Company, Remington Steele, Murder, She Wrote* and *Major Dad*. Bob

Hastings is, to this day, one of the busiest voice-over actors in films and on TV, and his voice has been heard in such cartoons as *The New Adventures of Superman, Batman, The Three Robonic Stooges,* and many other animated series. His younger brother, Don Hastings (1934–) is well known for his portrayal of The Video Ranger on the popular early television series *Captain Video,* and for his long-running stint on the soap opera *As the World Turns.*

Mann, Gloria b. circa 1924 – d. circa 1970s (Veronica Lodge)

Actress Gloria Mann, according to this author's research, appears to have had a rather limited show business career. When she was a child, Miss Mann appeared on Broadway in 1935 in the play, *The Old Maid,* and was featured in the play, *All in Favor* in 1942. A lovely, vivacious brunette, according to her *Archie Andrews* co-stars Bob Hastings and Hal Stone, she was occasionally heard playing supporting roles on radio soap opera series, such as *The Life and Love of Dr. Susan.* She enjoyed her longest tenure on radio, however, playing Veronica Lodge, the rich and beautiful girl who kept Archie Andrews' heart aflutter during the long Saturday morning run of *Archie Andrews.* In the 1950s, Gloria reportedly left New York City, where *Archie Andrews* was produced, and went to Hollywood to try to break into films. Thereafter, she seems to have had a rather low showbiz profile.

Rice, Rosemary b. 1928 (Betty Cooper)

Although Rosemary Rice is perhaps best known for playing Katrin, the girl who remembered her *Mama* on that very successful early-television series that was aired from 1949 until 1956, the actress made her acting debut on the stage and starred in such Broadway plays as *Junior Miss* (when she was thirteen years old), *Dear Ruth, Franklin Street, Brief Holiday, Love on Leave, Pick Up Girl, Mr. Roberts, The Naked Genius,* and *I Remember Mama.* Rosemary, who was born in Montclair, New Jersey, was also heard on Nila Mack's popular Saturday morning children's fairy tale anthology series, *Let's Pretend,* on CBS radio, for several years, and was featured on such radio programs as Fletcher Markle's dramatic anthology series, *Studio One,* playing leading ingenue roles in such award-winning adaptations as "A Tree Grows in Brooklyn" and "The Constant Nymph," both from best-selling novels. The actress was also a regular radio performer on the *Cavalcade of America, My True Story, Young Dr. Malone,* and *NBC Playhouse* programs, and for several years she played the sweet Kathy Cameron on the long-running soap opera, *When a Girl Marries.* One of her most memorable roles on radio, however, was as Archie Andrews' athletic-but-pretty friend, Betty Cooper, which she first started playing in 1946 and continued to play until the show ended its long radio run in 1953. In the 1970s, Rosemary returned to radio and was heard on 22 episodes of Himan Brown's valiant attempt to bring radio drama back to the airwaves, the *CBS Mystery Theater*, which was on the air from 1974 until 1982. Rosemary was also heard on another short-lived attempt to revive radio soap operas in the mid-1970s, *To Have and To Hold*, which was one of four fifteen-minute, five-day-a-week syndicated dramas that were part of an hour-long series called the *Radio Playhouse*. In addition to her tenure on the Mama television series, Rosemary also appeared on such series as *The Edge of Night, Search for Tomorrow, One Life to Live, Playhouse 90, The Kraft Television Theatre* (21 times), *Studio One,* and *As the World Turns.* Miss Rice also recorded more than 15 children's record albums for Columbia and RCA, including the Grammy Award-winning "Learn to Tell Time," "Hans Christian Andersen in Song and Story," "Hey Kids, Let's Sing," "Bedtime Stories and Songs," "The Wonderful World of Children's Songs," "Song and Games for a Happy Birthday Party," and "Holiday Fun for Children," to name just a few. Rosemary Rice was also a popular voice-over and onscreen TV commercial spokeswoman for such products as Lux soap, Prell shampoo, Exxon, Coca-Cola, and Life Savers.

(Credit: Courtesy of Rosemary Rice)

The lovely actress Rosemary Rice played Betty Cooper on the *Archie Andrews* radio program from 1946 until the show was canceled in 1953.

SMOLEN, VIVIAN B. 1920 (VERONICA LODGE)

Born in New York City, Vivian Smolen decided she wanted to become an actress while she was a student at Brooklyn College in the late 1930s. As soon as she graduated from college, Vivian landed roles in several of radio's most popular programs, because of her diction-perfect, attractive-sounding voice.

She made her radio acting debut as one of Doc Barclay's three daughters, Marce, on the *Doc Barclay's Daughters* soap opera series in 1938. Before long, Vivian was one of daytime radio's busiest performers and she had important, regular running roles on two of radio's most memorable soap operas, *Stella Dallas* and *Our Gal Sunday*. On *Stella Dallas*, Vivian played Stella's daughter, Laurel, or "Lolly Baby," as Stella called her, and, on Our Gal Sunday she played the title role of Sunday, the girl about whom the program's announcer said, "Can a girl from a small mining town out West find love and happiness as the wife of a wealthy and titled Englishman?" Smolen played the Sunday character until the program left the air in 1959. The actress also played the rich and beautiful Veronica Lodge, one of Archie Andrews' heartthrobs, on the original *Archie Andrews* radio series. She was also regularly featured on such radio programs as *Front Page Farrell, Grand Central Station, Radio City Playhouse*, and many other popular shows that were broadcast in the 1940s into the 1950s. After radio drama's demise, Miss Smolen remained active in show business throughout the 1960s and 1970s, appearing in numerous TV commercials. In 1980, Vivian made one of her few film appearances playing a supporting role in *My Bodyguard*. Thereafter, Vivian returned to her life as a suburban wife and mother, taking care of her husband and children in Connecticut.

STANG, ARNOLD B. 1923 (JUGHEAD JONES)

Arnold Stang, who was born in the Chelsea Section of Boston, Massachusetts, has an amusing nasal, squeaky-sounding voice that makes him sound like a perennial adolescent. It was his unusual vocal quality that gained him steady employment as a comic actor on radio. Stang began his career as a child on such programs as Nila Mack's *Let's Pretend* in the mid-1930s. Throughout the 1940s and 1950s, Stang played many humorous male teens, and then young adults, on such radio programs as *The Eileen Barton Show, The Goldbergs* (as Seymour Fingergood, which he also played on the television version), *The Milton Berle Show, The Henry Morgan Show* (as Gerard, which is probably his best-remembered radio role), and, in 1946–1947, and then again in 1952-1953, the *Archie Andrews* series (on which he played Archie's best friend, Jughead Jones). In addition to his radio acting career, Stang, who had as humorous an appearance as he did voice – he wore glasses, had a weak chin and a small frame – became a popular comic character in such films such as *My Sister Eileen* (1942), *They Got Me Covered* (1943), *So This is New York* (1948), *Two Gals and a Guy* (1951), *The Man With the Golden Arm* (1955, a rare chance at drama), *Dondi* (1961), and *Dennis the Menace* (1993), and many others. Between the 1940s and the 1990s, Stang was a regular on such TV series as *The Milton Berle Show*, and featured on such programs as *December Bride*,

Producer's Showcase, Playhouse 90, Wagon Train, Batman, Chico and the Man, Emergency!, The Cosby Show, and *Reading Rainbow.* Stang was also a frequent voice-over performer for numerous TV and film cartoon characters (Top Cat is his best remembered), as well as being a frequent spokesman on TV and radio commercials.

STONE, HAL (HARLAN) B. 1931 (JUGHEAD JONES)

When he was four years old, Hal Stone began an active career as one of the print industry's most sought-after child models. Hal continued to work as a model until he was twelve. During his modeling career, he posed for such top photographers of the day as Hesse and Keppler and illustrators like James Montgomery Flagg, being seen in hundreds of print ads in magazines and newspapers. Hal also appeared in many plays on the Broadway stage while he was modeling, including *Life With Father* (with Lillian Gish), *Peter Pan, Watch on the Rhine, Star Spangled Family, Lady in the Dark* (with Gertrude Lawrence), *This Rock* and *Tomorrow, the World!* While he was working on Broadway, Stone became active as a radio actor and he continued to work on radio from the age of 8 until he was 23. Hal

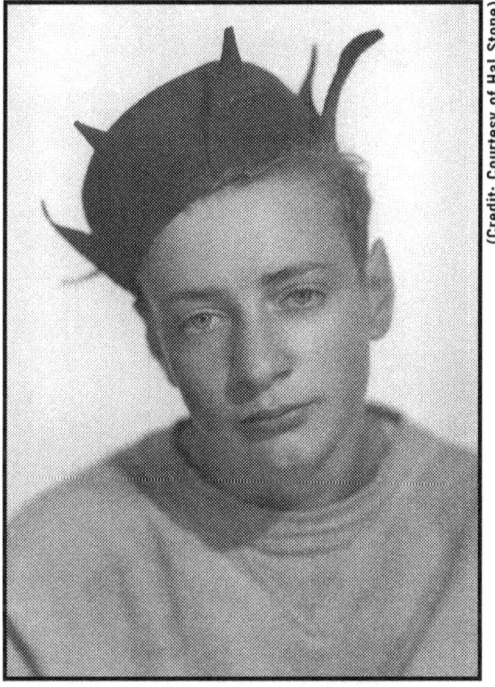

Harlan "Hal" Stone played "Jughead" Jones on the *Archie Andrews* program for ten years, with time out to serve in the U. S. Army. He is seen here in costume for his role as Archie's best pal.

had featured roles on such popular radio programs of the 1930s and 1940s as *Big Town, Death Valley Days, The Aldrich Family, The U. S. Steel Hour, The Henry Morgan Show, The Theater Guild of the Air, The Jack Benny Show, My True Story, Road of Life, The Right to Happiness, Portia Faces Life,* and many others. Hal's longest running radio role, however, was as Archie's pal, Jughead Jones, which he played for ten years, with a year or so off to serve in the U. S. Air Force during the Korean conflict. From 1956 until 1963, after Hal retired from radio acting, he worked at WNEM-TV in Michigan and WLOF-TV in Florida in television production, and from 1963 until 1970, he was the Principal Director and Board Chairman of Centrex Productions of New York, a company which specialized in TV commercial production. Hal continued to work in television production until he retired in 1980 and decided to concentrate on his longtime hobby of painting and sculpturing. He has also kept busy in recent years heading Dual Dimensions, Inc. and Bygone Days Press. Hal's art work is currently exhibited in various local art galleries in his hometown of Sedona, Arizona.

B

BLONDIE

When he was a boy, cartoonist Marat "Chic" Young was encouraged by his mother, who recognized his special artistic talent, to pursue a career as a professional artist when he finished his schooling. After graduating from high school, Young studied art in Chicago, New York and Cleveland, and began his career as a professional artist working for the Newspaper Enterprise Association drawing comic strips. His first comic strip was called *The Affairs of Jane,* which did not prove to be very popular with readers. In 1924, he applied for work at King Features Syndicate, and it was there that he created another comic strip called *Beautiful Babs.* This strip lasted only four months. In 1925, Marat began using his nickname "Chic," as his comic strip byline, and he created a strip for King Features called *Dumb Dora,* a feature lasting five years. All of the female cartoon characters Young created had been typical, free-spirited "flappers" of the 1920s. His next comic strip creation, *Blondie,* which made its newspaper comic strip debut in 1930, was no exception. *Blondie* became very popular with the comic strip-reading public. Young won the prestigious Reuben Award, which is given by the National Cartoonists' Society for his art work for *Blondie.* It wasn't, however, until the character Blondie, whose full name was Blondie Boopadoop, married her boyfriend Dagwood Bumstead in 1933, that the *Blondie* comic strip suddenly became one of the most popular newspaper comic strips in

Chic Young's popular Dagwood and Blondie Bumstead are seen here in one of their early comic strip panels.

the country. Before Dagwood and Blondie married, Blondie had been a free-spirited, somewhat déclassé, showgirl. Dagwood, who was the son of very wealthy Socialite-parents was disowned by his rich and snooty family when he married Blondie, because they disapproved of her rather "common" background. Dagwood then had to go to work for the first time in his life. He found employment as a clerk at the J. C. Dithers Construction Company. Mr. Dithers was a rather pompous, overbearing man and Dagwood was always in a state of nervous agitation in his company. In 1934, Blondie and Dagwood had a son they named "Alexander," nicknaming him "Baby Dumpling," and they later had a daughter they called "Cookie." With their little dog, Daisy, and later Daisy's large litter of puppies, Blondie and Dagwood Bumstead and their not-so-typical American family, became icons to millions of people who couldn't wait to read the next funny installment of their lives in their newspaper's daily comic strips, and then the comic books that followed. After Chic Young's death in 1973, his son, Dean, took over the *Blondie* comic books and strips and employed a succession of artists/writers that included Jim Raymond (cartoonist Alex Raymond's brother), Stan Drake, Michael Gersher and Dennis LeBrun to assist him with the comic book and strip series.

Because of the popularity of the *Blondie* comic strip, Columbia Pictures decided the characters would be perfect subjects for a series of second-feature comedy films. Between 1938 and 1950, Columbia produced 28 *Blondie* feature films with such titles as *Blondie Meets the Boss, Blondie Takes a Vacation, Blondie Brings Up Baby, Blondie Goes to College, Leave It to Blondie, Blondie's Anniversary, Blondie's Secret,* and *Beware of Blondie.* The stars of the film series were Penny Singleton and Arthur Lake, and they played the characters in all 28 features.

In 1938, *Blondie* made its on-air debut as a radio situation comedy series on the CBS network. Penny Singleton and Arthur Lake repeated their film roles of Blondie and Dagwood on the radio series and continued to play the roles on radio until 1950, when Singleton decided that she had had enough of the *Blondie* role and quit. She was replaced on radio by actresses Alice White, Patricia Van Cleve, and finally Ann Rutherford, but listeners could not accept any other actress but Singleton in the role and both the radio and the film series were canceled in 1950. Familiar characters who were heard on the radio show, as well as seen in the comic strips and *Blondie* films, were the Bumstead's next door neighbors, "Herb and Harriet Woodley," who were played on the radio series by Hal Peary (then Frank Nelson) and Mary Jane Croft; "J. C. Dithers" and his wife, "Cora," played on radio by Hanley Stafford and Elvia Allman; "Alexander Bumstead" (a.k.a. "Baby Dumpling)," played on radio by Leone Ledoux, and then Larry Simms (who also played Alexander in the films), Jeffrey Silver, and finally Tommy Cook; "Cookie

Bumstead," played by Marlene Ames, Joan Rae and Norma Jean Nilsson; "Alvin Fuddle," played by Dix Davis; and "Dimples Wilson," played by Veola Vonn, and then Lurene Tuttle. The announcers for the *Blondie* radio series were Bill Goodwin and Howard Patrie, who always began each program saying,

Penny Singleton and Arthur Lake played Blondie and Dagwood Bumstead on the successful radio version of Chic Young's *Blondie* comic strip, as well as in the popular *Blondie* films. They are seen here emoting during a broadcast of the show.

"Uh-uh-uh-uh.... Don't touch that dial! It's time for...!," and then Dagwood's voice would be heard bleating out, "B-l-o-o-o-o-o-n-d-i-e!!!!" The radio program was written by John L. "Johnny" Green and produced and directed by Don Bernard, and later directed by Eddie Pola. Among the titles of the *Blondie* radio program's classic episodes: "Dagwood Buys a Suit," "April Fool's Day," "The Gypsy Queen," "Dagwood Finds a $2,000 Fly," "Dagwood's Dream Comes True," and "Alexander Joins the Circus."

In 1957, a television series, starring Arthur Lake as Dagwood and Pamela Britton as Blondie, made its debut on the NBC network, but it failed to attract a sizeable enough audience to keep it on the air longer than one season. *Blondie* resurfaced on CBS in 1968 with Will Hutchins playing Dagwood and Patricia Harty playing Blondie, but this series also failed to click with TV viewers, and it was also canceled after just one season.

BLONDIE RADIO SERIES PERFORMERS

ALLMAN, ELVIA B. 1904 – D. 1992 (CORA DITHERS)

Born in Concord, North Carolina, comedienne/actress Elvia Allman became one of television's best-remembered performers when she appeared on the very successful situation comedy, *I Love Lucy*, playing the hard-driving supervisor in a chocolate factory where Lucy and her friend Ethel Mertz are hired to wrap candy and have difficulty keeping up with the ever-moving flow of chocolates on the conveyor belt. Allman's voice, by that time, was already very familiar to radio listeners, since she was heard as a regular on hundreds of radio programs throughout the 1930s and 1940s, usually playing overbearing, gushingly loud women on such popular series as *The Bob Hope Show*, *The Jack Benny Show*, *The Jimmy Durante Show*, and *Al Pearce and His Gang*. Allman was also an occasional performer on such radio shows as *Burns and Allen*, *Fibber McGee and Molly*, *The Abbott and Costello Show*, *Town Hall Tonight*, and *The Edgar Bergen/Charlie McCarthy Chase and Sanborn Hour*. She is well remembered by devotees of Radio's Golden Age as Cora Dithers on *Blondie*. Cora Withers was the overbearing wife of Dagwood Bumstead's boss, J. C. Dithers, but she was also a sympathetic friend to Dagwood's wife, Blondie. Allman also played Cora on the first television version of *Blondie*. The actress was seen in an impressive number of other TV series in addition to *I Love Lucy* and *Blondie* including *December Bride*, *Bachelor Father*, *The Bob Cummings Show*, *The Andy Griffith Show*, *Mister Ed*, *Perry Mason*, *Wagon Train*, *The Beverly Hillbillies*, *The Dick Van Dyke Show*, *Petticoat Junction*, *My Favorite Martian*, *The Addams Family*, *Green Acres*, *Bewitched*, *The Munsters*, *My Three Sons*, *Adam-12*, *The Odd Couple*, *Alice* and *Murder, She Wrote*. Miss Allman made her

(Credit: Photofest)

A frequent performer on radio and TV, character actress Elvia Allman, played Cora Dithers on the *Blondie* radio series.

onscreen film debut in the Bob Hope/Bing Crosby film *Road to Singapore* in 1940 and she subsequently appeared on the screen in such films as *The Kettles in the Ozarks* (1956), *Breakfast at Tiffany's* (1961), and *The Nutty Professor* (1963), among others.

KEARNS, JOSEPH B. 1904 – D. 1962 (MANY SUPPORTING ROLES)

Born in Salt Lake City, Utah, Joseph Kearns was one of show business' busiest supporting actors from the 1930s into the 1960s. Kearns, who began his career on radio station KSL in Utah, was heard on hundreds of popular radio shows during Radio's Golden Age. He was regularly featured on such memorable programs as *The Jack Benny Show, The Judy Canova Show* (as Count Benchley Botsford), *The Mel Blanc Show, Suspense* (as the host, the "Man in Black," and also as an actor in practically every drama presented on that series in the 1940s), *The Whistler, Lights Out, Honest Harold, A Date With Judy, Burns and Allen, The Phil Harris/Alice Faye Show, The Bob Hope Show, Let George Do It, Pursuit, Me and Janie,* and *Sherlock Holmes* (as Professor Moriarty). Kearns was also regularly featured on the *Blondie* radio series playing numerous supporting roles during the series' entire run. On television, Kearns was a regular on such series as *Dennis the Menace,* playing Dennis' neighbor, Mr. Wilson for three seasons from 1959 through 1961, *Our Miss Brooks* from 1953–1955, and *Peter Gunn* in 1958. The actor was also featured on episodes of such TV series as *Burns and Allen, The Jack Benny Show, December Bride, Screen Director's Playhouse, The General Electric Theater, The Real McCoys, The Court of Last Resort, How to Marry a Millionaire, Shower of Stars, Gunsmoke, Perry Mason,* and *The Donna Reed Show,* to name just a few. Kearns' film work included voice-over performances for Disney (he provided the memorable voice for the Doorknob in *Alice in Wonderland*), and he was the voice of the Chief Angel for the classic film *It's a Wonderful Life.* The actor also had supporting onscreen roles in such films as *Hard, Fast and Beautiful* (1951), *Our Miss Brooks* (1956), *Storm Center* (1956), *The Girl Most Likely* (1957), and *Anatomy of a Murder* (1959).

LAKE, ARTHUR B. 1905 – D. 1985 (DAGWOOD BUMSTEAD)

Arthur Lake was born in Corbin, Kentucky, where he parents performed as circus acrobats, joining their act when he was just five years old. The family eventually decided to retire from the circus and settle down in Hollywood in 1917. In the 1920s, Lake began acting in two-reel silent films, which were usually Westerns. In 1929, when "talkies" were the norm, Lake was featured in a series of college musicals usually playing rather dim, cow-eyed young swains. His roles, however, began to get smaller and smaller with each film he appeared in and the actor considered quitting show business. In 1938, he was cast in a film adaptation of Chic Young's successful *Blondie* comic strip. The film version of *Blondie* was, to everyone's surprise, an enormous success and made millions of dollars at the box office for Columbia Pictures. Lake was immediately signed to an exclusive contract with Columbia to play Dagwood Bumstead in a series of *Blondie* films. Lake, and his *Blondie* co-star, Penny Singleton, made 27 subsequent *Blondie* films over the next twelve years. Although he appeared in more than 100 films during his career as an actor, Arthur Lake is best remembered for playing Dagwood Bumstead.

In 1939, because of the success of the film series, Lake and Singleton starred on a radio series based on Chic Young's characters, presented on the CBS network. The radio series remained on the air for 11 years. In 1957, a *Blondie* TV series surfaced with Lake playing Dagwood, but it was not a success, mainly because Penny Singleton had opted not to continue playing the title character. The series was canceled after less than one full season. Lake, who was married to the niece of film star Marion Davies, retired from show business in the 1960s and settled down to a comfortably well off life as a real estate tycoon. Lake died in 1987 at the age of 82.

NELSON, FRANK B. 1911 – D. 1986 (HERB WOODLEY)

(Credit: Photofest)

Best known as the unctuous floorwalker and sales clerk on the *Jack Benny* radio and TV shows, actor Frank Nelson's long, drawn out, "Yeeeeeessssss?" as he greeted Benny always got one of the show's biggest laughs. Nelson, who was born in Denver, Colorado, began his career on radio as an announcer, but switched to acting in the mid-1930s because there was more work to be had as an actor. Nelson enjoyed a long and profitable career as a character actor on radio, as well as in films and on television. Among the many radio programs on which he was featured: *Blondie*

Two of radio's most successful characters actors, Hanley Stafford and Frank Nelson, were regulars on the *Blondie* radio program. Stafford played Dagwood's boss, Mr. Dithers, and Nelson played the Bumstead's next door neighbor, Herb Woodley.

(playing the Bumsteads' neighbor, Herb Woodley), *Flywheel, Shuster and Flywheel, The Life of Riley* (as Chester Riley's voice of conscience), *A Day in the Life of Dennis Day, The Eddie Cantor Show, Meet Me at Parky's, Lux Radio Theatre, Burns and Allen, The Danny Kaye Show, Baby Snooks,* and many other programs. Nelson made his motion picture debut in *Fugitives in the Sky* (1936), and was subsequently seen in such films as *Hold 'em Navy* (1937), *When You're Smiling* (1950), *The Milkman* (1950), *You Never Can Tell* (1951), *My Pal Gus* (1952), *Bonzo Goes to College* (1952), *Remains to be Seen* (1953), and *The Malibu Bikini Shop* (1985). The actor was also regularly featured on such TV series as *I Love Lucy, Petticoat Junction, Sanford and Son,* and *Alice,* among others.

SINGLETON, PENNY B. 1908 – D. 2003 (BLONDIE)
Some actresses become so identified with one particular role that they find it hard to become accepted as any other character by the public. Such is certainly true of Penny Singleton, who played *Blondie* in 28 feature films, as well as on a popular radio adaptation of Chic Young's successful comic strip. Singleton, the daughter of an Irish/American newspaperman named Benny McNulty, was christened Mariana Dorothy Agnes Letetia McNulty, in Philadelphia, Pennsylvania. As a child, Penny, as she was nicknamed, exhibited talent as a singer and often performed in movie theaters while the film projectionists changed their silent film reels. When she was in the sixth grade, she was asked to join a touring children's variety show that performed in various vaudeville theaters throughout the country. The kiddie show was called *Kiddie Kabaret* and also featured such later-to-be-famous performers as Milton Berle and Gene Raymond. In 1930, Dorothy McNulty, as Penny still billed herself, was discovered by a Hollywood talent scout and given a small role in the film musical *Good News*. She remained in Hollywood and had roles in such films as *After the Thin Man* (1936), *Vogues of 1938* (1937), *Swing Your Lady* (1938), *Boy Meets Girl* (1938), and *Hard to Get* (1938). Her big break came, however, when she was cast in the title role in the film adaptation of Chic Young's *Blondie* comic strip in 1938. The film was a big hit and Dorothy, who changed her name to Penny Singleton, continued to play *Blondie* in films from 1938 until 1950. Penny also starred on the successful radio program from 1939 until the late 1940s, when she decided to leave. Without Singleton playing Blondie, the radio series died a slow death and ended its radio run in 1950, the same year the last *Blondie* film was released. After leaving the Blondie film and radio series, Singleton only occasionally worked as an actress. In 1962, Penny was heard as the voice of Jane Jetson on the popular, long running animated television series *The Jetsons*. She was featured on television on such series as *Pulitzer Prize Playhouse, Death Valley Days, The Twilight Zone*

and, in 1984, Singleton appeared on an episode of the popular *Murder, She Wrote* TV series. She was elected President of the American Guild of Variety Artists Union in 1969, and she led the first strike of Radio City Music Hall's Rockettes, helping to improve working conditions for all variety show dancers. Penny died at the age of 95 in 2003.

STAFFORD, HANLEY B. 1900 – D. 1968 (J. C. DITHERS)

Hanley Stafford was born Alfred John Austin in Hanley, Staffordshire in Great Britain, using a variation of his birthplace as his stage name when he decided to become an actor. When he was a teenager, Hanley emigrated to Canada and after working at various odd jobs, became a radio announcer at radio station KFI in 1930. Eventually he joined a touring theatrical troupe and when the company performed in Hollywood, Stafford decided to remain there and began to work as an actor on various radio programs. Before long, he had become one of Hollywood's most sought-after radio actors, featured on such programs as *Thunder Colt* and *Big Town*. His most famous radio role, however, was as Baby Snooks' "Daddy" on *The Fanny Brice/Baby Snooks Show*, a role which he took over from film actor Frank Morgan who originated the role on the *Ziegfeld Follies of the Air* radio show. Stafford played the blustering Daddy Higgins to Fanny Brice's Baby Snooks, always exasperated due to Snooks' constantly asked question, "Why?" from 1939 until 1950, when the program left the air. The actor was also heard on the *Blondie* series from 1939 until 1950, playing Dagwood Bumstead's boss, J.C. Dithers. Stafford was also featured in such feature films as *Life with Henry* (1941), *Three Guys Named Mike* (1951), *Lullaby of Broadway* (1951), *A Girl in Every Port* (1952), *Just This Once* (1952), *Francis Covers the Big Town* (1953), and *The Go-Getter* (1956). He also made guest starring appearances on such series as *Maverick*, *Sugarfoot*, *Cheyenne* and *77 Sunset Strip*.

BLUE BEETLE

It was in 1939 that the *Blue Beetle* comic strip character first surfaced in four pages of the Fox Feature Syndicate's *Mystery Men Comics*. Created by artist Charles Nicholas (born Charles Wojtkowski), the *Blue Beetle* action hero had a very mysterious background. Unlike Superman, The Green Hornet, Batman, and other comic book superheros, The Blue Beetle did not have any other identity than that of the costumed, super-strong Blue Beetle character. The crime-fighting character simply turned up in his beetle costume and fought evildoers. *The Blue Beetle,* in spite of the fact that it was never quite clear who he was and why he did what he did, became a major comic book feature sensation by 1940. Charles Nicholas (1915 – 2001) began his career as a cartoonist working for Fox Comics. While he was at Fox, he created the Blue Beetle character. Nicholas drew *The Blue Beetle* comic strip until 1942, when he left Fox and went to work as an artist at Quality Comics. At Quality, Nicholas helped create the *Blackhawk* comic book character. After he left Quality, the artist worked at DC Comics, and drew the *Hawkman* and *The Incredible Hulk* newspaper comic strips with artist Larry Lieber.

The Blue Beetle, however, was the artist's most successful comic strip creation and the character was so popular with comic book readers that he appeared on the cover of the August 1940 issue of *Mystery Men Comics*. Later that same year, *The Blue Beetle* was featured in a comic book series of his own. In the early 1940s, *The Blue Beetle*, who was then being drawn by artist Jack Kirby, also became a daily newspaper comic strip character. By that time, however, he had an identity, other than that of a costumed crime-fighter; he had become a police officer named Patrolman Dan Garrett. Like Batman, The Blue Beetle was, when he first surfaced, a rather shadowy character, but by the time the comic strip appeared on the scene, he had a less questionable origin. The last issue of *Mystery Men Comics* was published in 1942, but *The Blue Beetle* character continued to appear in comics, and as a comic strip, until 1948 and then came back again in 1950 for several more Fox Feature Syndicate comics. In 1955, Charlton Comics reprinted several *Blue Beetle* comic books. As of this writing, there is still a Blue Beetle character being seen in DC's *Universe* comic book series. The comic strip and book's original cartoonist Charles Nicholas died in 2001 at the age of 86.

In 1940, Charles Nicholas' creation became the hero of a children's radio adventure series. The radio program unfortunately proved to be short-lived, and did not match the longevity of the comic book and comic strip incarnations. Actor Frank Lovejoy, who was, at the time, a busy radio actor and later became a successful motion picture actor, played the Blue Beetle/Dan Garrett character on the radio series for the first thirteen episodes. The actor who replaced Lovejoy was never identified on the program and remains anonymous. On the series, Patrolman Dan Garrett, a.k.a. "The Blue Beetle," had a rather plodding-but-amusing partner named Mike Mannigan. Like Clark Kent/Superman, Dan Garrett also had a girlfriend, Joan Mason, who was a newspaper reporter. Both Mike Mulligan and Joan were oblivious that Dan Garrett was indeed the crime-fighting Blue Beetle. On the radio series, it was finally explained that Garrett had used an experimental drug called Vitamin 2X, supplied by a druggist named Dr. Franz, which had given him his superhuman strength. Among several of the adventures that were heard on *The Blue Beetle* radio series were: "Smashing the Spy Ring" (the first show of the series), "Murder for Profit," "Invisible Ghost," "Frame Up," "Rounding Up the Payroll Bandits," "Saved by a Hair," "The Underworld Goes Underground,"

"The Dancing Ghost of Rocky Hill," and "The Jewel Mystery" (the last show of the series), among others.

After listening to two of the surviving episodes of *The Blue Beetle* radio series, it became apparent to this author why this series never caught on with the listening public, and disappeared from the airwaves after less than one year on the radio. The scripts for the series obviously lacked the excitement of many of the other serialized action dramas that featured superheros with superhuman strength. Although actor Frank Lovejoy was competent enough when he was playing Dan Garrett, when he became the crime-fighting *Blue Beetle,* he did not sound heroic or strong enough to do battle with the larger-than-life wicked villains he encountered on the radio series. Lovejoy's unidentified replacement, for the second and last thirteen-part episodes of *The Blue Beetle,* handled the less-than-vocally-demanding Beetle half of his role adequately, but was not nearly as convincing an actor to bring the Dan Garrett side of the character to life, as Lovejoy had.

BLUE BEETLE RADIO SERIES MAJOR PERFORMER

LOVEJOY, FRANK B.1912 – D.1962 (THE BLUE BEETLE/DAN GARRETT)

Actor Frank Lovejoy, who made a successful transition from radio to films, played *The Blue Beetle* on radio early in his career.
(Credit: Photofest)

Actor Frank Lovejoy was one of the few actors who began their careers as a radio actor and became a film star in Hollywood. Lovejoy, who was born in the Bronx in New York City, made his radio acting debut on the *Forty-Five Minutes From Hollywood* program, which showcased new and promising talent, in 1934. The actor had made his first less-than-triumphant acting debut on Broadway in the play *Judgment Day* in the mid-1930s. Lovejoy's distinctive voice soon made him one of radio's most sought-after performers by program directors. In the late 1930s into the 1940s, Lovejoy was heard on such popular programs as *The Amazing Mr. Malone* (a.k.a. *Murder and Mr. Malone,* as Malone), *Nightbeat* (as the series' hero, Randy Stone), *Calling All Detectives, Your Family and Mine, Stella Dallas, Just Plain Bill, Brave Tomorrow, Second Husband, Bright Horizon, The Shadow, Johnny Presents, The Columbia Workshop, The Adventures of Sam Spade, Mr. District Attorney, We Love and Learn,* and *The Adventures of Mr. Meek.* Throughout the 1930s and 1940s, Lovejoy continued to work on Broadway and was featured in such plays as *Chalked Out* (1937), *Censored* (1938), *The Greatest Show on Earth* (1938), and *Woman Bites Dog* (1946). In 1948, Lovejoy appeared in his first film, *Black Bart,* but it wasn't until the following year that the actor became a noticeable film presence in *The Home of the Brave.* For the remainder of his career, Lovejoy continued to work on radio, as well as appearing in such films as *South Sea Sinner* (1950), *In a Lonely Place* (1950), *The Sound and the Fury* (1950), *I Was a Communist for the FBI* (1951), *Goodbye, My Fancy* (1951), *I'll See You in My Dreams* (1951), *House of Wax* (1953), *The Hitch-Hiker* (1953), *Strategic Air Command* (1955), *Three Brave Men* (1957), and *Cole Younger, Gunfighter* (1958), among others. Lovejoy was also active on television in the 1950s, starring on two series, *Man Against Crime* in 1956 and Meet McGraw in 1957. He also made guest starring appearances on *Lux Video Theatre, Stage 7, Climax, A Letter to Loretta, Zane Grey Theater, The Ford Television Theater, Playhouse 90, The U. S. Steel Hour, The DuPont Show of the Week,* and other series. In 1961, Frank Lovejoy returned to his first love, Broadway, in the play *The Best Man,* in what was his most critically acclaimed performance. The following year, Lovejoy died suddenly, at the age of 50, while he was appearing in a touring production of *The Best Man* in New Jersey with his wife, radio actress Joan Banks.

BRINGING UP FATHER
(A.K.A. MAGGIE AND JIGGS)

One of the most popular and long-running comic strips of all time was *Bringing Up Father,* created by artist George McManus. McManus was already well known to newspaper comic strip fans as the artist who drew such popular features as *Nipsy the Newsboy in Funny Fairyland, The Merry Marcelene, Panhandle Pete, Cheerful Charley, Snoozer, The Ready Money Ladies, Let George Do It,* and the very successful *The Newlyweds and Their Baby,* when he created the enormously popular *Bringing Up Father* comic strip. Cartoonist George McManus (1882-1954) was born in St. Louis, Missouri. When McManus was an adult and a very successful, world-famous cartoonist, he told an interviewer that he could not remember a time in his life when he had not been drawing. He got his first job as a professional artist when he was sixteen years old with the St. Louis Republic newspaper, covering the crime scene in St. Louis.

He spent several years drawing hangings, murders, and suicide victims for the newspaper, finally deciding to ask for a change of assignments when he was asked to draw the hanging of a man who had to be hung twice because he didn't die the first time. Always interested in cartooning, McManus was delighted when the editors at the *St Louis Republic* asked him to draw a comic strip for them. The first strip he ever drew was called *Elmer and Oliver*, which was only relatively successful. When McManus won $3,000 betting on a horse in 1904, he pulled up stakes and moved to New York City, spending his winnings looking for the best job he could find. Within six months, he was hired by the *New York World* as a political cartoonist, and in time he began drawing a new comic strip he called *The Newlyweds* for the newspaper. This caught the attention of the prestigious newspaper publisher William Randolph Hearst, who asked McManus to continue *The Newlyweds*, now retitled *Their Only Child*, and to create new comic strips for his *American* newspaper. The result was several strips that became moderate successes: *Rosie's Beau*, *The Whole Blooming Family*, and *Spare Ribs and Gravy*. It was in 1913 that McManus came up with the comic strip he called *Bringing Up Father*, which became an immediate sensation and was eventually published in all of the Hearst newspapers, as well as the popular Sunday "Funnies" in 1916. The main characters in *Bringing Up Father* were an Irish/American couple named Maggie and Jiggs, a poor bricklayer and his laundress wife, who had suddenly become wealthy. McManus did not reveal how the couple had obtained their fortune until 1930, when he told his readers that Jiggs and Maggie had won the Irish Sweepstakes many years before. In its earliest years, the comic strip also featured Maggie and Jiggs' half-witted, shiftless son, Sonny, who had been kicked out of college and was put to work at his father's office. The comic strip's title referred to the fact that Jiggs' snobbishly overbearing wife, Maggie, and the couple's social-climbing

Frank McManus' popular comic strip character Jiggs, was first seen in *Bringing Up Father* in 1913. Jiggs became the main character in a short-lived radio series, based on the comic strip, in 1941.

(Credit: Author's collection. © King Features Syndicate, Inc.)

daughter, Nora, were constantly trying to make Jiggs more "refined," as they felt befitting to his newly acquired "moneyed" status. Throughout the many years *Bringing Up Father* was published, it was basically a one-joke comic strip that involved the ongoing conflict between the pretentious, status-seeking Maggie, and the lowbrow and somewhat common Jiggs. McManus continued to draw *Bringing Up Father* until the mid-1930s, when he hired an assistant named Zeke Zekley to help him. When McManus died in 1954, King Features Syndicate, who owned the publishing rights to the strip, hired a talented artist named Vernon Greene to take over the strip. Vernon Greene had begun his cartooning career as a staff artist at the Portland Telegram in Oregon, where he drew sports cartoons. In 1940, Greene began drawing comic strips and illustrated *The Shadow, Masked Lady* and *Perry Mason* pulp magazine novels. Greene then spent six years ghosting the *Polly and her Pals* comic strip before he took over the job of drawing of the Bringing Up Father strip. Greene continued drawing *Bringing Up Father* until he died in 1965; artist Frank Johnson then took over the drawing of the comic strip. *Bringing Up Father* continued to be published as a daily comic strip until May 20, 2000, when it was dropped from syndication.

In addition to being a comic strip feature, *Bringing Up Father* was also published as a Big Little Book, published by the Whitman Company in 1936, and as a *Jiggs and Maggie* comic book series that was originally published by Standard Comics in the late 1930s.

Because of its popularity, the *Bringing Up Father* comic strip was adapted into a musical comedy in 1914, and then shortly after, as a series of stage comedies that toured the country until 1921. In 1925, a second stage version of *Bringing Up Father* was presented on Broadway. From 1916 until 1918, there were 9 animated silent films based on the strip produced by William Randolph Hearst's International Film Service and in 1921, three two-reel, live-action *Bringing Up Father* short subjects were also produced by Hearst's company. In 1928, MGM released a full-length feature film that starred J. Farrell MacDonald as Jiggs, Polly Moran as Maggie, Jules Cowles played Jiggs' brother-in-law, Dinty Moore, and comedienne Marie Dressler played Jiggs' sister, Annie Moore. Four second feature *Bringing Up Father* films were also produced by Monogram: *Bringing Up Father* (1946), *Jiggs and Maggie in Society* (1947), *Maggie and Jiggs in Court* (1948), and *Maggie and Jiggs in Jackpot Jitters* (1949). Film star Mickey Rooney's father, Joe Yule, played Jiggs and Renie Riano played Maggie in these films.

In 1941, *Bringing Up Father* was presented as a radio series that was heard on NBC's Blue Network. The series starred stage comedian Neill O'Malley, and then Mark Smith, as Jiggs, and Agnes Moorehead as Maggie. Helen Shields, and then Joan Banks for the longest period of time, played their daughter, Nora, and Craig McDonnell played Maggie's brother, Dinty Moore. The short-lived series was produced by Cameo Broadcasting and Recording Studios in New York City and was supervised by the William Morris Agency. The radio series remained relatively faithful to George McManus' original comic strip and apparently the first episode in the series was actually based on an original McManus comic strip panel that was first published in 1919. Although the series was well produced, and several amusing episodes were aired, the *Bringing Up Father* radio program failed to capture the attention of the public and was canceled after less than one season on the air.

Listening to a short segment of one of the *Bringing Up Father* broadcasts today, it became obvious to this author why this series did not enjoy the long-running success of its comic strip inspiration. The Maggie character on the segment of the radio series that I heard, as played by actress Agnes Moorehead, seemed more brittle and mean spirited than the humorously pretentious Maggie was depicted in the comic strip, and the Jiggs character, as played by Neill O'Malley, had little more to do than mutter and grumble. *Bringing Up Father* was basically a one joke comic strip that depicted how the lower classes behave when suddenly given a great deal of money. Cartoonist George McManus had managed to make that one joke amusing in each and every daily strip he drew. Apparently, the half-hour radio program needed more than that one joke to make it succeed.

BRINGING UP FATHER RADIO SERIES PERFORMERS

BANKS, JOAN B. 1918 – D. 1998 (NORA)

Actress Joan Banks was born in Petersburg, West Virginia. Miss Banks became a professional actress soon after she graduated from Hunter College in the late 1930s. After appearing on the Broadway stage in several plays, she was cast as a "female stooge" on the popular *Stoopnagle and Budd* radio show. Within a short period of time, she was being heard on such popular radio programs as *Bringing Up Father* (playing the role of Maggie and Jiggs' daughter, Nora), *By Kathleen Norris, Deadline Drama, Ellery Queen, The Falcon, Gangbusters, Her Honor Nancy James, John's Other Wife, Portia Faces Life, Shorty Bell, This Day is Ours, This is Your FBI, We Love and Learn, Valiant Lady, Young Dr. Malone*. Miss Banks remained active on radio throughout the 1930s, 1940s and 1950s. In the late 1950s, the actress played the second lead, Jane Stacyon, on the popular situation comedy series *My Friend Irma*, when the actress who originated the role, Cathy Lewis, was ill for a few months. In addition to her roles on radio, Joan Banks appeared in such feature films as *Cry Danger* (1951), *Bright Victory* (1951), *The Washington Story* (1952), and *Return to Peyton Place* (1961). On television, in addition to being a regular on Ann Sothern's *Private Secretary* series, she also played supporting roles on such programs as *Stars Over Hollywood, The Medic, Alfred Hitchcock Presents, The Goodyear Theatre, Perry Mason, Wanted: Dead or Alive, Hawaiian Eye, Hazel, National Velvet, Bewitched*, and many others. A longtime cigarette smoker, the actress, who was married to actor Frank Lovejoy for many years before he passed away in 1962, died of lung cancer at the age of 80 in 1998.

MOOREHEAD, AGNES B. 1906 – D. 1974 (MAGGIE)

Few actresses have had longer or more distinguished careers than Agnes Moorehead. Certainly one of the finest performers on radio, Miss Moorehead also graced the Broadway stage, and the motion picture and television industries as an actress; her face, as well as her voice, became familiar to millions of people during her long and successful career in show business. Before she became an actress, Agnes Moorehead, who was born in Clinton, Massachusetts, had earned a doctoral degree in literature. She subsequently attended the American Academy of Dramatic Arts in New York City, where she studied acting. Although her career began on the stage, Miss Moorehead first gained national recognition as a radio actress in the early 1930s and continued to work regularly on radio throughout the 1940s. She was heard on such memorable radio programs as Orson Welles' *Mercury Theater on the Air, The Shadow* (as The Shadow's girlfriend, Margo Lane from 1937 until 1940), *The Adventures of Mr. Meek*,

Actress Agnes Moorehead, who was one of the movies' and television's most successful character actresses, first became well known as a radio actress in the 1930s. She played Maggie on the radio adaptation of George McManus' *Bringing Up Father* in the 1940s, and was also featured as Min Gump on the radio adaptation of Sidney Smith's comic strip, *The Gumps*.

The Aldrich Family, The Ben Bernie Show, The Phil Baker Show, This Day is Ours, Brenda Curtis, Life Begins, The March of Time Quiz, Bulldog Drummond, The Cavalcade of America, Dot and Will, Sherlock Holmes, Way Down East, The Mighty Show, The Orange Lantern, The Story of Bess Johnson, and many other programs. The actress was also the leading female character on three radio adaptations of popular comic strips, *Bringing Up Father* (as Maggie), *The Gumps* (as Min Gump) and *Terry and the Pirates* (as the treacherous Eurasian villainess, the Dragon Lady). Her most memorable radio performance, however, was given on *Suspense*, where she played the rich, whining invalid who, when alone in her New York City apartment, overhears a murder being planned on the telephone and gradually realizes that she is the intended victim. The radio play was Lucille Fletcher's "Sorry, Wrong Number." Agnes Moorehead's performance was so popular with the public that it was repeated seven times on *Suspense*. Miss Moorehead was also heard regularly on the long-running radio series *Mayor of the Town*, which was on the air from 1942 until 1949, and starred film actor Lionel Barrymore as the Mayor. On the *Mayor of the Town,* Moorehead played the role of the Mayor's housekeeper, Marilly. After her film debut in Orson Welles' *Citizen Kane* in 1941, Miss Moorehead appeared in many other memorable films including *The Magnificent Ambersons* (1942), *Journey Into Fear* (1942), *Jane Eyre* (1944), *Dragon Seed* (1944), *Since You Went Away* (1944), *Mrs. Parkington* (1944), *Tomorrow, the World!* (1944), *Our Vines Have Tender Grapes* (1945), *Dark Passage* (1947), *Summer Holiday* (1948), *Johnny Belinda* (1948), *Caged* (1950), *Show Boat* (1951), *The Story of Three Loves* (1953), *Magnificent Obsession* (1954), *The Conqueror* (1956), *The Swan* (1956), *The Revolt of Mamie Stover* (1956), *Raintree County* (1957), *The Bat* (1959), *Pollyanna* (1960), *How the West Was Won* (1962), *Hush...Hush, Sweet Charlotte* (1964), *Night of Terror* (1972), and many others, and she provided the voice for the character of the Goose in the animated film *Charlotte's Web*. On television, she is best remembered for playing Elizabeth Montgomery's mother, Endora, on the *Bewitched* series from 1964 until 1972. She was also featured on such television series as *Climax, Marcus Welby, MD, Matinee Theater, Love, American Style, Wagon Train, Playhouse 90, General Electric Theater, The Rebel, The Millionaire, Rawhide, The Twilight Zone, Burke's Law, The Wild, Wild West, The Virginian,* and *Night Gallery*. On the Broadway stage, the actress received critical acclaim for her performance in a staged reading of George Bernard Shaw's *Don Juan in Hell*, which also starred Charles Laughton and Tyrone Power. She was also featured in the stage version of the musical film *Gigi* on Broadway. Shortly before her death in 1974, Agnes Moorehead returned to the medium that had first brought her to the attention of the public – radio – when she was heard on Himan Brown's

CBS Mystery Theater series, which was a valiant, albeit unsuccessful, attempt to bring radio drama back to the airwaves.

O'MALLEY, NEILL B. CIRCA 1890 – D CIRCA 1960 (JIGGS)

The Irish/American bricklayer-turned-millionaire, Jiggs, on the *Bringing Up Father* radio series was originally played by actor Neill O'Malley when the series was first heard in 1941. O'Malley was primarily a character actor on the stage and was featured in such Broadway plays as *Easy Come, Easy Go* (1925), *Rendezvous* (1932), *Is Life Worth Living?* (1933), *Gentlewoman* (1934), *Stevedore* (1934), *Bury the Dead* (1936), *200 Were Chosen* (1938) and *Command Decision* (1948). O'Malley was also frequently seen in various regional theater productions throughout the 1920s, 1930s and 1940s. From the short excerpt from the *Bringing Up Father* radio program that this author heard, O'Malley was not a very effective Jiggs. His performance seemed to be more suitable for the stage than radio. He had given better radio performances on the *Bobby Benson's Adventures* series playing Tex Mason, who was originally called "Buck Mason" on that series, and on the *Howie Wing* series, playing Captain Harvey, in the 1930s. O'Malley was replaced as Jiggs, shortly before the series was canceled, by actor Mark Smith. There is no known recorded evidence to judge just how effective Smith was in the role of Jiggs.

BUCK ROGERS IN THE 25TH CENTURY

Buck Rogers in the 25th Century first appeared as a short story in *Amazing Stories* magazine in August 1918. Originally, the Buck Rogers character was called "Anthony Rogers," and he was the main character in a story written by Phillip Francis Nowlan that was titled "Armageddon 2419 AD." The story attracted the attention of newspaper syndicator John F. Dille, who became fascinated with the idea of a science fiction tale set in the distant future. Dille commissioned its creator, Phillip Nowlan, to adapt his short story into a comic strip. Although he loved the original story, Dille did not think the name of its main character sounded quite

After he became famous in the popular Dick Calkins' comic strip and comic books, Buck Rogers became the main character in a children's adventure series on radio.

right for a space traveling hero of the future, and he suggested that "Anthony" be changed to "Buck." Dille then hired artist Richard "Dick" Calkins to draw the new comic strip. Dick Calkins (1895 – 1965), who had studied at the Chicago Art Institute, got his first job as a professional artist drawing cartoons for the *Detroit Free Press*. In 1917, Dick was hired to be a staff artist at the *Chicago Examiner* newspaper, but his career was cut short when World War I broke out and he enlisted in the United States Army as an Air Service lieutenant. In 1919, Calkins returned to civilian life and went back to work as an artist for John F. Dille, who asked him to draw the new *Buck Rogers* comic strip for his newspapers. Nowlan continued to write the storylines for the new comic strip. That same year, Calkins was also working on a comic strip called *Skyroads* with writer Leslter J. Maitland. In 1940, when Phil Nowlan died, Calkins began to supply both the drawings and the storylines for the *Buck Rogers* comic strip, but he suddenly quit the series after a disagreement with his employer, John Dille. Calkins then began to write and draw a new comic strip he had created, *Red Ryder*, which he continued to draw until he retired in 1947. One of the artists who drew the *Buck Rogers in the 25th Century* comic strip, after Calkins dropped it, was Frank Frazetta. Frazetta is considered to be one of the best cartoonist/artists in the world by most authorities, and had begun his art career at 17 as an assistant to science fiction artist John Guinta. He was the "ghost artist" for several of the most famous comic strips in America after he drew the *Buck Rogers* comic strip and comic books, such as *Li'l Abner* and *Flash Gordon*. He was also the major artist who drew the comic book adaptation of the *Gangbusters* radio series, which was published by DC Comics. In the 1940s, Frazetta worked on the comic strip *Shining Knight,* and in 1952 and 1954 he created *Thun'da* and *Squeeze Play* for the comics. In 1966, Frank Frazetta won the Hugo Award as "Finest Illustrator." His art work for *Buck Rogers in the 25th Century* is considered to be among the best examples of science fiction cartoon art.

In the early *Buck Rogers in the 25th Century* comic strips, it was explained that Buck was a 20th Century American who had been overcome by fumes while trapped in a mine cave-in. The gas had a preservative, rather than a deadly, effect and Buck woke up from his deep sleep in the caved-in tunnel 500 years later. The America he found himself in had been overrun by wicked Asians, and Buck was recruited to fight them in a resistance force composed of other Americans from the future. Among the characters who Buck became involved with, in this America-of-the-future, was the lovely Wilma Deering and the scientist, Dr. Huer. In time, the Asian evildoers were overthrown, but Buck's adventures continued in a series of science fiction adventures, when he became a rocket ship pilot. Space travel was nothing new to readers of science fiction stories, but it was entirely new to comic strips; and within a short period of time the *Buck Rogers in the 25th Century* daily strip had become one of America's favorites. It was *Buck Rogers* that first introduced such things as rocket ships, robots, and ray guns to millions of people who had never even heard of "science fiction" before. Many imitators of *Buck Rogers in the 25th Century* soon followed, including such popular comic strips as *Flash Gordon* and *Brick Bradford*. Buck became one of the early stars of the *Famous Funnies* comic book along with such comic strip favorites as *Mutt and Jeff* and *Joe Palooka*. Eventually, in the late 1950s, veteran comic strip artist George Tuska took over the strip and the series continued to appear as a daily comic strip in various newspapers until 1967, when it was canceled. By that time, *Buck Rogers* and his fellow space travelers had, unfortunately, become tired, miserable imitations of themselves and readers had lost interest in the once popular comic strip.

In 1934, at the beginning of its comic strip popularity, a ten-minute *Buck Rogers in the 25th Century* short subject film was released. The inexpensive, poorly written film starred John Dille, Jr., the son of the newspaper syndicator who first published the *Buck Rogers* comic strip. It was universally panned by film critics and all but ignored by movie goers. Buster Crabbe played Buck Rogers in a fairly successful Universal 12-episode serial in 1939, but Crabbe had more success portraying Flash Gordon in three serials. Buck Rogers was first seen on television in a short-lived, one-season show on ABC in 1950; Kem Dibbs and Robert Pastene both played Buck, with Lou Prentis as Wilma Deering and Harry Southern as Dr. Huer. A feature film and a subsequent weekly series was seen on television in 1979, and the series, which starred Gil Gerard as Buck, Erin Gray as Wilma Deering and Tim O'Connor as Dr. Huer, remained on the air until 1981.

It was, however, the radio adaptation of the *Buck Rogers* comic strip, first heard in 1932, that enjoyed the longest other-than-comic-strip tenure in the performing arts. The program was on the air for fifteen minutes a day, four days a week, Monday through Thursday, and starred several actors as Buck over the years. Matt Crowley, Curtis Arnall, Carl Frank and John Larkin all played the role of Buck on the radio series at one time or another. Also heard on the program were Adele Ronson as Wilma Deering, Edgar Stehli as Dr. Huer, Ronald Liss as Buddy, Elaine Melchoir as Ardala, and William Shelley, Don Ocko, and Arthur Vinton, as the villainous Killer Kane. Also heard on the series at various times were Walter Tetley, Junius Matthews, Everett Sloane, Paul Stewart, Henry Gurvey, Dwight Weist, Walter Greasa, Fred Uttal, Walter Vaughn, Alice Frost, Jack Rosleigh, Joe Granby, Vicki Vola, John Monks, Frank Readick and Eustace Wyatt, among others. The show's announcers were Fred Uttal, Paul Douglas and Jack Johnstone. The plots of the radio adventures were similar to the comic strip stories with Buck, Wilma, and Dr. Huer

(Credit: Photofest)

Actor Matt Crowley, who played Buck Rogers on radio, is seen looking more like an elf than a sci-fi action hero in this publicity photo that was taken for the *Buck Rogers in the 25th Century* radio program.

attempting to keep the world of the future from destroying itself. The effective sound effects, created by using various electrical devices including a Shick electric razor, effectively brought death rays, incendiary missiles, gamma bombs, and even a mechanical mole that could burrow deep into the Earth, into millions of homes all across America. The program offered a wide variety of premiums that young listeners could obtain from the show's sponsor, including a map of the planets and cardboard space helmets, by sending in a metal seal from a can of Cocomalt, the show's sponsor. The radio series was written by Joe A. Gross, Albert G. Miller and Dick Calkins. Jack Johnstone was the series' longtime producer and director.

BUCK ROGERS IN THE 25TH CENTURY RADIO SERIES PERFORMERS

ARNALL, CURTIS B. 1898 – D. 1964 (BUCK ROGERS)

Before playing science fiction hero *Buck Rogers on Buck Rogers in the 25th Century*, actor Curtis Arnall was active on the stage and performed in many local amateur and professional productions in repertory in both California and Hawaii. As a young man, Arnall joined Mabel Talliferos' acting troupe in Honolulu, which brought him to the mainland in the 1920s, and he began to study acting at the famed Pasadena Playhouse in California. Aranll then went to New York, determined to work on Broadway. He obtained a role in the 1930 production, *Elizabeth the Queen* on Broadway and then was seen in the play *Devil in the Wind* in 1931. In 1931, while he was acting on Broadway,

Arnall took a job on a radio show to supplement his income as an actor. The role was the major role of Buck Rogers on a new CBS children's adventure series. Arnall remained with the radio series for a few years. Arnall also had the title role on the radio soap opera, *Red Davis*, which evolved into the popular, long-running series *Pepper Young's Family* after he left the series. In addition to *Buck Rogers* and *Red Davis,* Curtis Arnall was also featured on such radio programs as *Dick Tracy, Just Plain Bill* and *One Man's Family*, among others; but his heart was always in the theater. After radio drama's untimely demise in the late 1950s, the actor returned to the stage, which was his first love.

CROWLEY, MATT (SEE *JUNGLE JIM* FOR BIOGRAPHY)

LARKIN, JOHN B. 1912 – D. 1965 (BUCK ROGERS)

John Larkin was one of radio's and early television's most popular leading men. Larkin, who was born in Kansas City, Missouri, attended the University of Missouri. After he graduated from college, he went to Chicago, which, at the time, was the center of radio drama broadcasting, determined to become a radio actor. His strong, masculine baritone voice soon made him one of Chicago broadcasting's most sought after performers. Larkin was one of several actors who played Buck Rogers in the radio adaptation of the successful comic strip *Buck Rogers in the 25th Century,* and he also played Mark Trail, on the radio adaptation of the *Mark Trail* comic strip. The actor was also frequently heard on such Chicago-based radio shows as *The Chicago Theater of the Air, Helpmate, The Brighter Day,* and several other programs. In the late 1930s, he left Chicago and went to New York City, where he soon obtained roles on such important daytime soap opera series as *Backstage Wife, Lone Journey, Portia Faces Life, Ma Perkins, The Right to Happiness, The Road of Life, The Romance of Helen Trent, Perry Mason* (as Perry), and *Stepmother.* He was also heard on such evening programs as *The Radio City Playhouse* and *Under Arrest.* The actor also played numerous supporting roles on the radio adaptation of Chester Gould's *Dick Tracy* comic strip. As radio began to lose its hold on the nation as America's favorite home entertainment medium, Larkin made a successful transition to television and had major roles on such early TV series as *The Road of Life, Saints and Sinners,* and *Twelve O'Clock High.* He also played the major role of Mike Carr on the popular TV soap opera series *The Edge of Night* from 1956 until 1962, when illness forced him to leave the series. Before the actor died in 1965 at the age of 53, three films he had made after leaving *The Edge of Night* were released, *Seven Days in May, Those Callaways,* and *The Satan Bug.*

LISS, RONALD "RONNIE" B. 1930 – D. 1968 (BUDDY)

Another of the Golden Age of Radio's most popular juvenile performers was Ronald Liss, who was born in New York City. Liss began his professional acting career at the tender age of 7 on the *Peebles Takes Charge* and *Coast to Coast on a Bus* programs, and he became a regular cast member on Nila Mack's *Let's Pretend* children's fairy tale anthology show in 1939. As he grew older, he graduated from playing children's roles to playing teenagers on such programs as *Bright Horizon, Hilltop House, Portia Faces Life, Two on a Clue*, Fletcher Markle's *Studio One* and *Ford Theater* dramatic anthology series, and *Dimension X*. Liss is probably best remembered, however, for playing Batman's sidekick, Robin, on *The Adventures of Superman*, Scotty on *Mark Trail*, and Buddy on the *Buck Rogers in the 25th Century* series, which were all adapted for radio from popular comic strips and books. It has been reported, but not confirmed, that Ronald Liss died at the age of either 26 or 29 during the rebellious drug-culture years of the late 1960s.

RONSON, ADELE B. 1908 – D. 2000 (WILMA DEERING)

(Credit: Photofest)

One of radio's busiest actresses in the 1930s and 1940s, New York City native Adele Ronson attended Columbia University before deciding to become an actress. Miss Ronson appeared on Broadway between 1928 and 1930 in such plays as *Dorian Gray, The Legend of Leonora, Great Scott,* and *Gold Braid,* and she also had a major role in the exploitation film, *Her Unborn Child* (1930). In the early 1930s, Ronson began her radio acting career and played Wilma Deering on *Buck Rogers in the 25th Century,* a role she played until the show went off the air in 1947. She was also featured on such radio programs as *The Eno Crime Club, The Gibson Family, John's Other Wife, The March of Time Quiz, Meyer the Buyer,* and *We Love and Learn,* and many others.

In addition to playing Wilma Deering on the *Buck Rogers* radio series for many years, actress Adele Ronson was one of radio's busiest soap opera stars.

STEHLI, EDGAR B. 1884 – D. 1973 (DR. HUER)
Few actors enjoyed as long and distinguished a career as Edgar Stehli, who, for more than sixty years, was one of the busiest character actors in show business. Stehli's acting career included roles on the Broadway stage, on radio, in films, and on television. Edgar Stehli was born in Lyons, France and emigrated to the United States when he was a young man determined to become an actor. He made his Broadway debut in 1916 and was subsequently seen in over sixty plays on Broadway including *Six Who Pass, Those That Play the Clowns, While the Lentils Boil, He Who Gets Slapped, Hamlet, Eye on the Sparrow, Arsenic and Old Lace, The Happy Time, Mid-Summer* and *The Devils*, to name just a few. On radio, Stehli played Dr. Huer for many years on the *Buck Rogers in the 25th Century* radio serial drama. He was also featured on such radio programs as *The Crime Doctor* (playing D. A. Miller), *The Eternal Life, Life Begins, Thanks for Tomorrow, When a Girl Marries*, and many other series. Stehli's film work included roles in *Boomerang* (1947), *The Cobweb* (1955), *How to Steal the World* (1966), and *Loving* (1970). On television, he had supporting roles on *Suspense, Philco Television Playhouse, Kraft Television Theatre, Goodyear Playhouse, Armstrong Circle Theater, Lights Out, Studio One, Gunsmoke, The Restless Gun, Sugarfoot, Peter Gunn, Ben Casey, Dr. Kildare, I Spy*, and many other TV series.

BUSTER BROWN

One of the earliest comic strips to attract the attention of the American public was *Buster Brown*, which first appeared in print in the *New York Herald* newspaper in 1902. The mischievous little boy, Buster Brown, was the creation of cartoonist Richard Felton Outcault (1863-1928), who had created the very first cartoon comic strip character to appear in a daily newspaper and Sunday supplement newspaper, *The Yellow Kid*. Before he drew this comic strip, Outcault had drawn gag cartoons for various magazines. *The Yellow Kid* was an overnight sensation, and soon everyone in the United States was talking about the little cartoon character and his amusing antics. The comic strip generated numerous merchandising by-products such as *Yellow Kid* figurines, books, games, and rings, which increased the profits of *The New York Herald*. *The Yellow Kid* made Richard Felton Outcault one of the very first nationally known cartoonists in the United States. In 1902, Outcault created a second comic strip character that appeared for *The New York Herald*, which he called *Buster Brown*. It became even more popular with the public than *The Yellow Kid*, but in 1906, Richard Outcault suddenly left *The New York Herald*, and his popular *Buster Brown* comic strip began to appear in publisher William Randolph Hearst's chain of newspapers. Hearst had been quick to realize the financial potential of such a successful cartoonist as Richard Outcault and lured him to his newspaper syndicate with a lucrative contract that promised to make him a very wealthy man. *The New York Herald* sued Hearst, but the courts ruled that comic strip characters could go wherever the cartoonist who created them decided to work. *The New York Herald,* however, was permitted to continue to publish their own version of the *Buster Brown* comic strip with another artist drawing it. The *Herald's* version of *Buster Brown* did not appear in that newspaper for very long because the public preferred Outcault's *Buster Brown* cartooning, and bought the Hearst newspapers to read Buster's daily adventures. Once again, hundreds of *Buster Brown* by-products surfaced, just as they had when *The Yellow Kid* was so successful, and a shoe manufacturing company even obtained the rights to use *Buster Brown* as its brand name. Millions more people became familiar with the *Buster Brown* character and *Buster Brown* shoes when the shoes were introduced to the public at the 1904 World's Fair. Both *The Yellow Kid* and *Buster Brown* became legends in the comic strip world, and gained Outcault a permanent place in the history of American Popular Arts. A third comic strip by Outcault, *Buddy Tucker,* published in 1905, failed to attract the attention of the public. Although his Yellow Kid comic strip was dropped in the early 1900s, Outcault continued to draw *Buster Brown* until 1921, when various other artists took over the drawing of the strip. Outcault died a very wealthy man in 1928.

What was it that appealed to the public about Outcault's *Buster Brown* character? Buster Brown was a rich little boy who was always getting into trouble for his mischievous ways. In spite of his bad-boy antics, the public adored Buster for his cute impishness and people began to buy the various newspapers the *Buster Brown* comic strip appeared in, just to keep in touch with what Buster Brown, his little sister Mary Jane, and Buster's dog, Tige (who is said to have been America's first talking pet), were up to each day. Tige, who was one of the strip's most popular characters, always commented on Buster's behavior, via ballooned comments that appeared above his head, but human characters in the comic strip never heard his comments. Each of Hearst's *Buster Brown's* Sunday color supplement comics ended in a homily, with Buster always promising that he would never again do what it was that had gotten him into trouble that week. Buster, who was the son of well-to-do parents, unlike many of the more déclassé ethnic characters who appeared in other comic strips of the day, continued to delight the general public until the late 1920s. It seems ordinary people liked knowing that the children of the rich and privileged members of society could be as mischievous as their own children.

In the 1920s, a series of *Buster Brown* silent film shorts were produced with child actor Arthur Trimble playing Buster. A popular radio series called *Buster*

Brown, which was sponsored by Buster Brown shoes, surfaced in 1929, but proved to be short-lived, remaining on the air for just a few months. In 1945, however, the Buster Brown character returned to the airwaves for a long run on NBC in *The Buster Brown Gang/Smilin' Ed McConnell Show*. This program starred singer and master raconteur Ed McConnell and his sidekick, Buster

"Smilin' Ed" McConnell was the host of radio's and TV's *Buster Brown Gang* children's show, which was on the air in the1930s into the 1950s. The Buster Brown character had first been introduced to the public in Richard Outcault's successful *Buster Brown* comic strip in 1906.

Brown, who was played by midget/actor Jerry Maren. The program was heard on Saturday mornings from 11:30 to12 noon and was broadcast from Hollywood in front of a large live audience of screaming and enthusiastic kids. McConnell sang simple little songs and introduced comedy sketches that featured such characters as "Froggie the Gremlin" and "Squeakie the Mouse." With Buster asking numerous questions and commenting on the proceedings, and Buster's dog, Tige, barking and panting, as voiced by actor Bud Tollefson, McConnell also narrated stories that centered around four young heroes: "Baba," an Arabian boy and his horse; "Ghangi," a Hundu boy who had a pet elephant named Teelah; "Little Fox," an American Indian boy; and "Kulah," a boy who had a Genie who came out of a jug as a pal. The four heroes were played, at various times, by child actors Bobby Ellis, Tommy Cook, Tommy

Bernard, Billy Roy, Jimmy Ogg and Peter Rankin. Lou Merrill played Kulah's "Jug-Genie." The series' announcer was Arch Presby and the radio program was produced by Frank Ferrin and written and directed by Hobart Donovan.

BUSTER BROWN GANG RADIO SERIES PERFORMERS

MAREN, JERRY B. 1920 (BUSTER BROWN)

Three-foot-four-inch Jerry Maren, who was born Gerald Marenghi in Boston, Massachusetts, had studied dancing, and decided, in 1938, that he wanted to become a professional performer. Jerry, who was at the time an eighteen-year-old midget, made his professional acting debut a year later in the Our Gang short, *Tiny Troubles* (1939). That same year, he played one of the Munchkins in MGM's classic film *The Wizard of Oz* and Maren also had a role *At the Circus* with the Marx Brothers. Throughout the 1940s, Jerry was one of the busiest midget actors in Hollywood. He had roles in *Maisie Was a Lady* (1941), *Show Business* (1944), *Duffy's Tavern* (1945), *Samson and Delilah* (1949), *Planet of the Apes* (1968), *Bigfoot* (1970), *Under the Rainbow* (1981) and *Spaceballs* (1987), to name just a few of the films he appeared in. He also played the popular comic strip-based character, Buster Brown, on the *Buster Brown Gang* radio program, as well as being seen as Buster in numerous print and television advertisements. Jerry was also active on television and was frequently seen on *The Beverly Hillbillies, Bewitched, Get Smart, Here's Lucy, The Odd Couple, The Twilight Zone, Seinfeld,* and many other TV series.

MCCONNELL, ED "SMILIN' ED" B. 1892 – D. 1954 (HOST)

Well known to radio listeners as "Smilin' Ed," Atlanta-born singer, writer, philosopher and children's show host Ed McConnell entered show business against his parents wishes after he graduated from college. The stage-struck young McConnell, who had been a singer with a group of evangelists, was drawn to vaudeville and went on tour with a troupe of variety performers as a singer and comedy sketch actor. Vaudeville led him to radio and in 1922, McConnell was singing and playing the banjo on a radio show of his own on WSB in Atlanta. He signed a contract to make recordings in Orlando, Florida, and was asked to go on the air to promote his records. McConnell enjoyed working on radio more than he did recording his songs, and so he signed a contract to host a daily radio program at the Orlando station that was promoting his recordings. This led to talk and interview shows on WSM, WWJ, and WLW in Florida. The local shows, which contained a good deal of homespun McConnell philosophy, attracted the attention of NBC network officials and McConnell was given a contract by NBC to host a national program called *The Singing Philosopher.* McConnell's cozy, comfortable on-air-manner made him popular with listeners and NBC officials decided that he would make a perfect host for a regular children's program that was to be sponsored by the Buster Brown shoe company called the *Buster Brown Gang*. Buster Brown was the same mischievous boy, then played by midget Jerry Maren, who had been seen in Richard Outcault's successful *Buster Brown* comic strip for many years, and was a familiar character to most Americans because his likeness had been used for years by the Buster Brown shoe company in their print ads. In 1950, McConnell and his radio program gang took the show to television, where it was retitled first *The Buster Brown TV Show With Smilin' Ed McConnell and the Buster Brown Gang*, then the simpler, *Smilin' Ed's Gang*. Puppets of his radio show gang were seen. It enjoyed a memorable Saturday morning run on television. For a short time, the show was renamed Andy's Gang, when comic actor Andy Devine took over the hosting duties, upon McConnell's death in 1954.

Captain Midnight

Before he became a popular comic strip and comic book superhero, *Captain Midnight* was a very successful, fifteen-minute-a-day, five-day-a-week, radio adventure serial hero. The radio program was first heard on a local Mutual Broadcasting System station in Chicago in 1939. For a short time, *Captain Midnight* was heard on NBC as a national broadcast, and then it returned to the Mutual network as a nationally heard program. The radio series originally starred actor Ed Prentiss as Captain Midnight, and then Bill Bouchey for one year, with Prentiss returning to the role for next seven years, and finally, Paul Barnes, played the role until the series ended in 1949. The heroic Captain Midnight, who was identified as Agent SS1, was a member of the "Secret Squadron" of ace pilots who fought various evildoers. The series, which was sponsored nationally by Ovaltine, a chocolate "health" drink, was created for radio by Robert M. Burit and Wilfred G. Moore. The Captain Midnight character was, in reality, a World War I veteran named "Captain Albright," who served with a "secret" squadron of aviators, which was a covert operation sanctioned by the U. S. Government. The squadron fought subversives and tracked down spies and saboteurs. All of the Secret Squadron's pilots were adventurous men and women who were absolutely fearless in their desire to fight the bad guys. Fellow Secret Squadron

Ed Prentiss, seen above with actress Marilou Neumayer, was the original *Captain Midnight* on the popular children's radio adventure series.

(Credit: Photofest)

pilots, in addition to Captain Midnight, were: Agent SS3, Joyce Ramsey (also called "Patsy" at one time), who was played by actress Angeline Orr on the radio series, and then by Marilou Neumayer; Agent SS2, Chuck Ramsey,

Angeline Orr, Bill Bouchey, and Bill Rose, who played Joyce Ramsey (also called "Patsy" at one time), Captain Midnight, and Chuck on the *Captain Midnight* radio series in the early 1940s, are seen here in a publicity photo.

played by Bill Rose, and then by Jack Bivens and Johnny Coons; and Agent SS4, Icabod "Icky" Mudd, played by Hugh Studebaker, and then by Art Helm and Sherman Marks. Also heard on the radio series between 1939 and 1949 were: Boris Aplon, who played the villainous Ivan Shark; Rene Rodier and Son Grainger, who played Ivan's daughter, Fury; Earl George, who played Gardo; Marvin Miller, who played Rogart; Maurice Copeland, who played Dr. Glazer; and Olan Soule, who played Secret Squadron Agent SS11. The series' announcers were Pierre Andre, who had also introduced the *Little Orphan Annie* radio series for the program's sponsor, Ovaltine, and Don Gordon. *Captain Midnight's* directors over the years were Kirby Hawkins, Russell Young and Alan Wallace. Like Ovaltine's *Little Orphan Annie* program, the *Captain Midnight* became famous for the many premiums that could be obtained by listeners by sending in a label from a jar of Ovaltine and sometimes "a thin dime." These premiums included a Detect-O-Scope, a Code-O-Graph, a *Captain Midnight* watch, a flight patrol pin, a Secret Squadron Member Patch, a decoder-whistle and a *Captain Midnight* American Loyalty flag, to name just a few.

(Credit: Author's collection. © Whitman.)

"Captain Midnight!" Joyce exclaimed, "Look!"

Captain Midnight, first heard as a fifteen-minute a day, five-day-a-week children's adventure serial, became a comic book and comic strip character in the 1940s, due to his radio popularity.

Captain Midnight's first non-radio appearance was in a Big Little Book, published in 1941. That same year, the character made his comic book debut as a feature in Dell comics. In 1942, Columbia Pictures produced an adventure serial of fifteen episodes that featured the Captain and his Secret Squadron, and starred actor/stuntman Dave O'Brien as Captain Midnight. That same year, *Captain Midnight* was seen as a newspaper comic strip feature, continuing until 1945, and a comic book series, published by Fawcett Publishing Company, lasted from 1942 until 1948, with 67 issues being released. The character also appeared in issues #76 through #78 of Dell's *Popular Comics* series. Artists Leonard Frank, who drew the comic strip and comic book character for the longest period of time, and Clem Weis-Becker, Lincoln Cross and Al Bare were among the many cartoonists who drew the *Captain Midnight* character for the comics. The storylines for the comic strip and comic book versions of *Captain Midnight* were for the most part written by Otto O. Binder.

CAPTAIN MIDNIGHT RADIO SERIES MAJOR PERFORMERS

BOUCHEY, BILL B. 1907 – D. 1977 (CAPTAIN MIDNIGHT)

Actor Bill Bouchey, who was born in St. Clair, Michigan, was one of radio's busiest leading men. Bouchey played the title role of *Captain Midnight* on the popular radio adventure serial for several years in the 1940s. In addition, Bouchey, who had a deep, resonant, heroic-sounding voice, also played numerous husbands, boyfriends, and professional men on such daytime soap opera series as *Arnold Grimm's Daughter, The Barton Family, The Woman in White, Backstage Wife, Betty and Bob, The Guiding Light, The Right to Happiness, The Romance of Helen Trent, One Man's Family,* and *Kitty Keene*. He was also often featured on the popular *First Nighter* prime time radio drama series. Bouchey was also in more than 150 movies and television series between 1951 and 1977. He had supporting roles in such films as *Million Dollar Mermaid* (1952), *Pickup on South Street* (1953), *From Here to Eternity* (1953), *Executive Suite* (1954), *A Star is Born* (1954), *The Bridges of Toko-Ri* (1955), *The Long Gray Line* (1955), *The Spoilers* (1955), *The Last Hurrah* (1958), and *The Horse Soldiers* (1959). On television, he was seen on such TV series as *The Great Gildersleeve, Dragnet, General Electric Theater, A Letter to Loretta, You Are There, Have Gun, Will Travel, Sea Hunt, 77 Sunset Strip, Bat Masterson, Bonanza, Wagon Train, The Andy Griffith Show, Thriller, McHale's Navy, The Beverly Hillbillies, F Troop, The Munsters* and *Gunsmoke.*

MILLER, MARVIN B. 1913 – D. 1985 (ROGART)
Marvin Miller, who was born in St. Louis, Missouri, worked at his college's radio station as an announcer when he was a student at Washington University, and decided that when he graduated he would to become a professional radio announcer. Upon graduation, he got a job at radio station KMOV. In the late 1930s, Miller moved to Chicago and was soon heard as an announcer and an actor on most of the radio shows that originated in that city at that time including *The First Nighter, The Chicago Theater of the Air, Today's Children, The Woman in White, Jack Armstrong, The Guiding Light, Backstage Wife, Ma Perkins, The Affairs of Anthony, Captain Midnight, Harold Teen, Judy and Jane, Scattergood Baines, Lonely Woman, That Brewster Boy, The Buster Brown Gang,* and *The Romance of Helen Trent* (as Helen's love interest, Gil Whitney), and many others. In the early 1940s, Miller relocated to Los Angeles, where he continued to work on most of the radio shows were broadcast from Hollywood including *The Coronet Storyteller, The Whistler, The Andrews Sisters Show, The Billie Burke Show, Beulah, The Cisco Kid, A Date With Judy, One Man's Family, The Old Gold Show, The Railroad Hour, The Red Skelton Show, Stars Over Hollywood, The Don Ameche Show, Family Theater, The Dreft Star Playhouse, Irene Rich Dramas, Lassie,* and many, many others. It was on television in the late 1950s, however, that Marvin Miller became one of America's most recognized performers when he played the personal secretary who delivered one million dollars to some lucky, unsuspecting person on the popular series, *The Millionaire.* His voice was heard on such television shows as *Space Patrol* and the *Mr. Magoo* cartoon series, and he was seen on *The Jack Benny Show, Perry Mason, Make Room for Daddy, Adam-12, Mission: Impossible, Kolchak the Night Stalker, Wonder Woman,* and other TV series. Miller was often cast as Oriental characters in such films as *Blood on the Sun* (1945), *Peking Express* (1951), *The Golden Horde* (1951, as Genghis Khan), and *Hong Kong* (1952), but he also

played characters of other ethnic backgrounds in the films *Just Before Dawn* (1946), *Without Reservations* (1946), *Forbidden* (1953), *The Story of Mankind* (1957), *When the Girls Take Over* (1962), *The Naked Ape* (1973), *I Wonder Who's Killing Her Now* (1975), *Swing Shift* (1984), *Hell Squad* (1985), and numerous others.

PRENTISS, ED B. 1908 – D. 1992 (CAPTAIN MIDNIGHT)

For eleven years, from 1938 through 1949, actor Ed Prentiss played one of radio's most popular children's adventure show heroes, Captain Midnight. Prentiss, who was born in Chicago, Illinois, was one of that city's most successful radio actors throughout the 1930s and was featured on hundreds of radio programs that were broadcast from Chicago in those years, including *The Woman in White, The Romance of Helen Trent, Armstrong of the FBI, The General Mills Theater, Arnold Grimm's Daughter, The Barton Family, The Guiding Light, A Tale of Today, The Right to Happiness, Today's Children, Painted Dreams, Silver Eagle, Mountie,* and others. Beginning in the late 1940s, and throughout the 1950s, 1960s, and into the 1970s, Prentiss worked on television and in films. On early television, Prentiss was a regular on such series as *Action Autographs, Dr. Fix-um, The Majority Rules, The Guiding Light, As the World Turns,* and he played supporting roles on *Dragnet, Maverick, Cheyenne, Broken Arrow, 77 Sunset Strip, Perry Mason, A Letter to Loretta, Zane Grey Theater, Ben Casey, Laramie, Leave it to Beaver* and *F Troop*. The actor also appeared in such films as *Westbound* (1959), *Sunrise at Campobello* (1960), *Morning Star* (1965), *Project X* (1968), and *The Marriage of a Young Stockbroker* (1971). Prentiss played the regular, running-role of the Banker on the *Bonanza* TV series for the entire run of that series. Ed Prentiss retired from acting in the late 1970s and died at the age of 84 in Los Angeles.

SOULE, OLAN B. 1909 – D. 1994 (SS11)

One of the movies and television's most active character actors, Olan Soule was also one of radio's busiest leading men in the 1930s and 1940s. For many years, the thin, rather anemic-looking Soule played all of the leading male roles opposite actress Barbara Luddy on the weekly, half-hour dramas that were heard coming from the fictional "Little Theater Off Times Square" on the popular *First Nighter* radio program. Soule, who was one of Chicago's busiest radio actors in the 1930s, had a warm, attractive sounding baritone voice, and was often featured on such popular radio programs as *Bachelor Children, Captain Midnight* (as agent SS11), *Chandu the Magician, The Chicago Theater of the Air, The Couple Next Door, We Are Four, Grand Hotel, Houseboat Hannah, Jack Armstrong, Midstream, Today's Children,* and many other shows. Soule, who was born in La Harpe, Illinois, began his career as a performer with the touring *Jack Brooks' Tent Show* in the 1920s. In 1923, he became a radio actor and in 1933, he joined the cast of the *Little Orphan Annie* program, which had been adapted from the popular Harold Gray comic strip, playing the character of Aha, the Chinese cook. In 1943, Soule moved to Los Angeles, where he became the leading male actor on the *First Nighter* radio program, on which he performed from 1943 until 1952. He was also heard on many other Hollywood-based radio shows including *Grand Marquee*, another dramatic anthology series. As early as 1949, Soule made a successful transition from radio to films and television. Among the many films in which he appeared: *Beyond the Forest* (1949), *Ma and Pa Kettle Go to Town* (1950), *You Never Can Tell* (1951), *Monkey Business* (1952), *Call Me Madam* (1953), *Prince of Players* (1955), *Queen Bee* (1955), *North by Northwest* (1959), *Days of Wine and Roses* (1962), *The Towering Inferno* (1974), *Homicide* (1991), and others. On television, he was featured on such series as *Captain Midnight, Arnie, Dragnet* (as a regular), *The Millionaire, Front Row Center, Alfred Hitchcock Presents, You Are There, Mister Ed, Mayberry, R.F.D.* (as a regular), *Mission: Impossible, Ellery Queen, Battlestar Gallactica, Little House on the Prairie, Gunsmoke,* and practically every other TV series that was produced in Hollywood between 1950 and 1994, when the actor, who was a lifelong cigarette smoker, died of lung cancer at the age of 85.

(Credit: Photofest)

Olan Soule was one of the radio's busiest actors. One of his first roles on radio was SS-11 on the *Captain Midnight* radio series.

CHARLIE CHAN

Novelist Earl Derr Biggers' Oriental Hawaiian private detective, Charlie Chan, was the main character in Biggers' successful mystery novels before he was featured in a series of films, comic books and comic strips, as well as on several radio programs.

Earl Derr Biggers' private detective, *Charlie Chan*, first appeared in print in a mystery novel in 1925, and almost overnight became one of the world's most popular fictional detectives and the main character in a series of subsequent *Charlie Chan* mysteries. Biggers' *Charlie Chan* character, who was of Chinese extraction, was a private detective whose home base was Honolulu, Hawaii. Charlie had a wife and a very large family who lived in Honolulu, but Charlie was an internationally famous PI, with a reputation for solving difficult crimes, and therefore he traveled all over the world investigating cases for his various clients. Charlie's assistant and constant companion, was his firstborn son, Lee Chan, who he called his "Number One Son." Over the years, in addition to his appearances in Biggers' novels, Charlie Chan was the main character in the numerous film adaptations. At different times Charlie was played by actors Warner Oland, Sidney Toler and Roland Winters in the film versions produced by 20th Century-Fox and Monogram. Charlie was also the hero of several radio adaptations of Biggers' novels, and was also the main character in a short-lived 1958 television series that starred J. Carrol Naish as Chan, and the Hanna-Barbera cartoon, *The Amazing Chan and The Chan Clan,* which ran on CBS from 1972 until 1974, with Keye Luke ("Number One Son" in several of the Chan movies) voicing Charlie Chan. Biggers' novels are still in print in the 21st Century, almost eighty years after they were first published, which certainly attests to the character's perennial appeal to the public.

On October 30, 1938, *Charlie Chan* was first seen as a Sunday comic strip feature in several newspapers in the U. S. The comic strip was drawn by the talented artist Alfred Andriola. Andriola (1912 – 1983), who knew from childhood that he wanted to be an artist, was thirty years old and working in a newspaper office when he decided to apply for a job as a cartoonist at a studio that produced comic strips. The studio liked Andriola's art portfolio and hired him to assist artist Milton Caniff with his drawing of the popular *Terry and the Pirates* comic strip panels. Andriola also drew the *Dan Dunn* and *It's Me Dilly* comic strips for a while. The *Charlie Chan* Sunday comic strip contained the same humor and astute intelligence that the original *Charlie Chan* novels featured and Andriola's wonderful artwork was first-rate as well. The original comic strip ran in various newspapers' Sunday supplement comics sections from October 30, 1938 well into the 1940s. Andriola also drew a *Charlie Chan* comic book series for Quality Comics, as well as for various other publishers in the early 1940s. A full year of *Charlie Chan* Sunday supplement comic strips, originally published from October 30, 1938 through November 13, 1939, was recently published in a large trade paperback edition, released by the Pacific Comics Club.

A sample Sunday *Charlie Chan* comic strip is pictured above.

(Credit: Author's collection. © Quality Comics.)

In 1932, long before *Charlie Chan* appeared in comic strip or comic book form, the first *Charlie Chan* radio series was heard on the NBC Blue network. The series starred actor Walter Connolly as Charlie and featured Leon Janney as his Number One Son, Lee Chan. *Charlie Chan* was the same Oriental private detective that solved every crime he investigated, just as he did in the Biggers novels and Andriola's comic strips, and remained on radio on and off from 1932 until 1948. Walter Connolly, Santos Ortega and Ed Begley all played the Chan role at different times, and all three actors often quoted ancient Oriental proverbs to his clients and son. The radio series was produced and directed by Alfred Besser and Chick Vincent at different times, and the various episodes for the series were written by Bester, John Cole, Judith Bublick and James Erthein.

CHARLIE CHAN RADIO SERIES PERFORMERS

BEGLEY SR., ED B. 1901 – D. 1970 (CHARLIE CHAN)

Although two other actors, Walter Connolly and Santos Ortega, also played the part of Chinese private detective Charlie Chan on radio, actor Ed Begley played the role for the longest period of time and is perhaps the best remembered Charlie Chan on radio. Begley, who was born in Hartford, Connecticut, began his acting career when he was a child and appeared on the Broadway stage in such productions as *The Red Mill* and *The Passing Show* of 1913. As a young man, he appeared on Broadway in *Ewind of the Hills* and *Land of Flames*, and in the early 1930s, Begley began to work on radio and soon became one of that medium's busiest character actors. Throughout the 1930s, 1940s, and 1950s, Begley was a regularly featured actor on such radio programs as *The Aldrich Family*, *Stella Dallas*, *Joyce Jordan*, *Girl Intern*, *Big Sister*, *The Fat Man*, *Life Can Be Beautiful*, *Ethel and Albert*, *The Mysterious Traveler*, *The Saint*, *Richard Diamond*, and *Private Investigator*.

In addition to his work on radio, Begley continued to appear on the Broadway stage and was featured in the plays *All My Sons*, *Inherit the Wind*, and *Zelda*, during these years. The actor was also active in films and on television and had important roles in such films as *Boomerang*, *Sorry, Wrong Number*, *The Great Gatsby*, *12 Angry Men*, *Sweet Bird of Youth*, and on television in *Armstrong Circle Theater*, *Lights Out*, *Goodyear Television Playhouse*, *Robert Montgomery Presents*, *Kraft Television Theatre*, *The Alcoa Hour*, *Ben Casey*, *The Dick Powell Show*, *Naked City*, *Route 66*, *Burke's Law*, *Wagon Train*, *Dr. Kildare*, *Bonanza*, and *Gunsmoke*.

ORTEGA, SANTOS B. 1899 – D. 1976 (CHARLIE CHAN)

New York City-born actor Santos Ortega was the last actor to play *Charlie Chan* on radio. In addition to playing Charlie Chan on radio, Ortega was also a frequent performer on *The Adventures of Superman* radio series and was often heard on such diverse radio series as *This is Your FBI*, *The Man I Married*, *The Adventures of Nero Wolfe* (as Nero Wolfe), *Bright Horizon*, *Bulldog Drummond* (as Bulldog Drummond), *Dimension X*, *Big Sister*, *Hannibal Cobb* (as Hannibal Cobb), *Quick As a Flash*, *Ellery Queen* (as Ellery's police inspector/father), *Portia Faces Life*, *Gangbusters*, *Myrt and Marge*, and many, many other radio programs. Ortega was also featured as Will "Grandpa" Hughes on the *As The World Turns* television soap opera series from 1956 until 1976, and was also frequently seen on the *Studio One* dramatic anthology TV series, as well as many other TV series.

CHARLIE MCCARTHY
(ALSO THE EDGAR BERGEN/CHARLIE MCCARTHY SHOW)

One of the most fondly remembered programs of Radio's Golden Age is *The Edgar Bergen/Charlie McCarthy Show*. Bergen was a ventriloquist and Charlie McCarthy was the name of his dummy. As strange as it may seem to have a "dummy" (a doll with a moveable mouth) as one of the "stars" of a nonvisual radio program, the show worked. Millions of people enthusiastically tuned in to hear Edgar Bergen's, and especially Charlie's, voices each week. Bergen's two voices…his own mellow voice and the high, squeaky voice he used for Charlie…proved to be an irresistible combination to radio comedy show listeners. Edgar Bergen began his career as a ventriloquist in vaudeville and soon after he made his stage debut, he had become a headlining act. Bergen toured the entire country and in 1936, he was asked to make a guest starring appearance on singer Rudy Vallee's popular *Fleischmann's Yeast Hour* radio variety show. Bergen

Edgar Bergen's "Charlie McCarthy" character, seen here as he appeared in a popular comic strip and comic book series, first appeared on the vaudeville stage and was eventually heard on the very successful Edgar Bergen/Charlie McCarthy radio program, as well as seen in films and on television.

and his dummy, Charlie McCarthy, were an immediate hit on radio and became semi-regulars on Vallee's show. In 1937, Bergen was delighted when he was asked to become the star of NBC's *The Chase and Sanborn Hour*, which was hosted by Don Ameche. A clever advertising campaign conducted by NBC soon let everyone in America know what Bergen and his dummy, Charlie McCarthy, with his top hat, tuxedo and monocle in one eye, looked like. Eventually The Chase and Sanborn Hour changed its name to *The Edgar Bergen/Charlie McCarthy Show*, and Don Ameche left the show to concentrate on a career as a motion picture star. The clever, wicked playboy Charlie was

Actress Elvia Allman, who was one of radio's busiest performers, is seen with Charlie McCarthy and Edgar Bergen during a rehearsal for the *Edgar Bergen/Charlie McCarthy Chase and Sanborn Hour* show in the early 1940s.

an irreverent wise guy who exchanged quips with such big name movie stars of the 1930s as W. C. Fields and Mae West, and also flirted on the air with such Hollywood glamour girls of the 1930s and 1940s as Deanna Durbin, Lana Turner, Rita Hayworth, and Dorothy Lamour. By the end of the 1930s, Bergen and Charlie had become the stars of several films themselves and Charlie's image was seen on spoons, cups, dolls, paper dolls, dummies for budding ventriloquists, games, comic books and a comic strip.

In 1938, artist Carl Buettner, who drew comic book and comic strip versions of Walt Disney's characters such as *Dumbo, Bambi,* and *Snow White and the Seven Dwarfs,* met ventriloquist Edgar Bergen, who asked him to take over the drawing of the *Charlie McCarthy* comic strip and comic books, which were already being marketed and drawn by several other artists. Carl Buettner (1903-1965), who was born in Minneapolis, Minnesota and was of German/American parentage, studied at the Federal School of Art in the late 1920s and early 1930s. In 1935, Buettner drew illustrations and cartoons for the *Captain Billy's Whiz Bang* magazine. In the late 1930s, Buettner moved to California and was an artist at the Walt Disney Studios for several years before joining former Disney artists Hugh Harman and Rudolph Ising at their animation studio. It was in 1938 that Buettner took over the drawing of the syndicated comic strip version of Bergen's celebrated Charlie McCarthy character, sometimes sharing his duties with artist Charles Craig, with whom he would later create the short-lived *Hollywood Hams* cartoon series. In 1942, Buettner and Craig became artists for the Western Publishing Company and drew comic books of popular Warner Brothers film cartoon characters. Buettner remained active as a comic book artist until his death in 1965 at the age of 62. The original *Charlie McCarthy* comic book series had been published by the Whitman Publishing Company, who called it, "the only 'living' comic book character!" All subsequent *Charlie McCarthy* comic books were published by Dell in the late 1930s and throughout the 1940s and Dell published a special issue (#527) of the *Charlie McCarthy* comic book in 1953. Two of the most popular *Charlie McCarthy* comics were published by Dell, and they have become collectors' items, "Charlie McCarthy and the Twenty Thieves" and "Charlie McCarthy and the Haunted Hideout."

EDGAR BERGEN/CHARLIE MCCARTHY RADIO SERIES PERFORMER

BERGEN, EDGAR B. 1903 – D. 1978 (HIMSELF/CHARLIE MCCARTHY)

Although he created the actual ventriloquist's dummy, Charlie McCarthy, and was that character's voice on the stage, in films, and on radio and television for well over fifty years, ventriloquist/comedian Edgar Bergen did not draw Charlie when he became the main character of a popular comic book series and newspaper comic strip. In the artist Carl Buettner's comic book, Charlie was the same playboy, mischief–making, clever brat the public had grown to love over the years on the stage and radio. In the comic books, Buettner also drew the other dummies that were heard on the popular radio show and were also voiced by Edgar Bergen, the country bumpkin, Mortimer Snerd, and the old maid, Effie Klinker. In the 1930s, 1940s, and 1950s, Edgar Bergen was the star of *The Fleischmann's Yeast Hour* and *The Chase and Sanborn Hour* on radio, which eventually became *The Edgar Bergen/Charlie McCarthy Show*. Certainly, Edgar Bergen's comedic vocal talents made his radio shows the most popular programs on the air for more than thirty years.

Edgar Bergen was born on a farm in Decatur, Michigan. He attended Northwestern University, where he became interested in performing and decided that when he graduated from college, he would become an entertainer. Bergen developed an act for the vaudeville stage that used his talent as a ventriloquist and several wooden dummies that he constructed himself. The dummy that became a favorite with audiences was a wisecracking, bon-vivant, boy-about-town, who always wore a monocle in one eye and a tuxedo and top hat was, of course, Charlie McCarthy. Before long, Bergen's act became one of the most popular attractions in vaudeville theaters all across the United States. In 1936, Bergen made several guest appearances on music and variety radio shows, and his success on that medium led to a show of his own. Listeners adored the wicked-tongued Charlie and his sharp wit, as voiced by Bergen, who was also a notorious flirt. At the height of his radio fame, Bergen and

Charlie also appeared in several motion pictures, including *A Letter of Introduction* (1938), *Charlie McCarthy, Detective* (1939) and *Here We Go Again* (1942). After his radio show left the air, Bergen proved himself to be a capable dramatic actor and appeared without Charlie in the film *I Remember Mama* in 1948. In the 1950s and 1960s, Bergen and Charlie, were also frequent guest stars on several of TV's most popular variety shows including Ed Sullivan's *Toast of the Town* program. Edgar Bergen retired in the late 1960s and lived a comfortable life in retirement until his death in 1978. He was survived by his wife of many years, Frances, and their daughter, actress Candace Bergen, who was born in 1946 and always joked that her "brother's" name was "Charlie" and that he had a room in the family home that was much bigger than hers.

THE CISCO KID

Short story writer O. Henry's "Robin Hood of the old Southwest," The Cisco Kid, was first heard as a radio series on the Mutual Broadcasting System's network of stations in 1943. It didn't take long for the series to become one of radio's most popular children's adventure serials. *The Cisco Kid* was a Mexican/American character whose Wild West activities involved saving damsels in distress, tracking down outlaws, and flirting with pretty girls. The series had two different openings. In one, Cisco's voice is saying, "Of all the senoritas I have known…you are the most beautiful," and then, as a devoted champion of the ladies, he sets about to assist the damsels in any way he can. The second opening had Pancho calling out, "Cisco, the sheriff he is getting closer," and then Cisco would answer, "This way, Pancho, follow!" *The Cisco Kid* and his faithful companion, Pan Pancho, remained on Mutual for two years using the first opening. It was off the air from 1944 until 1947, and then it resurfaced as a new, syndicated series. *The Cisco Kid* series remained on the air for nine more years, using the second opening, until 1956. During these years, *The Cisco Kid* was heard on various stations through the United States. Jackson Beck, and, for a short time, Jack Mather, played *The Cisco Kid*, and Louis Sorin, Harry Lang, and finally Mel Blanc played as Pancho. The shows' announcers were Marvin Miller, who also played various supporting roles on the series, and Michael Rye (a.k.a. Rye Billsbury), who frequently was also heard playing a supporting role on the show. *The Cisco Kid* was written by John Sinn, Ralph Rosenberg, and Kenny Lyons and directed by Jock MacGregor, Jeanne K. Harrison and Fred Levings.

In the1940's, and into the1950's, Dell published a *Cisco Kid* comic book series. *The Cisco Kid* comic strip was, for most of the years it was published, drawn by artists Jose Salinas, Alberto Giolitti, and Bob Jenney. Cartoonist Jose Luis Salinas (1908 – 1985) was born in Argentina, and as a young artist, he worked for some of that country's major advertising agencies before creating the comic strip *Hernan el Corsario*. This strip was followed by Salinas' *Captain Tormenta, La Costa de Marfil*, and *Los Mosqueteros*, which were very popular comic strips in Argentina and other Latin American countries. In 1949, Salinas moved to the United States and went to work as a staff artist for King Features Syndicate, where he drew the comic strip adaptation of writer O. Henry's short story character *The Cisco Kid* from 1951 until 1968. In 1968, Salinas left the comic strip and comic book field and began devoting his time to oil painting and magazine story illustrations. *The Cisco Kid* comic strip and comic book series was then taken over by Italian artist, Alberto Giolitti (1923 – 1993), who immigrated to the United States in 1949. Giolitti drew *The Cisco Kid* comics for the Dell Publishing Company, which had taken over the character, after he drew the *Zorro* and *Tarzan* comics for Dell for a short time. In 1960, Giolitti moved back to his native Italy, where he founded Giolitti Studios, employing over fifty artists and producing hundreds of comic strip pages for Italian publications each month. *The Cisco Kid* was, in its later years, one of the King Feature's Syndicate's most popular comic strips. The character was first seen on screen in *In Old Arizona* (1928), which won actor Warner Baxter an Oscar for his portrayal of the Mexican bandit, and it was followed by numerous other films featuring The Cisco Kid. It was also seen as a television series in 1950, starring Duncan Renaldo. *The Cisco Kid* comic books, as drawn by various artists, still appear periodically on news stands throughout the country.

THE CISCO KID RADIO SERIES PERFORMER

BECK, JACKSON B. 1912 – D. 2004 (CISCO KID)

Jackson Beck, who was the son of silent film star Max Beck, was born in New York City. In the mid-1930s, after working for a short time as an elevator operator when he finished his schooling, Beck began his career in radio as a producer for radio stations WINS and WHN in New York. His deep, sonorous voice soon landed him work in front of the microphone as an announcer, and by the time he was 30, he had worked on practically every radio show produced in New York. Among the many radio programs on which he was either the announcer or an actor were *Death Valley Days, Easy Aces, The Witch's Tale, Dimension X, The FBI in Peace and War, The Mysterious Traveler, Big Sister, Grand Central Station, Life Can Be Beautiful, This Day Is Ours, The Shadow, Believe It Or Not, The Man I Married, The Man Behind the Gun, Myrt and Marge, Quick As a Flash*, and *Mystery Theater*. Beck also played the title roles on *The Cisco Kid* and *Philo Vance* radio series. Besides *The Cisco Kid*, among the other radio show adaptations of popular comic strips and comic books on which he

(Credit: Photofest)

One of radio's busiest radio announcers, Jackson Beck, played the title role on the *Cisco Kid* radio series. Beck's voice also became well known as the announcer on the very popular *Superman* radio program.

was featured were *Mark Trail* (as the show's announcer), *Popeye the Sailor* (as Bluto), *Hop Harrigan* (as Tank Tinker), and *The Adventures of Superman* (as the show's announcer).

After network radio drama disappeared from the airwaves in the early 1960s, Beck continued to remain active as a voice-over performer. He dubbed foreign films and provided voices for many animated characters. His voice also became famous as the spokesman for the Little Caesar pizza restaurant chain, Kellogg's Frosted Flakes, and many other products that were advertised on television and radio. Beck also remained active in The American Federation of Radio and Television Artists, the radio and TV actor's union, and was on that organization's Board of Directors for many years. Beck retired in the late 1990s.

Radio's Golden Age

Dan Dunn
(a.k.a Dan Dunn, Secret Operative #48)

The *Dan Dunn* comic strip first appeared in various Publisher's Syndicate newspapers throughout the country in 1933. The character was the creation of cartoonist Norman Marsh (1901–1981). The hero of the strip, *Dan Dunn*, was a U. S. Secret Service agent, who looked suspiciously like Chester Gould's police detective *Dick Tracy*, which had made its comic strip debut one year earlier, in 1931. Dan had the same profile as Tracy, wore the same kind of clothes, and used many of the same expressions that Tracy did. At the time *Dan Dunn* appeared on the scene, *Dick Tracy* had already become one of the most popular comic strips in the United States and cartoonist Norman Marsh simply sued Gould's *Dick Tracy* as his guide of *Dan Dunn*. Marsh had already "ripped off" the popular *Little Orphan Annie* comic strip character in 1929. Annie had first appeared in print in 1924. In his 1929 comic strip, which he called *Little Annie* Rooney, Marsh introduced a similar little poor girl heroine for King Features Syndicate. In his *Dan Dunn* comic strip, Dan had a dog companion, like

A promotional comic book for *Crackajack Funnies* featured several characters who were heard on the radio.

Annie, who Marsh called "Wolfe" and for the *Dan Dunn* strip, Marsh had Dan adopt a waif called "Babs," who wore an outfit that looked suspiciously like the clothes Little Orphan Annie wore. Little Orphan Annie had a red dress with a white collar, and so did Babs. Orphan Annie had a yellow dog named "Sandy" who was her constant companion. Babs had Dan's dog, Wolfe, and Babs and Wolfe often became the main characters in the *Dan Dunn* comic strip. At times, Dan wasn't seen on the strip for weeks on end and Babs and Wolfe dominated the story lines of the strip, thus capitalizing on the popularity of both the *Dick Tracy* and the *Little Orphan Annie* comic strips. In 1935, *Dan Dunn* appeared as a feature in the *Crackerjack Funnies* promotional giveaway comic book that also featured the *Buck Jones, G-Man, Clyde Beatty, The Nebbs, Major Hoople* and *Freckles* comic strip characters. Dunn was also featured in three Big Little Books between 1934 and 1940, and was also featured in two special issue magazines. In 1942, shortly after World War Two broke out, artist Norman Marsh, who drew the *Dan Dunn* comic strip, was drafted into military service. When he was discharged from the service in 1946, Marsh resumed his cartooning career but not with the *Dan Dunn* character. The new cartoon character he drew after the war was called "Danny

One needs only to glance at the above *Dan Dunn* comic strip panel to see just how much Norman Marsh's Dunn was influenced by Chester Gould's popular *Dick Tracy* comic strip character. Both had the same squared-jawed facial features and wore similar hats and coats.

Hale." The *Danny Hale* comic strip appeared in newspaper until 1962 but was not particularly popular with either the public or with newspaper comic strip syndicators. Marsh spent a good deal of time thereafter campaigning to have comic strips sold to independent newspapers, rather than sold to newspaper chains by comic strip syndicators. It was a losing battle. Marsh valiantly pursued his career as a cartoonist until, his death at the age of eighty in 1981.

Marsh's *Dan Dunn* was heard as a syndicated radio series called *Dan Dunn, Secret Operative #48*, in 1937. The radio series starred actor/announcer Lou Marcelle as Dan Dunn. Marcelle had previously been heard on the *Fu Manchu* radio adventure serial on the CBS network, playing the title character. On the fifteen minute, five-days-a-week syndicated radio series, Dan had a female partner Special Agent #185, Kay Fields, who was played by actress Lucille Meredith, who was also featured on CBS's *County Seat* drama series in 1938. Also frequently featured on the *Dan Dunn, Secret Operative #48* radio series were Gerald Mohn, Hans Conried, David Sterling, and Myron Gary. The radio *Dan Dunn* series' scripts were written by Maurice Zimm, and Paul and Ruth Henning. According to radio historian Jack French in his book *Private Eyelashes*, only four of the seventy-eight episodes of *Dan Dunn, Secret Operative #48* have survived and are being circulated among old time radio program collectors.

Dan Dunn Radio Series Performer

Marcelle, Lou b. 1909 – d. 1994 (Dan Dunn)

Radio actor and announcer Lou Marcelle entered radio shortly after he graduated from college in the late 1920s. His most significant radio role was as *Dan Dunn* on the syndicated radio adaptation of Norman Marsh's comic strip. Marcelle was also featured on the *Fu Manchu* radio series, among other programs, and his voice narrated the opening of the classic film, *Casablanca*. in the early 1940s. Throughout the 1940s, Lou Marcelle's voice was also heard as the narrator and announcer for hundreds of documentaries and short subject films and he was also heard narrating in the feature films *Cross Country Detours* (1940), *Background to Danger* (1943), *Thank Your Lucky Stars* (1943), *Wagon Wheels* (1943), *Destination Tokyo* (1943), *The Doughgirls* (1944), and *Musical Moveland* (1944). Lou Marcelle appeared on the screen in the feature films *Never Say Goodbye* (1946), *Riders of the Pony Express* (1949), and he was also seen as a television announcer in the film *Perfect Strangers* (1950), before departing the show business spotlight in the early 1950s to work in the private sector.

Dick Tracy

(Credit: Author's collection. © Tribune Media Services, Inc.)

Chester Gould's comic strip character, Dick Tracy, became one of America's favorite fictional heroes and was not only seen in the comics but appeared in films and on TV and was the main character on a long-running radio series which was on the air from 1935 until 1948.

Chester Gould's *Dick Tracy* made its debut as a newspaper comic strip feature in 1931 and within a year, it had become America's favorite daily newspaper and Sunday supplement favorites. Cartoonist Chester Gould was born in Pawnee, Oklahoma and his first commercial illustrations were published in local newspapers in Pawnee when he was seven years old. When he was nineteen, Gould was a student at Oklahoma A&M, but left this college to attend Northwestern University in Chicago in 1921. After he graduated from Northwestern in 1924, Gould got a job as a cartoonist with the Hearst Syndicate newspapers drawing several comic strips including *The Girlfriend*, which became one of the most popular comic strip features in Hearst's Chicago Tribune newspaper. At the time, mobsters like Al Capone, John Dillinger, and Bonnie and Clyde, had become well known, almost heroic characters to the public and many of these criminals were as famous as stars of the silver screen and the world of politics. Gould decided that it might be a good idea to do something to dispel the positive images the public was having of criminals by drawing a comic strip that featured a hero who brought down the crooks and exposed them for what they really were, evil-doers. Gould showed his new comic strip idea, which he called *Plainsclothes Tracy,* to his editor at the *Chicago Tribune,* Joseph Patterson, who liked the idea but suggested that Gould should change the detective's name to "Dick Tracy," "Dick" being a nickname that was used for detectives at the time. The comic strip was an overnight sensation and soon various imitators began to appear on the scene including *Dan Dunn* and *Red Barry,* who, in spite of their coat-tail popularity, couldn't hold a handle to Gould's *Tracy*. The *Dick Tracy* comic strip, and a later *Dick Tracy* comic book series, centered around the police detective and his tireless campaign to rid the world of various oddball criminal elements. The strip continued to delight comic strip and comic book readers for the next seventy-plus years, and it is still being seen in newspapers throughout the United States. In the strip, Tracy was surrounded by a group of cohorts that included fellow-detective, Pat Patton, his girlfriend, newspaper reporter, Tess Trueheart, his nephew Junior Tracy, a ham actor named "Vitamin Flintheart," the sweet, young Snowflake, the long, gray-haired harridan, Gravel Gertie, the flea ridden vagrant, B. O. Plenty, and later, Gertie and B.O's darling daughter, "Sparkle" Plenty, who was given her name by a fan in a contest run by the comic strip's publishers. Also appearing in the strip were a weird assortment of strange looking crooks who Tracy and his friends brought to justice, included such oddball evil-doers as the rodent-like Mole, the shifty-eyed Flattop, Shakey, Pruneface, Little Face Finney, the Brow, the Blank, Pear Shape, Boris Arson, Stooge Viller, Doc Hump, BB Eyes, and many others. These villains kept people breathlessly waiting for each installment of the *Dick Tracy* daily comic strip panel to appear as they eagerly awaited the apprehension of each of the bad guys. Even though the *Dick Tracy* character had several imitators over the years including *Secret Agent Dan Dunn,* as stated above, it was Tracy who remained America's favorite over the years. Chester

By 1962, the *Dick Tracy* comic strip had begun to venture into the world of science fiction, which did not make his many fans very happy, since they preferred that he chase oddball criminals like Pruneface, Flattop, and BB Eyes.

Gould employed an unusual, for the time it first surfaced, artistic cartooning technique when drawing his comic strip. He used large patches of black ink and areas of white space, and his style was totally unique. The *Dick Tracy* comic strip is also remembered for several technological devices that Gould invented, such as the two-way wrist radio, which was, in the strip, invented by a Gould character named "Diet Smith" in 1946, and the somewhat preposterous "Space Coupe," which transported people back and forth from the Earth to the Moon.

In 1977, artist Chester Gould, who was seventy-seven years old, decided that it was time to retire and he turned his *Dick Tracy* comic strip over to his assistants, Max Allen Collins and Rick Fletcher. Chester Gould died at the age of eighty-five, eight years after he had retired. The *Dick Tracy* comic strip, in more recent years, was drawn by the Pulitzer Prize winning cartoonist, Dick Locher, who teamed up with writer Michael Kilian to produce the strip.

In 1938, seven years after the comic strip first appeared as a daily newspaper feature, *Dick Tracy* became one of the features in a comic book series, *Super Comics*. *Dick Tracy* also appeared in a series of Whitman and Big Little Book novels in the late 1930s – early 1940s. Tracy's popularity also led to a feature length *Dick Tracy* film that starred actor Ralph Byrd as Tracy, in 1937, and a subsequent half-hour TV series was seen during the 1950–1951 season that also starred Ralph Byrd as Tracy. A pilot for a second *Dick Tracy* TV series was aired in 1967, with actor Ray Mac Donnell playing Tracy, but the series never materialized as a regular running program on television. In

(Credit: Photofest)

Actors Alan Reed (a.k.a. Teddy Bergman) and Walter Kinsella are seen congratulating actress Mercedes McCambridge after a broadcast of their popular situation comedy series *Abie's Irish Rose* in 1942. Miss McCambridge played Snowflake and Walter Kinsella was featured as Pat Patton on the *Dick Tracy* radio series in the 1940s.

Radio's Golden Age

1990, a big-budget action film surfaced with motion picture star Warren Beatty playing Tracy, but it was not the success the film's producers had hoped it would be and it failed to attract much of an audience.

The only entertainment medium, however, that produced as popular a version of *Dick Tracy* as Chester Gould's successful comic strip, was Radio. In 1935, a five-day-a-week, fifteen minute *Dick Tracy* radio series surfaced on the Mutal Broadcasting System's network of stations. The series later moved to the NBC Blue network, and then it was finally heard on the ABC network until it left the air in 1948. For many years, the *Dick Tracy* radio series was sponsored by the Quaker Oats, Quaker Puffed Wheat, and Quaker Puffed Rice cereals. On radio, *Dick Tracy* was played by actor Ned Wever from 1940 – until 1945, and then Matt Crowley, and Barry Thompson, until the series left the air. It also featured Andy Donnelly, and then Jackie Kelk, as Junior Tracy, Walter Kinsella as Pat Patton, Howard Smith as Chief Reardon, Helen Lewis and Tess Trueheart, Beatrice Pons as Tania, Mercedes Cambridge as Snowflake (using a broad imitation of film actress Katherine Hepburn), Thelma Ritter as Gravel Gertie, and John Griggs, Craig McDonnell, Gil Mack, James VanDyke, Ralph Bell, Curtis Arnall and John Larkin, among others. The Dick Tracy program's announcers were Don Gardner, George Gunn, Dan Seymour, and Ed Herlihy. The radio series was directed by Mitchell Grayson and Charles Powers and written by Sydney Slon and John Wray. Various titles for some of the adventures that were heard over the years were as intriguing as "The Case of the Black Pearl of Osirus," "The Case of the Firebug Murders," "The Case of the Dark Corridor," "The Purple Rider Returns," "The Case of the Blood Ruby," "The Case of the Broken Window," "The Case of the Graveyard Watch," "The Case of the Low-Hi Jacks," "The Case of the Book of Four Kings," The Case of the Poisonous Timber," which certainly kept listeners listening to the series over the years.

On February 15, 1944, the U. S. War Department produced a special, hour-long musical called *Dick Tracy in B-Flat, or Will Dick Tracy Ever Marry Tess Trueheart?* that was heard on the *Command Performance* radio program that was broadcast to members of the Armed Forces during World War Two. This show was never heard by most Americans. The hilarious musical comedy starred such celebrated stars as Bing Crosby as Dick Tracy, Dinah Shore as Tess Trueheart, Bob Hope as Flattop, Judy Garland as Snowflake, Frank Morgan as Vitamin Flintheart, Cass Daley as Gravel Gertie, the Andrews Sisters as The Summer Sisters, and Frank Sinatra, Jimmy Durante, Jerry Collona, and radio announcer, Harry VonZell. Recordings of this program have become prized collector's items among hundreds of Old Time Radio show buffs.

Dick Tracy Radio Series Performers

Crowley, Matt (Dick Tracy) See *Jungle Jim* for biography

Kelk, Jackie (Junior Tracy) See *The Gumps* for biography

Kinsella, Walter b. 1900 – d. 1975 (Pat Patton)

Before he decided he wanted to become an actor, Walter Kinsella, who was born in New York City, was an Arrow short model and an amateur track star. In 1924, he was cast in a role in the play *What Price Glory* on Broadway, which was a popular success. Kinsella subsequently appeared on Broadway in such plays as *The Road to Rome* (1928), *Ladies of the Jury* (1929), *It's A Grand Life* (1930), *Arrest That Woman* (1936), *Mrs. O'Brien Entertains* (1939), and the musical comedy *Juno* (1959). It is for his work on radio, however, that Kinsella is best remembered by the public. Among the many radio programs on which he was featured were *Abie's Irish Rose* (as Patrick Joseph Murphy, Rose's father), *Circus Days* (as the General Manager), *Joe and Mabel*, *Leave It to Mike*, *Martin Kane, Private Eye*, *Mr. and Mrs. North*, *Peewee and Windy*, and *Stella Dallas*. Kinsella also played Dick Tracy's faithful police department partner, Pat Patton, on the long running *Dick Tracy* children's adventure series, which was adapted to radio from Chester Gould's successful comic strip. Kinsella also had featured roles on such television programs in the 1950s as *Martin Kane, Private Eye*, *Naked City*, *Perry Mason*, *Brenner*, *The Tall Man* and *Car 54, Where Are You?* In the late 1940s, Walter Kinsella was also a frequent spokesman for various TV commercial products and was seen as "Happy McMahon," who operated a tobacco shop in the U. S. Tobacco Company's early TV advertisements.

McCambridge, Mercedes b. 1916 – d. 2004 (Snowflake)

Academy Award winning and Tony nominated actress Mercedes McCambridge began her career as a professional performer when she was still a college student at Mundelein College in Chicago. Born in Joliet, Illinois, Miss McCambridge was signed to an exclusive acting contract by the NBC Blue network when an executive from that company heard her perform with Mundelein's Verse speaking choir. In the late 1930s, Miss Cambridge was heard on hundreds of Chicago-based radio shows including *Girl Alone*, *The Guiding Light*, *Lights Out*, *Betty and Bob*, and many other programs. In 1941, the actress moved to Hollywood where she was heard on popular radio programs that starred such celebrated performers as Jack Benny, Bob Hope, Bing Crosby and Rudy Vallee, and she was also featured also on Carlton E., Morse's successful *I Love a Mystery* series as a regular member of the cast. She was also frequently featured on and *The Adventures of Red Ryder*, playing many supporting roles including, at one time, Red's Indian boy companion, Little Beaver. In 1942, Miss Cambridge joined the cast of the successful situation comedy series *Abie's Irish Rose* which was being broadcast from New York City, playing the title role of Rose on that NBC series. Before long, she became one of the busiest radio actresses in New York and was featured on hundreds of programs including *Big Sister* (as Ruth Wayne, the "big sister" of the series' title), *Bulldog Drummond*, *The Falcon*, *The Romance of Helen Trent*, *Inner Sanctum Mysteries*, *This is Nora Drake*, *Gangbusters*, and Fletcher Markle's *Studio One* and *Ford Theater* dramatic anthology series, to name just a few. Miss McCambridge also

(Credit: Photofest)

Actress Mercedes McCambridge played the regular running role of Snowflake on the *Dick Tracy* radio program, using a voice that was imitative of film star Katharine Hepburn. Miss McCambridge was one of radio's most active performers and was heard on hundreds of radio program during Radio's Golden Age.

played the part of "Snowflake" on the radio adaptation of Chester Gould's *Dick Tracy* comic strip, using a voice that sounded exactly like film star Katherine Hepburn, for several months. The actress starred on two radio programs of her own, *Family Skelton* and *Defense Attorney* in the 1950s. In 1949, Mercedes made her film debut in *All the King's Men* and won a Best Supporting Actress Academy Award for her work in that film. She was subsequently featured in such films as *Lightning Strikes Twice*, *The Scarf*, *Johnny Guitar*, *Giant* (for which she was nominated for a second Academy Award), *Suddenly Last Summer*, *Angel Baby*, *Cimarron*, *A Farewell to Arms*, and as the voice of the Devil for the 1973 film *The Exorcist*. Mercedes McCambridge was also very active on the stage. She starred in the original Broadway production of *Who's Afraid of Virginia Wolfe* (replacing actress Uta Hagen in the role of Martha), and received critical acclaim for her performance in that play. She also starred in the play *Love Suicide at Schoffield Barracks* on Broadway (for which she was nominated for a Tony Award) and in 1991 she starred in Neil Simon's play, *Lost in Yonkers* on Broadway and on a national tour. Mercedes McCambridge was also featured on many television series throughout her long career including *Bonanza, Gunsmoke, Bewitched, Studio One, The Kraft Television Theater,* and numerous other TV programs, as well as on her own TV series *Wire Service* in 1956–1957.

WEVER, NED B. 1899 – D. 1984 (DICK TRACY)

Ned Wever played the *Dick Tracy* character on radio for several years. A very successful radio actor, Wever also played radio's *Bulldog Drummond*.

The versatile actor Ned Wever had a long and prosperous acting career on the stage, on radio, in films, and on television. Wever, who was born in New York City, began his performing career as a cabaret singer and song writer. In the 1920s, Wever wrote songs for showmen Billy Rose and Ed Wynn and he was featured in such Broadway plays as *The Second Little Show* (1930), *Days to Come* (1936) and *Case History* (1938). Wever also began working on radio in 1929 and was heard on such early radio programs as *True Detective Mysteries, Pages of Romance, True Story* and Himan Brown's *Little Italy*. Eventually, Wever became one of the busiest leading men on radio and throughout the 1930s, 1940s and 1950s, he was heard on such popular series as *Bulldog Drummond* (as Drummond), *Valiant Lady, Betty and Bob, Big Sister, Her Honor Nancy James, Grand Central Station, Young Widder Brown* (from 1938-1956), *Laura Lawton*, and hundreds of other programs. Wever also played *Dick Tracy* on the radio adaptation of Chester Gould's popular comic strip from 1935 until 1944. After radio drama all but disappeared from the airwaves in the late 1950s, Wever became active in films and on television. He had featured roles in such films as *Slaughter on 10th Avenue* (1957), *The Joker is Wild* (1957), *Some Came Running* (1958), *Anatomy of a Murder* (1959), and *The Prize* (1963), and was seen on such TV series as *Bonanza, Get Smart, Alfred Hitchcock Presents, Perry Mason, The Lawman, Petticoat Junction* and *The Big Valley,* among others.

Don Winslow of the Navy
(a.k.a Don Winslow, Trouble Shooter)

Frank V. Martinek's adventure-filled comic strip, *Don Winslow of the Navy*, was first published in various newspapers throughout the country in the late 1930s and was subsequently seen in a Fawcett comic book series from 1943 until 1955. He continued to appear in reprints as well as several new comic books which continued to surface into the 1990s. Frank Martinek (1895 – c. 1970), who was actually a writer and not a cartoonist, created *Don Winslow of the Navy* because of his life long interest in the Navy. Martinek was a Lieutenant Commander in the U. S. Naval Reserve when he conceived an idea for a comic strip about a Naval officer/hero who he decided to name Don Winslow. The comic strip was unlike any other panel strip of the time, because it was not a "gag" or "slap-strip" comic, as were most of the successful comic strips of the mid 1930s. It was an adventure serial that proved to be educational, as well as entertaining. Before long, *Don Winslow of the Navy* was being printed in hundreds of newspapers all across the United States and made Marinek one of the most influential men in the comic strip business. In *Don Winslow of the Navy*, Martinek introduced such interesting and inventive devices as a master barometer that photographed hurricanes like an infra-red camera and projected the storm center as a map on a motion picture screen. He also introduced a man-carrying bat wing glider in the comic strip that became a prototype for an actual glider used by the Navy. The comic strip made Frank Martinek a very wealthy man, even though he never drew the comic strip himself. The art work for the *Don Winslow* comic strip was done by two very talented cartoonists named Carl Pfeufer and John Jordan. They continued to draw the strip well into the 1950s, when Martinek decided to retire.

The hero of Martinek's comic strip, Don Winslow, was a top United States Navy troubleshooter. With his sidekick, Red Pennington, Winslow broke up smuggling rings, sought out purloined secret documents for the U.S. government, and went undercover to break up a band of thieves preying on sailors on shore leave in Turkey. At one time, Don and another buddy named Lance O'Casey solved the mystery of "The Bandit Birds," which was one of Don Winslow's most memorable adventures. *Don Winslow of the Navy* also became the main character of several *Big Little Books* and was also seen in a Universal Pictures film series in the 1940s. The twelve part serial, which was released in 1942, starred Don Terry as Don Winslow and Walter Slade played Lt. Red Pennington.

The first radio adaptation of *Don Winslow of the Navy* was produced in Chicago in 1937 and was heard on the NBC Blue network. This series starred

Robert "Bob" Guilbert as Don Winslow and featured Betty Lou Gerson as Mercedes Colby, Betty Ito as Lotus, and Ruth Barth as Misty. From 1938 until 1939, actor Karl Weber replaced Guilbert as Don Winslow. The series left the air in 1939, but resurfaced in 1942 with Raymond Edward Johnson playing the role of Don Winslow. This second series which was produced in New York and was set during World War Two with Winslow working for the United States Coast Guard. The wartime series was sponsored by Post Toasties. The program's inspirational and memorable theme music was "Columbia the Gem of the Ocean."

DON WINSLOW OF THE NAVY RADIO SERIES PERFORMERS

GERSON, BETTY LOU B. 1914 – D. 1999 (MERCEDES COLBY)

Actress Betty Lou Gerson, who played Mercedes Colby on the popular radio adventure series *Don Winslow of the Navy*, was born in Chattanooga, Tennessee. In 1934, after studying drama at the Goodman School in Chicago, Miss Gerson became a staff actress at NBC's Blue network in Chicago and throughout the 1930s, she was heard on such popular radio series as *Arnold Grimm's Daughter, Aunt Mary, The Chicago Theater of the Air, The First Nighter, Flying Time, Girl Alone, The Guiding Light, Lonely Woman, Midstream,* and *Today's Children*. In the 1940s, Gerson continued to remain active on radio in New York, and was heard on *The Woman in White, The Saint, The Road of Life,* and then on the *One Man's Family* series, and many other Hollywood-based radio programs.

Betty Lou Gerson was also active in films and on television in the late 1940s, 1950s and 1960s. In films, she had featured roles in *The Red Menace* (1949), *Undercover Girl* (1950), *The Fly* (1958), *The Miracle of the Hills* (1959), and *Mary Poppins* (1964). Her most memorable film work, however, was done behind the camera as a voice-over actress. She was the narrator for Disney's *Cinderella* (1950), the voice of "Frances" for *Cats Don't Dance* (1997), and most memorably, she was the voice of the evil Cruella De Vil/Miss Birwell, for Disney's *One Hundred and One Dalmatians* (1961). Betty Lou Gerson also had supporting roles on many television series including the *Schlitz Playhouse of Stars, A Letter to Loretta, Four Star Playhouse, Perry Mason,* the *Bob Cummings Show, The Untouchables, The Rifleman, Wanted, Dead or Alive,* the *Dick Van Dyke Show,* and *The Twilight Zone*. Miss Gerson died at the age of eighty-five in 1999.

JOHNSON, RAYMOND EDWARD (DON WINSLOW) SEE *MANDRAKE THE MAGICIAN* FOR BIOGRAPHY

WEBER, KARL 1916 – 1990 (DON WINSLOW)

Actor Karl Weber was one of radio's most popular leading men during Radio's Golden Age (the 1930s-1950s) and was featured on numerous soap opera series throughout the 1930s and 1940s. Weber, who was born in Columbus Junction, Idaho, was a graduate of the University of Iowa. He began his acting career performing with various touring productions in Shakespeare's plays and with others, he founded the off-Broadway New Stages theatrical company in New York City. Weber began working in radio in the late 1930s in Chicago. In 1938-1939, he played adventure series hero, Don Winslow on the *Don Winslow of the Navy* radio series. Moving to New York in the early 1940s, Weber was heard on such popular radio programs as *The Story of Mary Marlin, The Woman in White, Cloak and Dagger, The Road of Life, The Guiding Light, David Harum,* and *Lora Lawton,* to name just a few. Weber also became well known to theater-goers and appeared in Broadway productions of such plays as *Tea and Sympathy* and *The Best Man.* A tall, good looking actor, Weber made a successful transition from radio to television in the 1950s and had major roles on the *Search for Tomorrow* and *Perry Mason* TV series. Karl Weber was also featured on such TV series as *Studio One, Hawaiian Eye, Maverick, Bronco,* and *Dr. Kildare.*

Karl Weber played *Don Winslow of the Navy* on radio during the 1938-1939 season. Weber was also featured as the leading man on such radio soap opera series as *Lorenzo Jones, The Romance of Helen Trent* and *When a Girl Marries.*

(Credit: Photofest)

WINKLER, BETTY B. 1914 (MERCEDES COLBY)

Betty Winkler had no idea she would become a professional actress when she was growing up in Berwick, Pennsylvania. After studying at Western Reserve, Betty and a friend decided to be backstage apprentices at the celebrated Cleveland Playhouse where she appeared and became stage struck.

Few actresses were busier on radio than Betty Winkler. Betty played Mercedes Colby on the *Don Winslow of the Navy* series and was also heard playing the title character on the soap opera series *Rosemary, Joyce Jordan* and *Girl Alone*, among others.

On a dare in 1933, Betty auditioned for a role on a radio soap opera that was called *Vivan Ware* at WTAM in Cleveland and, to her surprise, she got the part. At the time, Chicago was the center of radio drama activity and so Betty decided to move to Chicago where she soon became one of the busiest contracted radio actresses at the NBC Blue network. While she was in Chicago in the mid-to-late 1930s, Miss Winkler was heard on such popular programs as *Girl Alone, Betty and Bob,* the *Chicago Theater of the Air, Lights Out, The Man I Married, Welcome Valley,* and the popular comic strip that had been adapted to radio, *Don Winslow of the Navy,* on which she played Don's girlfriend, Mercedes Colby. In the early 1940s, Betty Winkler relocated to New York City which had replaced Chicago as the center of radio drama broadcasting and once again, she became one of that city's busiest radio actresses. Major roles on such programs as *Abie's Irish Rose* (on which she was the original Rose Murphy), *Knickerbocker Playhouse, The O'Neills, Joyce Jordan Girl Intern* (as Joyce Jordan), *Rosemary* (as Rosemary from 1944 until 1955), *Just Plain Bill, Curtain Time, Inner Sanctum Mysteries, This Life Is Mine,* and many other radio shows, kept her busy throughout the 1940s and 1950s. With the demise of radio drama in the late 1950s – early 1960s, Betty decided to retire from show business. In 1976 she came out of retirement to work on Himan Brown's CBS Mystery Theater in a radio play called, "The Ghostly Private Eye." Miss Winkler regularly taught classes in sensory awareness at The New School in New York City in the 1970s and 1980s.

F

Flash Gordon

Because of the tremendous success of the *Buck Rogers in the 25th Century* science fiction comic strip series which first attracted the public's attention in 1928, a young artist named Alex Raymond convinced King Features Syndicate to release a science fiction comic strip of their own that Raymond had been working on. In 1931, Alex Raymond (1909 – 1956), after studying at the Grand Central School of Art in New York City, had been hired as an assistant to cartoonist Russ Westover, who drew the very popular *Tillie the Toiler* comic strip. Raymond, who was born in New Rochelle, New York, had known that he wanted to be a professional artist from the time he was a boy, and he was thrilled when Westover chose him to be his assistant over the many other young artists who had applied for the job. After working for Westover for several years, Raymond went to work for Chic and Lyman Young and assisted them with drawing of their *Tim Tyler's Luck* and *Blondie* comic strips until 1933. Late in 1933, Raymond began to work on his new comic strip about a space traveler that would be similar to the very successful *Buck Rogers in the 25th Century* comic strip, which had taken the country by storm several years before in 1928. The result was a character Raymond called *Flash Gordon*. The comic strip, whose story lines were written by Don Moore, almost immediately replaced *Buck Rogers* as America's favorite science fiction comic strip. Shortly after *Flash Gordon* surfaced, Alex Raymond teamed up with mystery writer Dashiel Hammett, to create another comic strip which they called *Secret Agent X-9*. Raymond was a very talented artist who was expert at drawing the human form. He used a dry brush technique that made his comic strip characters unique and eventually he became one of America's most admired cartoon artists. Raymond's work, according to comic strip authority Harvey Kurtsman, had a sensual quality to it that appealed to comic strip readers, especially young men, and his *Flash Gordon* strip became second only to George McManus' very popular *Bringing up Father* as a Sunday supplement comic strip feature and appeared on the second page of the Sunday Funnies, which was a very prestigious place for comic strip to be. In the early 1940s, Alex Raymond began to spend less and less of his time drawing the *Flash Gordon* and in 1944, Raymond joined the service and served in the Pacific on the USS Gilbert Islands until the end of World War Two. When he was released from active military service, Raymond held the rank of Major. Returning to the United States after the war, Raymond launched a new comic strip project, *Rip Kirby*, that centered around a scientific detective. Much admired by his peers, Alex Raymond served as the president of the National Cartoonist's Society for two years from 1950 and 1951. Raymond's untimely death in an automobile accident at the age of forty-seven in 1956, cut short the artist's successful career, but *Flash Gordon* continued to be published. Over the years, the *Flash Gordon* daily comic strip and comic books were drawn by such talented artists as Austin Briggs, who had been Raymond's assistant since 1940 and began drawing the daily *Flash Gordon* strip in 1940 and drew it until 1944. Briggs continued to draw the *Flash Gordon* comic books until 1948. Daniel Barry, who had previously drawn the *Captain Marvel* comic strip, drew a new version of *Flash Gordon* comic strip in 1951 and Emmanuel "Mac" Raboy, began drawing the *Flash Gordon* comic books in 1948. Artist Al Williamson (1931–) took over the drawing of the *Flash Gordon* comic book series in the 1960s, when he was in his twenties. Williamson often collaborated with artists Frank Frazetta and Angelo Torres but preferred doing pencil work and was "deathly afraid" of inking his work. Frazetta often took over the inking of his comic art for him. Williamson's fluid and almost cinematic style is evident in his *Flash Gordon* comics. *Flash Gordon* comic strips and comic books have remained popular with readers, right up to the present.

When the *Flash Gordon* series first appeared as a comic strip feature, Flash was a world-famous polo player who had safely parachuted from an aircraft that was wrecked by a falling meteor. As he parachuted from the damaged

(Credit: Author's collection. © King Features Syndicates, Inc. and Nostalgia Press.)

Numerous talented artists drew the *Flash Gordon* comic strip and comic books and all of them were particularly adept at drawing the human figure, as can be seen on the comic strip frames above.

airplane, Flash grabbed a fellow passenger, the beautiful Dale Arden, moments before it crashed to Earth and when Flash and Dale regained consciousness, they were sometime in the far distant future. Flash and Dale had reached the ground near the place a rocket ship heading for outer space was about to take off for the planet Mongo, which about to try to destroy the planet Earth. The leader of the expedition to Mongo was a Dr. Hans Zarkoff. Flash and Dale, who found themselves trapped in a futuristic world, joined Zarkoff's the expedition to Mongo and thus began the thrill-a-minute outer space adventures of Flash Gordon. Flash and Dale were immediately embroiled in the intrigues on the planet Mongo, which was ruled by an evil warlord named Ming.

In addition to the successful *Flash Gordon* comic books and the daily comic strip, several movie serials, commercial products such as games, toys and adventure novels, and a radio series based on Raymond's creation surfaced. Swimming champion-turned actor, Buster Crabbe, played Flash in no less than three movie serials that were produced between 1936 and 1940. In 1957, a full length feature *Flash Gordon* film was released that starred actor Steve Holland in the title role. A second *Flash Gordon* feature film was released in 1980 with Sam Jones playing Flash and the character even appeared in an animated cartoon TV series which was aired from 1979 through 1981. In 1987, Flash was seen with his fellow King Features superheros, *The Phantom* and *Mandrake the Magician*, in a Saturday morning TV cartoon series called *Defenders of the Earth*.

The Amazing Interplanetary Adventures of Flash Gordon was first presented as a radio series on the Mutual Broadcasting System's network in 1935 and was heard on Saturday mornings. The radio series was directed toward a juvenile audience and the series aired for just one year, ending its radio run in 1936. Produced by Himan Brown, the *Flash Gordon* radio series starred actor Gale Gordon, and then James Meighan, as Flash, and featured Maurice Franklin as Dr. Zarkoff, and Bruno Wick as the mean Ming character. Also heard regularly on the series regularly were Alan Reed (a.k.a. Teddy Bergman), Everett Sloane, Charles Cantor, and Ray Collins. The titles of some of *Flash Gordon's* exciting radio series episodes included "On the Planet Mongo," "Imprisoned by Hawkmen," "Blue Magic Men Capture Flash," "Dr. Zarkoff to the Rescue," "Flash Charges the Ice Barricade of the Hawkmen," "Dr. Zarkoff is Thawed Out," "Flash, The Avenging Shadow," "Pit of Fire," and "Flash and Dale Married in the Jungle," to name just a few.

FLASH GORDON RADIO SERIES PERFORMERS

CANTOR, CHARLES B. 1898 – D. 1966 (MANY ROLES)

Charles Cantor, who was born in Russia, immigrated to the United States with his parents and siblings, when he was a small boy. Cantor grew up in New York City and he began his career in show business when he was in his teens performing as a blackface comedian and dialectician on the vaudeville stage. Cantor made his radio performing debut playing the banjo on a small, local radio station in Brooklyn, New York in the late 1920s. In the early 1930s, because of his talent to perform in numerous ethnic dialects Cantor began to get acting jobs on various radio programs and his vocal versatility led to playing a wide variety of characters on such radio series as *Flash Gordon* and *Terry and the Pirates*. He was also heard regularly on such radio programs as *Grand Central Station* and *The Fred Allen Show* in the 1930s. In the early 1940s, Cantor went to Hollywood where he soon became a regular performer on such popular comedy programs as *Duffy's Tavern*, playing the hilarious, dim-witted Clifton Finnegan the waiter, *The Eddie Cantor Show, The Amazing Mr. Smith, The Alan Young Show* (as Zero), *The Life of Riley, The Adventures of Mr. Meek,* and *The Philip Morris Playhouse*.

Charles Cantor repeated his Clifton Finnegan role in the film adaptation of *Duffy's Tavern* and was subsequently in the film *Stop, You're Killing Me* (1952). On television, Cantor was a regular performer on *The Jack Benny Show* throughout the 1950s, and was also seen on *December Bride, The Bob Cummings Show, The Dick VanDyke Show,* and *Bob Hope Presents the Chrysler Theater* TV series.

FRANKLIN, MAURICE B. 1885 – 1955 (DR. ZARKOFF)

One of radio's busiest character actors, Maurice Franklin began his acting career on the stage appearing in such Broadway plays as *His House in Order* (1906), *On the Eve* (1909), *The Next of Kin* (1909), *Julius Caesar* (1912), and *A Tailor Made Man* (1929). On radio in the 1930s and 1940s, Franklin had running roles on most of the major soap opera series including *Aunt Jenny, Ellen Randolph, Her Honor, Nancy James, Perry Mason,* and *The Right to Happiness,* as well as on such prime time programs as *Mr. District Attorney*. Franklin also played Dr. Zarkoff on the adventure series *Flash Gordon* for several seasons and was also a regular performer on two other comic strip based radio series, *Jane Arden* and *Archie Andrews*.

GORDON, GALE B. 1906 – D. 1995 (FLASH GORDON)

Although he became best known for playing a blustering, often irate character on many radio and television shows, actor Gale Gordon's first major role was as the title character on the *Flash Gordon* radio series in the 1935. Gale Gordon's mother was character actress Gloria Gordon, whose voice later became familiar to radio program listeners as Mrs. O'Reilly on the popular situation comedy series *My Friend Irma* in the 1950s, therefore Gale had been born into a show business family and was a performer from the time he was a small child. Gale Gordon's list of radio program credits is formidable and includes regular, running roles on such popular radio series as *Big Town, Burns and Allen, The Case Book of Gregory Hood, Fibber McGee and Molly, Glorious One, The Great Gildersleeve, Johnathan Trimble, Esq., The Judy Canova Show, Junior Miss, My Favorite Husband, Our Miss Brooks* (as Madison High School Principal Osgood Conklin), *Stories of the Black Chamber, Those We Love, The Fabulous Dr. Tweedy, Irene Rich Dramas, The Phil Harris/Alice Faye Show, Halls of Ivy, Mr. Blandings Builds His Dream House,* and *The Penny Singleton Show,* to name just a few. The actor's list of television credits is equally as impressive. He had regular supporting roles on such TV series as *Our Miss Brooks, Pete and Gladys, Dennis the Menace, The Lucille Ball Show* (a.k.a. *The Lucy Show*), *Here's Lucy,* and *Life With Lucy.* He also made appearances on such TV shows as *I Love Lucy, The Real McCoys, Playhouse 90, Studio One, The Danny Thomas Hour, Hi Honey, I'm Home,* and *The New Lassie Show,* among others. Gordon also appeared in many films including *Here We Go Again* (1942), *Woman of Distinction* (1950), *Our Miss Brooks* (1956), *Rally 'round the Flag* (1955), *Don't Give Up the Ship* (1959), *Visit to a Small Planet* (1960), *Dondi* (1961), *Speedway* (1968), and *The Burbs* (1989), to name just a few. Gale Gordon died of lung cancer at the age of eighty-nine in 1995.

MEIGHAN, JAMES B. 1906 – D. 1970 (FLASH GORDON)
One of Broadway's and radio's most prolific leading men, James Meighan who was born in New York City, graduated from Carnegie Institute of Technology in that city. Meighan had a long and distinguished acting career that began when he was fifteen years old. Meighan appeared on Broadway in the play *The Hand of the Potter* in 1921 and he had major roles in such Broadway plays as *Montmartre* (1922), *God of Vengeance* (1922), *Antony and Cleopatra* (1924), *The Ancient Mariner* (1924), *The Saint* (1924), *SS Glencaim* (1924), *Paolo and Francesca* (1924), *The Emperor Jones* (1925), *Michael Auclair* (1925), *Love For Love* (1925), *Hamlet* (1925), *My Maryland* (1927), *These Few Ashes* (1928), *The Octoroon* (1929), *Under the Gaslight* (1929), and *Privileged Car* (1931). Meighan's well trained, deep baritone voice and his perfect diction made him a logical choice to play leading male roles on radio and in the early 1930s, he became one of the first leading men on one of one of the first soap operas series heard on radio. The program was called *Marie, the Little French Princess,* and it was produced and directed by Himan Brown. Meighan also played the title character on the short-lived *Flash Gordon* children's adventure radio serial, which had been adapted to radio from Alex Raymond's popular comic strip. Throughout the 1930s and 1940s, Meighan was also featured on such radio programs as *Against the Storm, Backstage Wife* (as leading man Larry

Noble), *By Kathleen Norris, City Desk, Dot and Will, The Falcon* (as the Falcon, Mike Waring), *Lora Lawton, I Love Linda Dale, Just Plain Bill, Lone Journey, Orphans of the Storm, The Romance of Helen Trent, Second Husband, Special Agent, The Helen Hayes Theater, Alias Jimmy Valentine, Death Valley Days, The Mohawk Treasure Chest,* and too many other radio programs to list here. After the demise of radio drama in the late 1950s, Meighan toured the country in stage plays, but ill health caused him to curtail his acting career in the 1960s. The actor died in 1970 at the age of sixty-four.

GANGBUSTERS

Each week, for twenty-two years, at the beginning of each *Gangbusters* radio drama episode, the announcer's voice began each program saying, "Gangbusters! With the cooperation of leading law-enforcement officials of the United States, Gangbusters presents facts in the relentless war of the police on the underworld...authentic case histories that show the never-ending activity of the police in their work protecting our citizens." Originally called *G-Men* when it first aired, Gangbusters was produced by Phillips H. Lord and directed over the years by Paul Monroe, Harry Frazee, Jay Hanna, George Zachery, Bill Sweets and Leonard Bass. The program was narrated at different times by Phillips H. Lord, Colonel H. Norman Schwartzkopf (the father of the General who led the U. S. Desert Storm action against Iraq in the 1990s), John C. Hilley, and Dean Carlton. The Chief Investigator who was heard on the show was played by actor Lew Valentine. Among the well known familiar voices that were heard on the series regularly were those belonging to frequent radio performers Art Carney, Richard Widmark, Elspeth Eric, Alice Reinheart, Bryna Raeburn, Mercedes Cambridge, Don MacLaughlin, Santos Ortega, Robert Dryden, Joan Banks, Leon Janney, Grant Richards, Larry Haines, Roger DeKoven, Bill Lipton, Raymond Edward Johnson, Anne-Marie Gayer, Mandel Kramer, Ralph Bell, Ethel Owen, Adelaide Klein, James McCallion, Helene Dumas, Linda Watkins, Frank Lovejoy, and many others.

In the 1950s, a series of *Gangbusters* comic books mostly drawn by the talented artist Frank Frazetta (see *Buck Rogers in the 25th Century* entry), surfaced and proved to be very popular among comic book readers. On the cover of the Gangbusters comics, which cost ten cents and were published by DC Comics in bold letters it said, "**BRAND NEW ADVENTURES OF RADIO'S COAST-TO-COAST FAVORITES.**" The comics were almost too realistically drawn by artist Frazetta and many parents complained that the art work in the comic were too violent and bloody for young readers to see and were "gritty" and contained the often brutal actions that could only be heard on the radio series. The *Gangbusters* comic books remained in print for a relatively short period of time, but while they were being released, they sold extremely well. The *Gangbusters* comic book series disappeared from the newsstands a few years before the radio program was canceled in 1957.

(THERE WERE NO REGULAR PERFORMERS IN THIS SERIES)

GASOLINE ALLEY

One of the most successful and longest running comic strips ever published in America is Frank King's *Gasoline Alley*. When he was eighteen years old, artist Frank King (1883-1969), got his first job as a professional cartoonist at the Minneapolis Times. King moved to Chicago in 1910 and found employment as a staff artist at The Chicago American newspaper. He then went to work as a cartoonist at the Chicago Examiner and finally worked at the Chicago Tribune. In 1915, King, inspired by the success Winsor McCay's *Little Nemo* comic strip, created his own *Little Nemo*-like comic strip *Bobby Make-Believe*. *Bobby Make-Believe* was not as successful as McCay's strip, but his next comic strip, *Gasoline Alley*, which was first published in 1918, took American by storm and soon become one of the country's favorite comic strip features. The first panel of the *Gasoline Alley* comic strip was published on November 24, 1918 in *The Chicago Tribune* newspapers. In their Sunday Funnies section, *The Chicago Tribune*, at that time, ran a page they called "The Rectangle," which was divided into little boxes where its staff artists would contribute black and white cartoons. Some of the artists used ongoing themes and others chose to

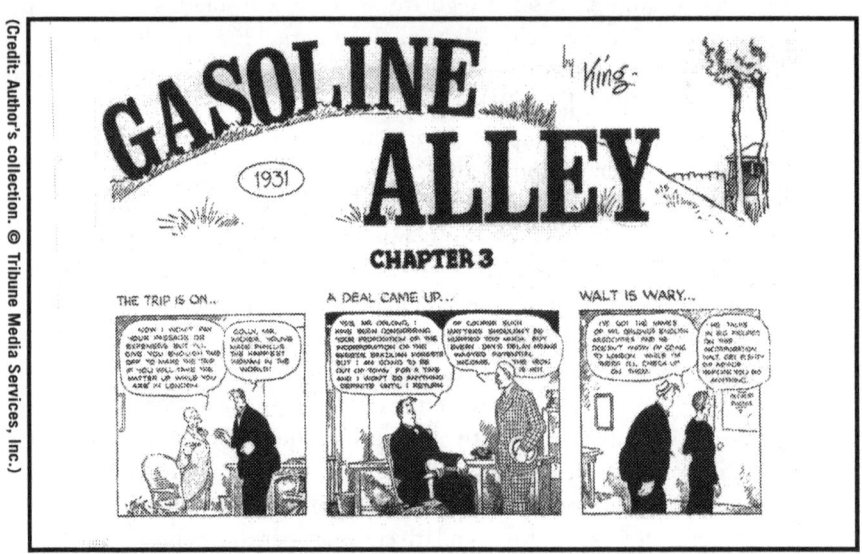

In 1941, Frank King's very successful *Gasoline Alley* comic strip, which was first published in 1918, made its debut as a radio series. The program remained on the air for eight years.

have different cartoon themes each week. King used his small section of "The Rectangle" to feature a regular cast of characters, Walt, Doc, Avery and Bill, who got together each week in the cartoon and discussed automobiles. Thus his title, "Gasoline Alley" emerged. On August 25, 1919, a *Gasoline Alley* panel began appearing regularly in the *Daily Tribune* and shortly after that, the panel developed into a regular, full-scale comic strip and then a weekly Sunday Funnies color comic strip. A few years later, *Tribune* Editor Joseph Patterson decided that the strip should try to more more to women and he suggested that if there was a baby in the strip, women might read *Gasoline Alley* more than they did. The major character of the strip, Walt Wallett, was a confirmed bachelor, so Frank King had Walt find an abandoned baby on his doorstep. From then on, the *Gasoline Alley's* characters aged normally, as they would in real life, which was the first time that was ever attempted in comic strips. Over the years that followed, he baby, who was named "Skeezix," grew up, became a teenager and then a young man and even fought in World War Two. At the present time, since the strip is still being published, Skeezix is now a grandfather. Walt Wallet did eventually marry in the strip and he had many more children of his own, who also grew up, had families of their own, and often occupied the major story line of the strip. Reading *Gasoline Alley* each day, and especially on Sundays, and then talking about it on Monday morning, became a national pastime. Because he was ready to retire by the 1950s, cartoonist Frank King hired Bill Perry to assist him with the drawing of his comic strip and in 1951, Perry took over the drawing the *Gasoline Alley* comic strip. Perry then hired an assistant, Dick Moores, who had assisted Chester Gould on the *Dick Tracy* strip in 1956, to help with the strip and eventually Moores took over the *Gasoline Alley* strip. Frank King died in 1969, but Perry and Moores had continued to produce *Gasoline Alley's* high standard of good story lines and drawing and the comic strip retained its popularity with the public. In 1975, Perry retired, but Moores continued to draw the strip until his death in 1986. Currently, *Gasoline Alley* is drawn by artist Jim Scancarelli (1941–), who has a deep respect for the history and quality of *Gasoline Alley's* past. Before he began drawing the *Gasoline Alley* comic strips, Scancarelli had assisted George Breisacher with the Mutt and Jeff comic strip and before that he had worked in the art departments of several broadcasting companies. *Gasoline Alley's* popularity continued as Scancarelli drew it and in 1988, Scancarelli offered a free Wallet family family tree to its many readers. The response was overwhelming. Over 100,000 people from all fifty states, Canada and the Philippines requested copies of the family tree. Scancarelli, who currently resides in Charlotte, North Carolina, continues to draw *Gasoline Alley* as of this date, and in addition to his comic strip activities, he is an avid amateur bluegrass fiddler.

It was inevitable that the *Gasoline Alley* comic strip should eventually turn up as a radio series, as indeed it did in 1941. The series, which remained on the air until 1949, was first heard in a fifteen minute a day, five-day-a-week format and then as a half-hour, once a week program. Episodes centered around various members of the *Gasoline Alley* community and individual episode had such intriguing titles as "Hypnotized Hero," "Rat Race With Rice," "Fortune's Fool," "The Defective Detective," "Ancient Autobox," "Agitated Announcer," "Feminine Touch," and "Fighting and Feuding." It was King's "Skeezix" character who usually dominated the radio program's episodes. Featured on the program were Jimmy McCallion, and then Billy Idelson and Bill Lipton, as Skeezix, Janice Gilbert, and then Jean Gillespie as Nina Clock, Irna Phillips as Aunt Blossom, Clifford Soubier as Skeezix's boss, Mr. Wumple, Hazel Dopheide as Idaho Ida, Junius Matthews as Ling Wee, the Chinese waiter, and many other talented radio actors. The series was written by Kay Chase and Kane Campbell and directed by Charles Schenck and John Cole.

GASOLINE ALLEY RADIO SERIES PERFORMERS

IDELSON, BILLY B. 1920 (SKEEZIX)

Although he is probably best remembered for playing Vic and Sade's son, Rush, which he first played in 1932 when he was twelve years old, on the very popular *Vic and Sade* radio series, Billy Idelson appeared on numerous other radio programs. Idelson, who was born in Forest Park, Illinois, was also featured on such radio series as *The Truitts, Those Websters, Secret City, That Brewster Boy* and as Skeezix on the radio adaptation of the popular comic strip *Gasoline Alley*. When he was twenty-two years old, Idelson temporarily left *Vic and Sade* and entered military service during World War Two. When the war ended in 1945, Idelson returned to radio and, in addition to rejoining the *Vic and Sade* cast, in the early 1950s also played Hank Murray on Carlton E. Morse's long-running *One Man's Family* series. In the mid 1950s, Idelson decided that he needed a better education and attended and graduated from Northwestern University, using the GI Bill for veterans of World War Two. He returned to his show business career and began working on television after attending college, and was featured on such TV series as *One Man's Family* (as Cliff Barbour), *The Twilight Zone, The Last Time I Saw Archie, Get Smart,* and *Gomer Pyle, USMC.* He also provided the voice of "Mickey" for *The New Schmoo* and *Barney Meets the Schmoo* animated cartoon TV series. Idelson also wrote scripts for several TV series such as *The Bob Newhart Show, The Andy Griffith Show, Bewitched, The Mothers-in-Law, The Ghost and Mrs. Muir, Love, American Style, The Odd Couple, M*A*S*H, Anna and the King* and *Happy Days*.

LIPTON, BILL A.K.A. BILLY B. 1924 (SKEEZIX)

Few juvenile actors who performed on radio during its Golden Age were busier than Bill a.k.a. "Billy" Lipton. Bill, who was born in Brooklyn, New York, was twelve years old when he made his radio debut on the Mutual Broadcasting System's *Rainbow House* program in 1937. Lipton was subsequently heard on the *Coast to Coast on a Bus* and *Let's Pretend* children's shows and was featured on the *Hearts in Harmony* and *The Story of Mary Marlin* radio series. We he became a teenager, and then as a young man, Bill continued to remain active on radio and was regularly heard on such popular programs as *The Columbia Workshop, The March of Time, Everyman's Theater, Gangbusters, Mick Carter, Master Detective, The Right to Happiness, The Road of Life, Rogue's Gallery, Young Dr. Malone,* and *Your Family and Mine* series. He also played the major roles of "Skeezix" on the radio adaptation of the *Gasoline Alley* comic strip and he played the title role of Chick Carter on the *Chick Carter, Boy Detective* series. As radio began to lose ground to television in the 1950s, Bill was featured on *The Road of Life* TV series, but he continued to work on radio on such series as *X-Minus One* and *Dimension X*. When he was still a relatively young man, Bill was stricken with Parkinson's disease and the debilitating illness made him less able to continue working in the performing arts. Although he retired from acting, Bill continued to remain active as a member of the Board of Directors of the Oregon chapter of the American Parkinson's Disease Association.

MCCALLION, JIMMY B. 1919 – D. 1991 (SKEEZIX)

Jimmy McCallion was one of several very talented young performers who were heard on hundreds of radio programs throughout Radio's Golden Age, the 1930s and 1940s, and then disappeared from the show business scene when radio drama, comedy and variety programs left the airwaves in the late 1950s. McCallion played the leading role of "Skeezix" on the radio adaptation of Frank King's popular comic strip Gasoline Alley in the 1930s, and was regularly featured on such radio shows as *Billy and Betty, The Children's Hour, City Desk, The Light of the World, One Man's Family, Three Men on a Horse, Wilderness Road,* and *Young Widder Brown.*

GENE AUTRY

Cowboy Movie Star, Gene Autry, was one of the Twentieth Century's most famous performers. Autry appeared in hundreds of short subject, as well as feature length Western films and he was also seen on his own popular television series, as well as heard on his very successful *Gene Autry's Melody Ranch* radio program, which was on the air from 1940 until 1956. The *Melody Ranch* program, which featured songs by Gene and a weekly dramatic Western adventure story, was extremely popular with youngsters. In addition to Gene and his sidekick, comedian Pat Buttram, who was co-starred in his films, the radio series often featured such talented radio performers as Jim Boles, Wally

One films' most successful singing cowboy stars, Gene Autry, had a popular radio series called *Gene Autry's Melody Ranch* on the air for sixteen years. Gene was also a major character of a popular comic book and comic strip series when he was at the height of his popularity. Gene is pictured above with his comic sidekick Smiley Burnette.

Mayer and Tyler McVey in the regular supporting casts of Gene's serial adventure dramas. In these adventures, Gene tracked down outlaws and assisted people who needed a helping hand, while singing a cowboy song or two in between the action. Also featured on *Melody Ranch* were the Cass County Boys, the Pinafores, the Gene Autry Blue Genes, Alvino Ray, Carl Cotner's Melody Ranch 6, Johnny Bond, the King Sisters, and singer Mary Ford. Lou Crosby and Wendell Niles were the show's announcers during the years the program was aired. Gene's theme song, "Back in the Saddle Again," became familiar to millions of loyal listeners who tuned in to hear the show each week.

Because of his enormous popularity, Gene Autry, whose recordings of cowboy songs, as well as his very successful renditions of "Rudolph, the Red-Nosed Reindeer," "Here Comes Santa Claus" and "Peter Cottontail," sold in the millions of copies. Gene also endorsed numerous products such as games, toys, dolls, and adventure novels, Little Golden books and several comic book series. For a time, a daily *Gene Autry* comic strip was featured in many newspapers that were published throughout the country. The *Gene Autry* Dell comic book series, which were mainly drawn by artists Nat Edson, Pete Alvarado, and Jesse Marsh, was published in the late 1940s and well into the 1950s and 1960s. Many of these comic books have become popular and valuable collector's items. All three of the major artists who drew the Gene Autry comic books and comic strips, were fine caricaturists who drew excellent likenesses of the cowboy star. When Nat Edson (1909–2001) was a boy, he was handicapped and spent seven years in a hospital where he drew caricatures of staff members and visitors at the hospital to pass his time away. In 1927, Edson went to work as an office boy for the King Features Syndicate, where he hoped to eventually join the company's staff of cartoonists. When it didn't happen, Edson left King Features Syndicate and went to work as an artist for Disney Comics and worked on Disney's comic book versions of *Tonka, Toby Tyler, Kidnapped, Indentured Servants, Pollyana, Hans Brinker,* and many other films. He also moonlighted as an artist with DC/National and Pines and Standard comic book publishers throughout the 1940s. For Dell, Edson also drew many of the *Gene Autry* comic books issued by that company, as well as a comic book that featured the self proclaimed "King of the Cowboys," Roy Rogers. Edson continued to work in the comic book field for the next forty years. Before he began drawing comic books and comic strips, artist Pete Alvarado (1920–) was a film animator who worked at the Walt Disney, Hanna-Barbera, and Warner Brothers Studios. At Disney, Alvarado, like Nat Edson, also drew Disney character comic books such as *Donald Duck* and *The Rescuers*. He also provided comic strip panels for several Disney cartoons that were featured in daily and Sunday Funnies comics. At Warner Brothers, Alvarado drew a comic book version of their popular *Road Runner* cartoon character and also, like Edson, drew the *Roy Rogers* comic books for a while. From 1948 until 1952, he was the major artist on the *Gene Autry* comic books published by Dell and also drew the *Mr. McGoo* comic book series. Pete Alvarado remained active in the comic book field until he retired in the 1980s. Artist Jesse Marsh (1907 – 1966) drew the *Gene Autry* comic books until 1950, working with both of the above mentioned artists. Marsh had a long and distinguished career in cartooning. He was one of several artists who drew Edgar Rice Burrough's popular *Tarzan* character for both the comic book series and as a daily newspaper comic strip. Like Alvarado, Marsh, who was a self-taught artist, worked as an animator at the Walt Disney Studios in 1939. He assisted in the drawing of the cells and story lines that were prepared for Disney's *Pinocchio* and *Fantasia* animated film features. In 1947, Marsh left the Disney Company to work for Dell/Western publishers, where he first began to work on the *Gene Autry* comic book series. Throughout the 1950s, Marsh worked on other comic book, but throughout his career, he continued to work on the *Tarzan* comic strip and comic books until 1965, one year before he died, when he turned the *Tarzan* strip over to his friend, Russ Manning.

It was Gene Autry's remarkable ability to market himself during his long and lucrative performing career that led to the many by-products, including the *Gene Autry* comic books and comic strips, that surfaced over the years. The very first *Gene Autry* comic book, which depicted the same character Autry played in films and on the radio, was published by Fawcett in 1941. Dell subsequently published the *Gene Autry* comics, and released 121 issues in that series. The first issue of the Dell Gene Autry comic book in that series is one of the most prized comic books currently being offered to collectors in the nostalgia market and one copy recently sold for $7,000.

GENE AUTRY'S MELODY RANCH RADIO SERIES PERFORMER

AUTRY, GENE B. 1907 – D. 1998 (GENE AUTRY)

Throughout the 1940s and 1950s, there were no bigger All-American cowboy stars on earth than Roy Rogers and Gene Autry. Both Roy and Gene were major stars in motion pictures and had their own radio, and later television, series. It wasn't, however, until they had established themselves as big-time film and radio stars, however, that their characters began to appear in comic strip and comic books.

Gene Autry was the son of a rancher and was born in Tioga, Texas. Autry began his career as a singing cowboy on KVOO radio in Texas in 1929, and he then performed on station WLS in Chicago. Autry became nationally known when he first sang his cowboy songs on the very popular country-and-western radio variety show *The Grand Ole Opry* in the 1930s. His subsequent guest starring appearances on that and other radio variety programs in the 1930s, as well as his successful cowboy song recordings, led him to Hollywood in 1932. Autry appeared in a series of cowboy films beginning in 1932 including the feature film *Boots and Saddle* in 1932, and starred in a twelve chapter film serial entitles *Phantom Empire* in 1934. These were followed by over fifty similar multi-part serials and films from *Melody Ranch* in 1940 to *The Big Sombrero* in 1949. By 1939, Gene had become the star of his own weekly radio show, *Gene Autry's Melody Ranch,* which featured music and a weekly western adventure story. As a recording artist, Gene Autry recorded three of the most popular recordings of all time; "Peter Cottontail," "Here Comes Santa Claus," and "Rudolph the Red-nosed Reindeer." His performing career was interrupted when World War Two broke out and Gene volunteered to serve in the

United States Army Air Force. When the war ended in 1945, Gene resumed his performing career. The cowboy star retired from show business in the 1960s, one of the wealthiest men in America. A millionaire many times over because of the many wise investments he had made during his long career, Autry was the owner of several radio and television stations, the Continental Hotel in Los Angeles, the Mark Hopkins Hotel in San Francisco, the California Angeles baseball team, and a motion picture and television program production company.

THE GREEN HORNET

One of the Golden Age of Radio's most memorable programs was *The Green Hornet* adventure series, which was created by George W. Trendle and Fran Striker, who were also responsible for giving the world the very popular *Lone Ranger* radio series. After the tremendous success of *The Lone Ranger* radio series in 1933, Fran Striker was asked to develop another, more modern, but similar, action hero for George W. Trendle's WXYZ radio station in Detroit, Michigan. Striker came up with the *Green Hornet* character, which was one the air from 1936 until 1952 and almost rivaled *The Lone Ranger*, which was on the air from 1933 until 1955, in popularity. Fran Striker, according to James Jewell, the oft-time director of both the *Lone Ranger* and *Green Hornet* radio series, once said that Fran Striker was "the greatest hack writer who ever lived." Jewell estimated that Striker had written about 60,000 words a week and was responsible for 156 *Lone Ranger* and 1004 *Green Hornet* shows during their hey-days, as well writing as 12 *Lone Ranger* novels and the story lines for 355 *Lone Ranger* comic books and newspaper strips. Striker also wrote the *Challenge of the Yukon* and *Ned Jordan, Secret Agent* radio series, and made invaluable contributions to several *Lone Ranger* movie serials and feature films over the years. Unfortunately, George W. Trendle retained all of the rights to both *The Lone Ranger* and *Green Hornet* and Striker, who was always a salaried employee, never shared in any of those show's enormous profits. Fran Striker died in 1962, and was inducted into the Radio Hall of Fame on September 4, 1962.

The premise of the *Green Hornet* series, which made its on-air debut on January 31, 1936, was simply that it was a modern-day version of the *Lone Ranger* series, which, like *The Green Hornet* aired from the studios of W.X.Y.Z. in Detroit, Michigan. The main character on *The Green Hornet* was a young man named Britt Reid, who published the *Daily Sentinel* newspaper and whose crime-fighting alter ego was an action hero named "The Green Hornet." Britt was the great-nephew of the Lone Ranger and, like his great-uncle, he was determined to rid the world of criminal elements. While The Lone Ranger character had his "great white horse, Silver" to transport him from place to place in the American West of the late 1800s, Britt had his high-powered car, which he called "Black Beauty," to take him around town. Like his great uncle, who had an Indian companion named Tonto who helped him fight outlaws, Britt had a Japanese valet (who became a Filipino when World War Two broke out) named Kato, to help him fight the bad guys. The Lone Ranger was often thought to be an outlaw, because he always wore a black mask to keep his true identity a secret, and Britt Reid made it seem that the Green Hornet was a villain, while actually fighting crime in the big city. Wearing his "Green Hornet" mask and costume, Britt would often actively make the police think that he was the mastermind behind a crime and then lead the authorities to the real criminals, escaping capture only minutes before the police arrived on the scene. Working only during the darkness of night, The Green Hornet and his pal, Kato, put away hundreds of nasty criminals during the sixteen years the program was aired. The radio episodes ran for thirty minutes and were usually heard two times a week. In the middle of its long run, the program aired for thirty minutes just once a week, but during the series' last season in 1952, the series reverted to its twice-a-week schedule. *The Green Hornet's* adventures were written by Fran Striker, the same man who was responsible for writing *The Long Ranger* scripts. Four actors played the Green Hornet/Britt Reid role on radio over the years. Actor Al Hodge originated the role in 1936 and played the part until 1943. (Hodge later became television's *Captain Video*) Donavan Faust played The Green Hornet in

(Credit: Photofest)

Al Hodge, later well known as *Captain Video*, one of television's earliest action heroes, was the original actor who played *The Green Hornet* on radio in 1936.

Radio's Golden Age

1943, and then Bob Hall played the role from 1944 until 1951. Finally, Jack McCarthy played the part in 1952, the year the last episode was aired. Also heard on the radio series over the years were Raymond Hayashi, Rollon Parker, and Mickey Tolan as Kato, Lee Allman as Reid's faithful secretary Lenore Case (called "Casey" by Reid), Jim Irwin and then Gil Shea, as reporter, Michael Axford, Jack Petruzzi as ace reporter, Ed Lowry, and Rollon Parker as the newsboy. Also frequently heard on the series were Paul Hughes and John Todd, both of whom were regulars on *The Lone Ranger*. *The Green Hornet's* announcers were Charles Woods, Mike Wallace, Fielden Farrington, Bob Hite and Hal Neal and the series was directed by Charles Livingstone. Fans of *The Green Hornet* remember that the show's unforgettable theme music was Rimsky-Korsakov's "Flight of the Bumble Bee." In the 1960s *The Green Hornet* became a TV series and starred Van Williams as the Hornet/Reid and Bruce Lee, who later became a popular action film star, as Kato.

Because of the popularity of the radio series, *The Green Hornet* became a comic book in 1940. The series of comics were published by Holyoke and six issues were released from December, 1940 until August, 1941. From 1942 until September, 1949, *Harvey Family Comics* included the Green Hornet character as one of its features and The Hornet also appeared in two issues of Harvey's "All New" comics in 1946 and 1947. Dell Comics published one issue of *The Green Hornet* in 1953 and Gold Key published three issues of *Green Hornet* comics from November 1966 through August 1967. New *Green Hornet* comics were also published in the 1980s into the 1990s.

GREEN HORNET RADIO SERIES PERFORMER

HODGE, AL B. 1912 – D. 1979 (THE GREEN HORNET/BRITT REID)

Al Hodge, who played The Green Hornet/Britt Reid role on radio from 1936 until 1943, was born into a show business family in Rovena, Ohio. Al's father was a rider with the *Buffalo Bill Wild West Show*. Al attended the University of Miami in Oxford, Ohio, where he majored in Drama and was a successful track star. After graduating from college, Hodge acted in various summer stock productions and went on tour with the Casford Drama Troupe, which toured the country, before becoming a radio announcer in the early 1930s. Hodge worked as an announcer on several radio station in New England before he joined the staff at WXYZ in Detroit, Michigan. The station produced several radio shows that received national attention including the popular *Lone Ranger* and *Bobby Benson's Adventures* series. In addition to writing scripts for these series and announcing and directing those and other radio series at WXYZ, Hodge starred on the successful *Green Hornet* series as the title character for seven years. He also played Tex Mason on the *Songs of the B-Bar-B Show* from 1936 until 1943. In 1943, while World War Two was raging in Europe and the South Pacific, Hodge enlisted in the Navy. When the war ended, he resumed his career on radio in New York City where he was heard on such programs as *Gangbusters, Mr. District Attorney, Mr. Keen, Tracer of Lost Persons,* and many other series. In 1951, Hodge was cast in what became his most famous role, Captain Video, on the early television afternoon adventure series, *Captain Video,* which was presented on the now defunct Dumont Television network. When *Captain Video* left the air, Hodge had a difficult time getting other acting assignments, because he had become so identified with the role of Captain Video in the public's minds. Hodge went to Hollywood where he managed to get small supporting roles on several TV series such as *Alfred Hitchcock Presents, Tightrope, Hawaiian Eye, Naked City, M-Squad,* and *Mannix.* The parts he got, however, were few and far between and the actor found it difficult making a living in his chosen profession. Al Hodge died alone and almost destitute in 1979. At the time of his death, Hodge was living on his $63 a week Social Security check.

THE GUMPS

One of the longest-running comic strips in the United States was a series called *The Gumps,* which was first published in 1917 and remained in print until 1959. The main character in the comic strip was Andy Gump, who became somewhat of a national hero, in spite of his goofy appearance and awkward demeanor. Andy had absolutely no chin, and a brush of a mustache and beady little eyes, but readers loved Andy and couldn't wait to read each installment of the comic strip. The basic idea for *The Gumps* comic strip came from Captain Joseph M. Patterson, the editor and publisher of *The Chicago Tribune* newspaper, who claimed he based the Gumps on his own family. Patterson was also responsible for the *Moon Mullins, Winnie Winkle* and *Little Orphan Annie* comic strips. Patterson said he wanted to feature a strip in his newspaper that was a "domestic comedy" about ordinary people who were not too bright, not good looking and certainly not rich. He even came up with the name "Gump" for the family, which was a term he personally used for members of "the uneducated masses." Patterson hired the talented cartoonist Sidney Smith to draw *The Gumps,* which made its debut on February 12, 1917. It was Smith who decided what Andy, his wife Min, their son, Chester, their wealthy uncle, Bim, and his maid, Tilda should look like, although it is likely the opinionated Patterson had something to say about that as well. Smith began the strip by drawing the ordinary things that happened to the Gump family during their everyday lives but he gradually developed more complicated story lines for the family. *The Gumps* was popular with the comic strip reading public from the moment it appeared in *The Chicago Tribune* and it was soon being seen in *The New York Daily News,* and other newspapers throughout the country. Before long, there were Andy Gump song sheets being published and sung all across America, an Andy Gump board game, and numerous Gumps toys and books, as well as a series of *Gumps* animated film cartoons, which were released in 1931.

The Gumps was the very first comic strip to be adapted to radio and the series was first heard on the local radio station WGN in Chicago in 1931. An actor named Jack Boyle played the Andy Gump role on the local Chicago series, Dorothy Denver played Min Gump, Andy's wife, Charles Flynn played Chester, and Bess Flynn played Tilda, the maid. In 1934, *The Gumps* made its debut as a national network series and was heard for fifteen minutes a day, five days a week, on the CBS network. Stage and silent film comedian Wilmer Walter starred as Andy Gump on the program, and Agnes Moorehead played his wife, Min Gump. Also heard on the series was child actor Jack Grimes playing their son, Chester Gump. *The Gumps* announcer was Ralph Edwards. The Columbia Broadcasting System's *Gumps* series was written by Himan Brown and Irwin Shaw and enjoyed a three year run on CBS.

THE GUMPS RADIO SERIES PERFORMERS

KELK, JACKIE B. 1922 (CHESTER GUMP)

Jackie Kelk made a successful transition from being a child actor to playing teenager roles on radio and on the Broadway stage. He seldom found himself out of work as a performer during the first thirty years of his life. Born in Brooklyn, New York, Jackie attended the Professional Children's School in New York and in 1933, when he was twelve years old, he appeared in no less than three plays on the Broadway stage; *Bridal Wise, The Perfect Marriage,* and *Goodbye Again.* In 1936, Kelk had a role in the play *Jubilee,* in 1943 he was in *Flare Path,* and in 1947 he was featured in the play *Tenting Tonight* on Broadway. While he was performing on Broadway, Jackie made his debut as a radio actor on *The Chase and Sanborn Hour* and then played several spoiled brat kid roles on radio shows that starred George Burns and Gracie Allen, Eddie Cantor, Bert Lahr, and Jack Benny. He also had regular running roles on such popular children's radio shows as the popular Saturday morning programs *Coast to Coast on a Bus* and *The Gumps* (playing Andy and Mind Gumps' son, Chester Gump). In the late 1930s into the 1940s, Kelk was also a regular performer on the *Hello Peggy* and *The Aldrich Family* (as Henry's friend, Homer Brown) radio programs and was frequently heard on such programs as *Amanda of Honeymoon Hill, Hilltop House, Mother of Mine,* and *Valiant Lady.* In addition to his role on *The Gumps,* Jackie had the distinction of playing roles on three

Jackie Kelk played Chester Gump on the less-than-successful radio adaptation of Sidney Smith's *The Gumps* comic strip. A popular juvenile actor on many radio programs in the 1930s and 1940s, Jackie is seen above with actress Mary Rolfe during a broadcast of *The Aldrich Family* radio show.

other successful comic strips that were adapted to radio: Jimmy Olsen on *The Adventures of Superman*, Terry Lee on *Terry and the Pirates* and Junior Tracy on *Dick Tracy*. In 1949, Kelk repeated his Homer Brown on the television version of *The Aldrich Family* series. When *The Aldrich Family* TV show was canceled in 1951, the producers of the series developed a new TV show for Kelk that was called *Young Mr. Bobbins*, but the series failed to attract of audience and was canceled after only a few episodes were aired. Of all of the radio and TV shows Kelk was featured on, the actor later said that one of the highlights of his career was when he appeared on the *Theater Guild on the Air* hour-long radio program's adaptation of Eugene O'Neill's classic play "Ah Wilderness." In 1954, Kelk returned to Broadway when he appeared on the musical comedy *Me and Juliet*. In the 1950s, he also had featured roles in the films *Somebody Up There Likes Me* (1956) and *Pajama Game* (1957), but roles on TV and in films and on the stage had, by this time, become less and less frequent. Kelk eventually decided to retire from show business to pursue a less pubic life in the private sector.

MOOREHEAD, AGNES (SEE *BRINGING UP FATHER* FOR BIOGRAPHY)

WALTER, WILMER B. 1884 – D. 1941 (ANDY GUMP)

Little has been uncovered about the life and career of actor Wilmer Walter, who played Andy Gump on the radio adaptation of the popular Sidney Smith comic strip, *The Gumps*, when it was heard on the CBS network in 1934. Mr. Walter is known to have appeared in such silent films as *The Fair Pretender* as early as 1918, and had a featured role on Broadway in the play *For Better or*

Worse in 1927. In addition to playing Andy Gump on radio, Walter also had the title role on the original broadcasts of what became a long-running radio series *David Harum,* which made its radio debut in 1936, but apparently he did not work on that series very long. The actor died in 1941, which was five years after *David Harum* was first broadcast, and two years after *The Gumps* left the airways.

H

HAROLD TEEN

Years before there were teen age media idols like Archie Andrews, Andy Hardy, and Henry Aldrich, there was Carl Ed's comic strip teen hero, *Harold Teen*. In the 1930s, when cartoonist Carl Ed was asked why he had started drawing what eventually became the popular, long-running comic strip *Harold Teen* in 1919, he said, "Twenty years ago there was no comic strip on adolescence. I thought every well-balanced comic sheet should have one." The Harold Teen character was just like every typical teenager. He used teen slang words, and even originated some of the 1920s most popular teen expressions such as, "Yowsah," "Fan ma brow," "Pitch a li'l woo," and "pantywaist." Carl Ed's *Harold Teen* also popularized several teen fashions of his time, including bell-bottom pants and yellow raincoats. In the *Harold Teen* comic strip, Harold had a girlfriend named Lillums, a best friend named Shadow, and of course, he had trouble communicating with his parents who in turn found it difficult understanding their adolescent son. Harold and his friends often went to the neighborhood soda fountain, "Pop Jenks," to "sip sodas," and often got into trouble with his teachers at school. Harold was, however, basically a good kid and he became one of America's fictional characters in the 1920s into the 1930s. During those years, Harold Teen items seemed to be everywhere. There were *Harold Teen* toys, figurines, and *Harold Teen* Big Little Books, a *Harold Teen* released in 1928 which starred Arthur Lake (who later became famous as Dagwood Bumstead in the *Blondie* films and on the radio series) as Harold, and six years later in 1934, there was a second *Harold Teen* film that starred popular film comedian Hal LeRoy as Harold. In the 1930s, several *Harold Teen* comic books appeared in print in addition to Ed's daily and Sunday supplement comic strip series.

Artist Carl Ed's (1890 – 1959) first job as a cartoonist was for the sports pages of the Chicago American newspaper in 1912. The publisher of the newspaper was impressed with Ed's artistic talents and encouraged him to try his hand at drawing a comic strip for the newspaper. He wanted his comic strip to feature a typical American teenage boy as its main character. In 1918, Carl Ed's *Harold Teen* made its first appearance in the Chicago American and soon became one of the country's favorite comic strips, especially in the 1920s when the United States was enjoying widespread prosperity and economic growth. When the Great Depression descended upon America in 1929, the popularity of the comic strip about the carefree teen, Harold Teen, waned. The comic strip's became popular again for a short time during in the 1940s when the U. S. entered World War Two and Harold became a government spy in uniform. When the war ended, interest in Harold and his pals diminished and when artist Carl Ed died in 1959 at the age of sixty-nine, *Harold Teen* died with him and the character ceased to appear in the nation's newspapers.

In 1941, a *Harold Teen* radio series was produced that was broadcast from Chicago. The program's first episode was aired on August 5, 1941 and the series remained on the air for several years. Actor Charles Flynn originally played the role of Harold on radio, but Flynn was soon replaced by actors Willard Farnum, and then by Eddie Firestone, Jr. in the part. Bob Jellison played Harold's pal, Shadow, Loretta Poynton, and then Euince Yankee, played Lillums, Harold Waterman played Harold's father. Also heard on the series were Beryl Vaughn, Rosemary Garbell, Marvin Miller, and Jack Spencer. The series was directed by Blair Walliser and written by Walliser and Fred Kress.

HAROLD TEEN RADIO SERIES PERFORMERS

FARNUM, WILLARD B. 1916 – 1943 ? (HAROLD TEEN)

Willard Farnum was the second actor to play the title role of Harold Teen on the 1941 radio adaptation of Carl Ed's popular *Harold Teen* comic strip, but he had the longest tenure in that role. *Harold Teen* was America's first teenage comic strip hero, and he had been introduced to the American public in 1918. His teenage misadventures delighted comic strip readers for over forty years. Harold was the prototype for a succession of teenage boys who followed including *Archie Andrews* in the comics, *Henry Aldrich* on the radio, and Andy Hardy in films. Bill Farnum was, when he was cast as Harold Teen, one of the busiest young actors on radio. In the 1930s and 1940s, in addition to *Harold Teen,* Farnum was also heard on such Chicago-based programs as *Dan Harding's Wife, Flying Time, Midstream, A Tale of Today, Today's Children* and *The Woman in White.* When World War Two broke out in 1941, Farnum entered the U. S. military and his career as an actor appears to have come to an end. It has been rumored that Bill Farnum entered the private sector after his discharge from military service, but it has also been said, but never substantiated, that "Bill" Farnum was killed in action in Europe during the war.

FIRESTONE, EDDIE JR. B. 1920 (HAROLD TEEN)

One of America's most successful young character actors, Eddie Firestone Jr. began his career on radio when he was a child. He starred as the perennial teenager *Harold Teen* on radio, replacing the actors who had originally played the role, Charles Flynn and Willard Farnum. Firestone also played major characters on such popular radio programs as *The Goldbergs, Hawthorne House, One Man's Family* (as Pinky), *The Story of Mary Marlin, That Brewster Boy* (in the title role of Joey Brewster), and *The Woman in White*. In the 1950s, Firestone began to work in films and on television. In the movies he had supporting roles in such films as *The Jackpot* (1950), *With a Song in my Heart* (1952), *Good Morning, Miss Dove* (1955), *The Revolt of Mamie Stover* (1956), *Angel Baby* (1961), *Two for the Seesaw* (1962), *Panic in the City* (1968), *Dragnet-66* (1969), *Cry Panic* (1974), and *I Take These Men* (1983). On television, the actor was featured on almost every major series produced from the early 1950s through the 1980s including *Dragnet, Four Star Playhouse, The Millionaire, The Medic, The Untouchables, Bonanza, Death Valley Days, Ben Casey, Perry Mason, Dr. Kildare, Rawhide, Mannix, Cannon, Ellery Queen, The Rockford Files, Hawaii Five-O, The Streets of San Francisco, Quincy, The Night Riders*, and many other shows.

FLYNN, CHARLES (CHARLES J. FLYNN) B. 1921 (HAROLD TEEN)

Charles Flynn was the first of three juvenile actors to play *Harold Teen* on radio. Flynn's best remembered and longest role on radio, however, was as Jack Armstrong, the All-American boy on the *Jack Armstrong* radio series which he played from 1939 until 1943. Flynn then played the grown-up Jack Armstrong on the radio series *Armstrong of the SBI*. In the 1930s and 1940s, Flynn was also featured on such radio series as *Bachelor Children, Silver Eagle, Mountie* and *We Are Four*. Flynn had a less-than-distinguished film career as well, and appeared in numerous films, usually playing small, uncredited roles. His film appearances include roles in *Hot Steel* (1940), *Mystery Sea Raider* (1940), *Penny Seranade* (1941), *Remember Pearl Harbor* (1942), *The Great Impersonator* (1942), *San Quentin* (1946), *That Brewster Girl* (1946), *Smash-Up: The Story of a Woman* (1947), *I, Jane Doe* (1948), *Road House* (1948), *It Happens Every Spring* (1949), *Father Was a Fullback* (1948), *No Way Out* (1950), *Has Anybody Seen My Gal* (1952), and *Francis Covers the Big Town* (1953), among others. On television, Flynn was featured on the short-lived *So Many Partings* series in 1967.

HOP HARRIGAN

The character "Hop Harrigan" who became known as America's "Ace of the Airways" when the popular comic book series *Hop Harrigan* was adapted to radio, was first seen in an All American Publications comic book, *All American Comics* issue #1, in April. 1939. Hop Harrigan was created by artist Jon L.

Blummer, and he was the first aviation hero to appear in a comic book series, although such aviators as *Terry and the Pirates* and *Tailspin Tommy* had previously appeared in newspaper comic strips. Hop Harrigan was a young man who was orphaned as a boy when his father, a famous pilot, disappeared on a flight to South America where he was going to visit his estranged wife. The boy was raised by a greedy neighbor who falsely claimed legal guardianship of Hop, in order to obtain his inheritance. When the wicked neighbor, who treated Hop very badly, as the comic book series revealed over the years, tried to destroy an old biplane that Hop's father had put in storage for him years before he left for South America, Hop took off in the biplane and never returned home. When his airplane had a mechanical failure, Hop landed it in an air field many miles away from home, and made a friend for life with a mechanic named Tank Tinker who saved Hop's life and put out a fire, just as the biplane was about to explode. Hop and his pal, Tank, subsequently launched the "All American Aviation Company," with the help of an heiress named Gail Nolan, who became Hop's girlfriend. The company became the base for Hop and Tank's many exciting future adventures. When World War Two broke out Hop, Tank, and a pilot/friend who was nicknamed "Prop Wash" joined the U. S. Army Air Corps and for the several years (1941–1945) most of their comic book adventures involved adventurous wartime activities. Hop Harrigan's adventures continued to delight young readers throughout the 1940s in the All American comic book series and also in the Comic Cavalcade comics.

In 1942, *Hop Harrigan* became the main character on a children adventure radio adventure series which was heard first on the Mutual Broadcasting System's network of stations, and was then heard on the ABC radio network. On the very first episode of the Mutual radio series, Hop joined the United States Army Air Corps. The radio series, thereafter, rather closely followed the story lines that had been seen in the *Hop Harrigan* comic books. Actor

J. L. Blummer's character, aviator *Hop Harrigan*, who made his debut in a comic strip in 1939, became the hero of a radio series three years later in 1942. Actor Chester Stratton was the original Hop Harrigan on the radio series.

Chester Stratton, and then Albert Aley, played "Hop" on the series, and Ken Lynch, and then Jackson Beck, played Tank Tinker. Actress Mitzi Gould was Hop's girlfriend, Gail Nolan, on the series. The *Hop Harrigan* radio program was directed by Jessica Maxwell, Allen Du Covny, and Jay Clark and written by Albert Aley, who also played Hop for a time. *Hop Harrigan* had one of radio's most exciting openings. Announcer Glenn Riggs would begin each episode saying, "Presenting Hop Harrigan…America's Ace of the Airwaves." The sound of an airplane in flight was then heard and Hop's voice said, "CX-4 calling control tower! CX-4 calling control tower! Standing by! Okay, this is Hop Harrigan coming in!!!" One year after World War Two ended in 1945, so did the *Hop Harrigan* radio series. The show aired its last broadcast on August 2, 1946. That same year, Columbia Pictures released the first fifteen minute, short subject episode of a fifteen part film series with Hop Harrigan as its main character. William Bakewell played Hop in the serial and Sumner Getchell played Tank Tinker. Bakewell had previously played *Harold Teen* in a 1928 film adaptation of that popular comic strip.

HOP HARRIGAN RADIO SERIES PERFORMERS

ALEY, ALBERT B. 1919 – D. 1986 (HOP HARRIGAN)

A triple threat in radio, Albert Aley was a successful radio actor, writer, and producer. Born in New York City, Aley was a beautiful child who was of Dutch and Spanish ancestry and he became a professional model when he was just five years old. Albert attended the Children's Professional School in New York. Impressed with his looks and performing talent, the school's principal introduced him to CBS's successful children's show producer/director Nila Mack in 1929. Miss Mack immediately made him a regular cast member on her *Let's Pretend* fairy tale anthology show. The talented youngster even directed a *Let's Pretend* program and CBS billed him as "Radio's Youngest Director" in publicity releases. In addition to acting on *Let's Pretend* Aley was also regularly featured on *The American School of the Air* and *Sunday Morning's at Aunt Susan's* radio programs. When he was in his teens, Albert began to write radio show scripts for such popular series as *The First Nighter* and soon radio fans magazines were calling him "Radio's youngest writer." When he was only twenty-three years old, Aley became the head writer of three radio series: *Superstition, Don Winslow of the Navy* and *Hop Harrigan*. On *Hop Harrigan*, Aley even took over the leading role of Hop when actor Chester Stratton left the show because of other commitments. Upon radio dramas untimely demise in the 1950s, Aley turned to television and he became the executive producer and chief writer of the *Tom Corbett, Space Cadet* TV series. Tom Corbett was one of early television's most popular children's adventure programs. Throughout the

1950s and 1960s, Aley continued to write scripts for such television shows as *Cheyenne, Have Gun, Will Travel, The Rifleman* and *Laramie*. In 1966, Aley wrote the screenplay for the Walt Disney company's blockbuster hit, *The Ugly Dachshund* and also became the main writer of such TV series as *Ironsides* and *Cimarron Strip*. Aley's last major show business achievement was as the producer of the hit TV series *The Paper Chase* in 1970. He continued to remain active in television until the early 1980s, when he settled into a well deserved retirement.

RIGGS, GLENN B. 1907 – D. 1975 (ANNOUNCER)
Glenn Riggs, who was born in Pittsburg, became one of NBC's busiest announcers during Radio's Golden Age. Riggs began his radio announcing career at KDKA on the *Musical Clock* program, which was one of radio first early morning shows. Before working on radio, Riggs had worked at a Westinghouse factory but he decided to become an actor. Acting jobs failed to materialize, but his wonderful rich baritone voice and his perfect diction earned him a job as a staff announcer at KDKA when he auditioned for a role in a radio play. Riggs joined the staff of announcers at NBC in 1938 and became one of their busiest announcers. In the 1940s, Riggs moved to the newly formed ABC network. Some of the comic strip oriented programs Riggs read his always stirring announcements for were *Hop Harrigan, Mark Trail*, and *Jungle Jim*. Riggs was also the announcer for such popular programs as *The Thin Man, Boston Blackie, My True Story, The Bing Crosby Show, Ethel and Albert, The Dunninger Show, Olivio Santoro,* and *Vic and Sade*. Riggs retired from radio in 1972, after working for twenty-nine years at ABC. He spent his retirement years living in Malaga, Spain.

STRATTON, CHESTER B. 1910 – D. 1970 (HOP HARRIGAN)
Chester Stratton decided that he wanted to become an actor while he was a student at Rutgers University and got his first job as a radio actor on station WMCA in New York shortly after he graduated from college. His masculine voice and perfect diction made him a good choice to play leading male roles on radio. Stratton also appeared in several Broadway plays in the 1930s including *White Oaks* with Ethel Barrymore, *A Connecticut Yankee in King Arthur's Court* with Vivian Segal, and in the national tour of *The Barretts of Wimpole Street* with Katherine Cornell. Among the numerous radio series on which he had the leading male roles were *Against the Styorm, Pepper Young's Family, Amanda of Honeymoon Hill, American School of the Air, The O'Neills, Wilderness Road, Light of the World, Lorenzo Jones, By Kathleen Norris, Cimarron Tavern, Bright Horizon, Big Sister, Her Honor, Nancy James, Mickey of the Circus, The First Nighter* and *Cavalcade of America*. Stratton was also the first actor to

play the title role of Hop Harrigan on the *Hop Harrigan* children's adventure serial. Equally as successful on television and in films as he had been on the stage and on radio, Chester Stratton appeared in such feature films as *Julius Caesar* (1953), *Ask McCall* (1960), *Advise and Consent* (1962), *The Greatest Story Ever Told* (1965) and *Sweet Charity* (1969), to name just a few and he also appeared on hundreds of television series including *Captain Video and His Video Rangers* (as a cast regular), *The Kraft TV Theater, Robert Montgomery Presents, The Hallmark Hall of Fame, The United States Steel Hour, Broken Arrow, Perry Mason, Have Gun, Will Travel, Maverick, Hawaiian Eye, The Goodyear Theater, Wagon Train, Twilight Zone, Thriller, The Bob Cummings Show, Ben Casey, The Beverly Hillbillies, The Munsters, Green Acres, I Spy, The Andy Griffith Show, Hogan's Heroes, Bonanza, Marcus Welby, MD,* and other TV shows too numerous to mention.

J

JANE ARDEN

The comic strip, *Jane Arden,* created by Monte Barrett and Russell E. Ross, was first published in 1927. Although moderately successful in the United States, the comic strip became one of Canada's and Australia's most popular newspaper features. Jane was a spirited newspaper reporter whose daily adventures were often more like something that could be heard on a radio soap opera series than seen in a comic strip. Jane Arden was, however, the prototype for such newspaper employed ladies as Brenda Starr and *Superman's* Lois Lane, which followed. The colored Sunday Funnies and the daily black and white newspaper

Comic strip characters seldom became the main characters on long-running radio soap opera series. *Jane Arden*, who had a long and successful run on radio from 1938 into the 1950s, was certainly an exception.

strip, *Jane Arden*, were the work of Monte Barrett and Russell Ross and then of Walt Graham and Jim Seed. The Sunday Funnies version of *Jane Arden* was especially popular with young girls, because it featured a full-size paper doll and a dress for the doll to wear. The *Jane Arden* strip was published in various newspapers in Canada and Australia, and in some cities in the United States, from 1927 until 1968.

Jane Arden made its debut as a radio series on the NBC Blue network in 1938. The series was typical of the many soap operas that were being heard as a five day a week soap opera series throughout the 1930s, 1940s and 1950s. The radio series starred actress Ruth Yorke, who played one of radio's first soap opera heroines on the *Marie the Little French Princess* series, which is said to have been one of the earliest soap opera programs on the air. The Jane Arden character was an admirable heroine who fought all sorts of diversities over the years, both in the comic strips and on the radio series, including an unfaithful bunch of boyfriends, the Great Depression, and a struggle to earn equality with men as a reporter. The cast of *Jane Arden* included such seasoned radio performers as Florence Freeman, Frank Provo, Helene Dumas, Howard Smith, Richard Gordon, Betty Garde, Spencer Bentley, Bill Baer, Henry Wadsworth, and Maurice Franklin, among others. Although the radio series remained on the air for two seasons, unable to compete with the ever-growing number of soap operas that crowded the daytime airwaves in the late 1930s into the 1940s, the comic strip continued to be published long after the radio series departed the airwaves.

One year after the *Jane Arden* radio series was first aired, a motion picture titled *The Adventures of Jane Arden* was released. The film, starred a relatively unknown actress named Rosella Towne as Jane, but it was well received by the public. In the film, ace reporter, Jane Arden, goes undercover to try to expose a gang of jewel thieves and smugglers. Jane really gets into trouble when her undercover character, Maxine Brownkow, is almost discovered by the gang's leaders.

JANE ARDEN RADIO SERIES PERFORMER

YORKE, RUTH B. CIRCA 1915 – ? (JANE ARDEN)

Before she became one of radio soap opera's most popular leading ladies, Ruth Yorke was an actress on Broadway. Reported to have had one of the most perfect female voices on the air, Miss Yorke had major roles in the Broadway plays *Parnell* in 1935, *Plumes in the Dust* in 1936, *All the Way* in 1938 and *Morning Star* in 1940, before settling into a career as a successful radio actress. The actress was regularly heard playing long-running roles on such popular radio series as *Amanda of Honeymoon Hill, Aunt Jenny, John's Other Wife, The Eno Crime Club, Life Can Be Beautiful, Little Italy, Marie the Little French Princess* (as Marie, on what is said to have been one of the first soap opera heard on radio), *Mother of Mine,* and as Jane, the long suffering heroine of the *Jane Arden* soap opera series. Miss Yorke apparently retired from show business after radio's untimely demise in the late 1950s and there is no record of any further appearances by Miss Yorke in films, on TV, or on the stage, that this author could uncover.

JOE PALOOKA

It took sports cartoonist Hammond Fisher seven years, from 1920 until 1927, to sell his comic strip idea about a good natured, not very bright, "palooka," or prize fighter, which he called *Joe Palooka*, to a newspaper syndicate. The company Fisher was finally able to sell his comic strip to was the McNaught Syndicate, who he had been working for selling other people's comic strip ideas to various newspapers around the country. Hammond Edward Fisher who was nicknamed "Ham" Fisher, had exhibited an interest in art and drawing from the time he was a young boy. In 1919, when he was eighteen years old, he got his first job for a newspaper as an editorial and sports cartoonist. When *Joe Palooka* finally appeared in print, Fisher hired a talented cartoonist to assist

Ham Fisher's *Joe Palooka* comic strip arrived on radio in the 1930s and departed the airwaves after a short time on the air. Actor Alan Reed played the role of Joe on the radio adaptation.

him with the drawing of the strip. The artist's name was Alfred G. Caplin, who later changed his name to "Al" Capp and, on his own, and created the very successful *Li'l Abner* comic strip. At one time, *Joe Palooka* fought a hillbilly named Big Levitcus, and it was this character that led to Capp to develop a comic strip about a hillbilly of his own. After Capp left Fisher's employ, Fisher kept bringing the Leviticus back over and over again and this led to a feud between the two cartoonists that lasted for many years. At the height of their feud, Fisher spitefully took Capp to court, accusing him of using obscene material in his *Li'l Abner* comic strip. To support his claim, Fisher used fake examples of the Li'l Abner strip, which he had drawn himself, to try to prove his case. When the truth came out, Fisher lost the case and was expelled from the National Cartoonist's Society. Distraught by the outcome of the court case and humiliated that he had been exposed as a fraud, Fisher, whose *Joe Palooka* comic strip was dropped from syndication, ended his own life in 1955 at the age of fifty-four.

In addition to boxer Joe Palooka, other characters who appeared regularly in Fisher's strip were Joe's manager, an excitable Irishman named Knobby Walsh, his lovely fiancée, Ann Howe (who finally Joe married in 1948, much to the public's relief), a mute little boy named "Little Max," and Joe's odd friend, Humphrey Pennyworth. The *Joe Palooka* character not only fought in the ring, he also battled criminals, and even ghosts and then Nazi's during World War Two. Joe Palooka was the son most American parents wished they had. He was principled and had high moral standards and possessed a strong desire to combat the evil in the world. The *Joe Palooka* comic strip eventually led to *Joe Palooka* comic books which were published by Harvey Comic's in their *Feature Funnies* (as the comic books' cover boy) and in twelve issues of *Columbia Comics* from 1945 until 1961. Harvey also published a few of *Joe Palooka's* friends in comic books of their own. After Capp left Fisher, artist Mo Leff was hired to assist Fisher with the drawing of the comic strip and Leff remained with Fisher until 1959, when the artist committed suicide. Cartoonist Tony DiPreta took over the drawing of the strip after Leff departed. At the peak of its popularity, the *Joe Palooka* comic strip was being read by millions of people throughout the world and was being published in over one thousand newspapers, making Ham Fisher one of the wealthiest comic book creators in the field, until his feud with Al Capp ended his career. The last *Joe Palooka* comic strip appeared in newspapers in April, 1984.

Because of its popularity, *Joe Palooka* became the main character in a featured film that was released in 1934 and this led to several movie sequels. Joe Kirkwood, Jr. played Joe in most of these films, which continued into the 1950s. In the 1930s, a radio adaptation of Fisher's popular strip was produced in Chicago and starred actor Teddy Bergman as *Joe Palooka*. Later Bergman became better known as Alan Reed, and Reed's voice was world-famous as the voice of Fred Flintstone in the TV animated cartoon series. Norman Gottschalk, and then Karl Swenson, replaced Bergman as Joe on the radio series for short periods of time. Elsie Hitz played Joe's fiancée, Ann Howe, on the radio series and Hitz was then replaced by actress Mary Jane Higby. Knobby Walsh was played by veteran radio actor Frank Readick. The series did not enjoy the success, or the long run, of its comic strip inspiration, and left the airwaves in the late 1930s.

JOE PALOOKA RADIO SERIES PERFORMERS

HIGBY, MARY JANE B. 1915 – D. 1986 (ANNE HOWE)

One of the Golden Age of Radio's most successful actresses, Mary Jane Higby, was born in California and made her radio debut on such Hollywood-based shows as *Parties at Pickfair* (which starred silent film star Mary Pickford) and *The Shell Chateau*. In the late 1930s, Miss Higby moved east to New York, where she felt she would find better radio roles to suit her talents. In New York, she soon found herself constantly employed and she was heard on such programs as the radio adaptation of Ham Fisher's popular comic strip *Joe Palooka*, playing Joe's girlfriend, Anne Howe, and as the leading lady or a regular, running character on such radio soap operas as *When A Girl Marries* (as the title character, Joan Davis, from 1938 until 1956) and *This is Nora Drake* (as Nora from 1958–1959). She was also regularly featured on such series as *John's Other Wife, Joyce Jordan, Girl Intern, Linda's First Love, The Romance of Helen Trent, Stella Dallas, The Story of Mary Marlin, Thanks for Tomorrow,* and many other soap opera programs. Mary Jane Higby's radio acting was not limited to soap operas. She was also frequently heard on such prime time programs as *The Mysterious Traveler, Inner Sanctum Mysteries,* and *Nick Carter, Master Detective*. In the 1960s, when radio dramas had all but disappeared from the airwaves, Higby kept herself busy dubbing foreign films and doing voice over work for radio and television commercials. In the 1970s, Mary Jane was one of the many former Golden Age actresses who returned to radio on Himan Brown's *CBS Mystery Theater* series, on which she was heard on over thirty-five broadcasts. As far as this author could determine, Mary Jane Higby only made one appearance in a film. In 1970, she had a featured role in *The Honeymoon Killers*.

HITZ, ELSIE B. 1902 – ? (ANNE HOWE)

Actress Elsie Hitz, who was born in Cleveland, Ohio, began her professional acting career as a child. Elsie's parents took her to New York where they thought her exceptional talent as an actress would soon be recognized. They were proven right and after a few months in New York, Elsie, who was twelve years old, made her Broadway debut in a play called *Miss Daisy*. She subsequently appeared on Broadway in the 1920s in a play called in *Restless Women*, before beginning what would become a busy career as a radio actress. Elsie's first radio role was in an adaptation of the Broadway musical "Showboat" on *The Eveready Hour* which starred film and stage actor Lionel

Atwell. In 1932, Elsie was heard on a series of programs, *The Magic Voice, Follow the Moon,* and *Dangerous Paradise* which made her the talk of show business. On these fifteen minute programs, Elsie read romantic poetry and Nick Dawson announced the poems, narrated the shows and made appropriate comments. Elsie and Dawson's sexy readings and voices earned them reputations as Depression Era sex symbols and the shows became enormously popular all over the country. This led to Elsie's being heard on many daytime soap operas throughout the 1930s and into the 1940s including *Ellen Randolph, Life Can Be Beautiful,* and *Stella Dallas.* She also starred on such evening radio series as *An Evening in Paris, Barry Cameron,* and, later in her career, on *My True Story Hour with Mary and Bob.* One of her most memorable roles, however, was as Anne Howe, on the radio adaptation of Ham Fisher's *Joe Palooka* comic strip in the late 1930s. After the demise of radio drama in the late 1950s, Miss Hitz disappeared from the show business scene. It has been reported that she is still alive and well, and if this is true, she would be over one hundred years old. Other sources have said, however, that Elsie Hitz died in the 1970s, but no amount of research has revealed thus far which of these reports are true. Hopefully, it is the former.

READICK, FRANK (KNOBBY WALSH, SEE *SMILIN' JACK* FOR BIOGRAPHY)

REED, ALAN A.K.A. TEDDY BERGMAN B. 1907 – D. 1977 (JOE PALOOKA)
New York City born Alan Reed, who began his professional performing career as Teddy Bergman, decided he wanted to be an actor while he was majoring in Journalism at Columbia University. When he graduated from Columbia, he applied for an acting apprenticeship at the famed Provincetown Playhouse in New York. A talented dialectician, Teddy Bergman could perform in any dialect and this talent soon led him to the casting offices of The Theater Guild, which produced Broadway plays. The Guild was suitably impressed with Teddy's acting ability and he was cast in two Broadway plays; *Double Dummy* (1936), and *A House in the Country* (1937). He continued to appear on Broadway in such plays as *Love's Old Sweet Song, Hope for a Harvest* and *The Pirate* in the 1930s. Because of his versatility as a dialectician, became a radio actor. He had major roles on such radio series as *Abie Irish Rose* (as Papa Levy), *Meyer the Buyer, Big Sister, The Ford Theater, Pages of Romance, The Shadow, Valiant Lady, The Ziegfeld Follies of the Air, Harv and Esther, Ellery Queen, Myrt and Marge, The Tim and Irene Show, The Maxwell House Coffee Time* (as Baby Snooks' Daddy), *The Fred Allen Show* (as ham actor Flagstaff Openshaw), and many other programs including the title role on the radio adaptation of Ham Fisher's comic strip, *Joe Palooka,* as well as on the *Flash Gordon* series. In 1943, Reed, who had changed his professional name to Alan Reed, relocated to

Hollywood where he soon established himself as one of the West Coast's busiest radio, film, and later television performers. He was heard on such popular radio programs as *Duffy's Tavern, Life With Luigi* (as Luigi's boss, Pasquale), *The Mel Blanc Show, My Friend Irma* (as Irma's boss, Mr. Clyde), and many, many other programs. Reed was also active in films. He had supporting roles in such films as *Days of Glory* (1944), *The Postman Always Rings Twice* (1946), *The Redhead and the Cowboy* (1950), *Perfect Strangers* (1950), *Here Comes the Groom* (1951), *Viva Zapata* (1952), *I, the Jury* (1953), *Kiss of Fire* (1953), *The Desperate Hours* (1955), *The Revolt of Mamie Stover* (1956), *Marjorie Morningstar* (1958), *Breakfast at Tiffany's* (1961), *A Dream of Kings* (1969), and *The Seniors* (1978), among others. On television, Reed was regularly seen on such series as *Life With Luigi, Duffy's Tavern, Mr. Adams and Eve, Where's Huddles,* and he was the voice of Fred Flintstone on hundreds of *Flintstone* animated TV cartoons. He also provided voices for many other cartoon characters. The actor also made guest appearances on such TV series as *Your Show Time, The Goodyear Television Playhouse, Alfred Hitchcock Presents, The Gale Storm Show, The Bob Cummings Show, The Donna Reed Show, Have Gun, Will Travel, Michael Shayne, Bachelor Father, The Lucille Ball Show, The Dick VanDyke Show, The Beverly Hillbillies, The Addams Family, Dr. Kildare, Batman, Petticoat Junction,* and many other series. Alan Reed died at the age of seventy, after a long illness in 1977.

SWENSON, KARL B. 1908 – D. 1978 (JOE PALOOKA)

Few actors enjoyed longer or more diverse careers than Karl Swenson. Born in Brooklyn, New York, Swenson studied medicine, before being bitten by the acting bug and deciding he wanted to be an actor. From the early 1930s until the late 1970s, Swenson appeared in hundreds of plays, television series, and films and was heard on most of the major radio programs of Radio's Golden Age, the 1930s – 1950s. Swenson made his Broadway debut in the play *A Glass of Water* in 1939, and subsequently appeared on Broadway in the plays *Carrie Nation* (1932), *One Sunday Afternoon* (1973), *House of Remsen* (1934), *It's You I Want* (1935), *Panic* (1935), and *The Man Who Had All the Luck* (1944), which was Arthur Miller's first play on Broadway. Swenson's first major role on radio was as the dumb-but-heroic prizefighter *Joe Palooka* on the radio series adaptation of Ham Fisher's popular comic strip. This led to roles on such varied radio programs as *The Cavalcade of America, Our Gal Sunday* (on which he played the male lead of Lord Henry Brinthrope from 1935 until 1955), *Lorenzo Jones* (as Lorenzo from 1937 until 1955), *Mr. Chameleon* (as Mr. Cameleon from 1948–1951), *Great Novels, Linda' First Love, Portia Faces Life, Inner Sanctum Mysteries, Grand Central Station, There Was A Woman, Aunt Jenny's*

Real Life Stories, The Court of Missing Heirs, The March of Time, The Ford Theater, This is Your FBI, and many other programs. In the mid 1950s, as radio drama disappeared from the airwaves, Swenson moved to Hollywood where he soon became active in films and on television. He had featured roles in such films as *Four Boys and a Gun* (1957, his film debut), *Kings Go Forth* (1958), *One Foot in Hell* (1968), *North to Alaska* (1960), *Judgment at Nuremberg* (1961), *How the West Was Won* (1962), *The Birds* (1963), *The Sons of Katie Elder* (1968), *Hour of the Gun* (1967) and *Wild Country* (1971), and many others. His very active television acting career included regular roles on the series *The Little House on the Prairie* (from 1974 until 1978, as Lars Hanson), *Gus and the Pulpit* (1973, as Adams), *Howling in the Woods* (1971, as Apperton), as well as appearances on most of the other TV series there were aired between the mid-1950s and the late 1970s including *The Kraft Television Playhouse, The U. S. Steel Hour, Robert Montgomery Presents, Gunsmoke, Maverick, Leave It to Beaver, Sugarfoot, Alfred Hitchcock Presents, Cheyenne, Have Gun, Will Travel, Bat Masterson, The Jack Benny Show, Rawhide, The Rebel, The Rifleman, Hawaiian Eye, Bonanzo, 77 Sunset Strip, The Untouchables, Ben Casey, Perry Mason, The Andy Griffith Show, Laramie, Wagon Train, Lassie, Gomer Pyle, USMC, Wagon Train, Big Valley, Cannon,* and many other shows.

JUNGLE JIM

The *Jungle Jim* comic strip, which was created and written by Don Moore and drawn by Alex Raymond (See *Flash Gordon* for biographical information) was distributed by King Features Syndicate, and was first published in 1934 as King Features answer to United Features Syndicate's popular *Tarzan* comic strip. King Features also published the science fiction comic strip *Flash Gordon* to compete with United's *Buck Rogers in the 25th Century* comic strip. Unlike the *Tarzan* character, *Jungle Jim* did not wear a loincloth, consort with apes, or swing through the jungle on vines. Jim was a Caucasian hunter who wore jodhpurs and a pith helmet, used side arms, and lived in the jungles of Southeast Asia, not the jungles of Tarzan's Africa. Jungle Jim had a big, brawny native friend named Kolu, who assisted him in his plight to rid the jungles of bad guys. Later on in the series, a beautiful young lady named Lilli deVrille joined Jim and Kolu in the jungle. When the U. S. entered World War Two in the early 1940s, Jim turned his attention from tracking down slave traders, river pirates, and other menaces to his beloved jungle, to fighting the evil military forces of the Japan, our World War Two enemy. In 1944, artist artist Alex Raymond joined the Marines and several other cartoonists drew the *Jungle Jim* comic strip. The best of them was Paul Norris, who drew the strip beginning in 1948. *Jungle Jim* enjoyed a brief renaissance until 1952, when once again a series of other artists took over the strip. *Jungle Jim's* last comic strip newspaper panel was published in 1954.

In 1935, one year after *Jungle Jim* made its comic strip debut, Jim became the hero of a popular, fifteen minute, five-days-a-week radio adventure series. The radio series, which remained on the air for an impressive nineteen years, actually equaled the comic strips' long run. The syndicated radio show starred actor Matt Crowley for almost the entire time the series was aired, with Gerald Mohr briefly replacing Crowley for a short time in 1938. Juano Hernandez played Jim's sidekick, Kolu and Franc (pronounced France) Hale played the exotic Shanghai Lil. Also heard on the series over the years were Irene Winston as Tiger Lil (Shanghai Lili's replacement), Owen Jordan as Tom Sun, Arthur Hughes as Sigh-Lee and, at various times, Jack Lloyd, Vicki Vola, and Kenny Delmar, among others. Glenn Riggs and Roger Krupp were the program's announcers. The series was produced and written by Jay Clark and directed by Steve Buchanan and Irene Fenton. The plots of the *Jungle Jim* radio show were decidedly more adult than most children's adventure serials of the time. Typical of the many-episode adventures heard on *Jungle Jim* were "The Bat Woman" (which was the first adventure heard on the series in 1935), "Ghost of the Java Sea" (broadcast in 1937) "Chen Lu and the Island of Pearls" (1946),"Indo-China Expedition" (1948) "The Pirates of Pearl Island" (1949), and "Andura Island Gold Treasure" (1954).

Matt Crowley was a popular leading man on several radio series. In addition to playing Jim on the Jungle Jim radio series, he also played Buck Rogers on the *Buck Rogers in the 25th Century* program.

Jungle Jim was also the main character in a twelve-part movie serial that was produced by Universal Pictures in 1936. Actor Grant Withers played Jim in these films. Previously published *Jungle Jim* comic strips were reprinted in the back pages of King Features' *Ace Comics* in the late 1930s-into the 1940s. In 1948, Columbia Pictures released a series of *Jungle Jim* films starring filmdom's former *Tarzan,* Johnny Weissmueller, who had gotten a bit too stout to play the skimpily clad film *Tarzan.* The last of Weissmueller's *Jungle Jim* films was released by Columbia in 1952. Standard Comic Books published eleven issues of *Jungle Jim* comics from 1949–1951. The last original *Jungle Jim* comic books were published by Charlton in 1969–1970.

JUNGLE JIM RADIO SERIES PERFORMERS

CROWLEY, MATT A.K.A. MATTHEW CROWLEY B. 1904 – D. 1983 (JUNGLE JIM)

One of the Golden Age of Radio's busiest leading men, Matt Crowley had a masculine, attractive-sounding voice that made him a natural choice to play heroes on many radio programs. Crowley, who was born in New Haven, Connecticut, was a graduate of that city's Yale University where he had studied Drama. Crowley began his acting career on the Broadway stage in New York City and had featured roles in the plays *The Front Page* in 1928 and *Oh, Promise Me* in 1930. He soon discovered, however, that acting on radio was far more lucrative than acting on the stage. His well trained, pleasant-sounding voice made him one of the most sought after actors in radio. No other actor played more heroic comic strip characters on radio than Matt Crowley. In the 1930s and 1940s, he played Batman on *The Adventures of Superman* radio series, Mark Trail on the *Mark Trail* series, Jungle Jim on the *Jungle Jim* program, Dick Tracy on the *Dick Tracy* series, and Buck on the *Buck Rogers in the 25th Century* series. As if this was not enough to keep the actor busy, he also played leading male roles on such radio series as *John's Other Wife, Pretty Kitty Kelly, and The Road of Life, Myrt and Marge, Brenda Curtis, Amanda of Honeymoon Hill,* and *Perry Mason,* and many other programs . In spite of his active career on radio, Crowley continued to appear in such Broadway plays as *The Eve of St. Mark* in 1943 and *Decision* in 1944. As radio dramas became less and less frequent on the airwaves in the late 1950s, Crowley began to appear on television and in films. He had supporting roles in the films *The Mob* (1951), *Somebody Up There Likes Me* (1956), *April Love* (1957), and *The Young Doctors* (1961). On television, Crowley was seen on *The Edge of Night, The Patty Duke Show, The Defenders, Route 66, Car 54 Where Are You?, Naked City,* and *The Man Behind the Badge.* In 1968, Matt Crowley returned to Broadway and had a featured role in the play *I Never Sang for My Father.* The actor died in 1983 at the age of seventy-nine.

HERNANDEZ, JUANO B. 1901 – D. 1970 (KOLU)

Puerto Rican born African American actor Juano Hernandez was a self-educated man who spent much of his childhood in Brazil singing on the streets to earn money to buy food. Before he became an actor, Juano was a seaman and a circus performer. Hernandez immigrated to the United States in the early 1920s and his natural singing and dancing ability led to his performing on the vaudeville stage and eventually on Broadway in the musical *Show Boat*. Hernandez made his film acting debut in 1932 in *Harlem is Heaven* and he was subsequently featured in the films *The Girl From Chicago* (1932) and *Lying Lips* (1939). In the 1930s, while he was appearing on Broadway and in films, Juano Hernandez made his debut on radio and soon became one of the busiest African American actors on the airwaves. His deep, rich voice earned him roles on such radio programs as *African Trek, Amanda of Honeymoon Hill, Tennessee Jed,* and *We Love and Learn* and he played the major supporting roles of Kolu on the radio adaptations of Alex Raymond's comic strip *Jungle Jim* and Lothar and Lee Falk's and Phil Davis' popular comic strip *Mandrake the Magician*. Throughout the 1950s, Hernandez continued to appear in such films as *Young Man With a Horn* (1950), *Kiss Me Deadly* (1955), *Ransom* (1956), *The Pawnbroker* (1964), *The Reivers* (1969), *They Call Me Mister Tibbs* (1970, and other films. On television, Juano Hernandez had featured roles on such series as *Studio One, Alfred Hitchcock Presents, Adventures in Paradise, Route 66, The Defenders,* and *Naked City*. The actor died of a cerebral hemorrhage at the age of sixty-nine in 1970.

K

KING OF THE ROYAL MOUNTED

The popular hero of a comic strip created by novelist Zane Grey's *King of the Royal Mounted*, from his successful novel, was first aired as a radio adventure series in 1943.

The King of the Royal Mounted comic strip and comic book series had a Western setting that was different than the usual cowboy comics. These comics were set in the Canadian Northwest. *King of the Royal Mounted* first appeared in print as a Sunday Funnies newspaper feature on February 2, 1936. Although novelist Zane Grey was given credit for both the comic strip and comic books, he was only responsible for the first few panels of the comic strip. When *King of the Royal Mounted* first appeared in print, it was drawn by artist Allen Dean. Dean's drawings were unpretentious and even a bit primitive looking, but his cartooning style was never amateurish. He drew the Canadian landscapes that were seen in the strips beautifully, and his drawings of horses were especially praiseworthy. In 1936, artist Charles Flanders took over the *King of the Royal Mounted* comics, and is probably most associated with the *King of the Royal Mounted* comics. Charles Flanders (1907–1973) got his first job as an artist working for a silkscreen company in Buffalo, New York in 1919. While he was working in Buffalo, he began to attend art classes at the Allbright Art School. In 1928, Flanders moved to New York City and in 1932, he got a job as a staff artist with the King Features Syndicate. In 1935, Flanders drew the *Robin Hood* comic strip and then in 1938 he took over the *Secret Agent X-9* strip from artist Alex Raymond. His most successful comic strip and comic book, besides *King of the Royal Mounted*, was *The Lone Ranger*. Flanders continued to draw *The Lone*

Ranger daily comic strip and comic books until 1971. The artist died two years after he retired in 1973 well after the last *King of the Royal Mounted* comic strip had been published. It was, however, author Zane Grey who exerted the greatest influence over the *King of the Royal Mounted* comics and supervised the early comics. The title character of the *King of the Royal Mounted* strip was Sergeant Dave King of the Royal Canadian Mounties. Sgt. King fought all sorts of criminals one might expect to find in the great out-of-doors; poachers, overly zealous animal trappers, land thieves, escaping bank robbers, et al. Although *King of the Royal Mounted* cannot be rated with the best comic strips of its day, it was certainly worthy of the short-lived popularity it enjoyed with adventure strip readers, especially in Canada where it enjoyed its greatest success.

As early as 1935, one year before the comic strip appeared on the scene, the Whitman Company published Zane Grey's novel *King of the Royal Mounted* in an abbreviated, mostly picture book version in one of their Big Little Books. In 1940, one year after the comic strip was published in newspapers, Dell Comics began publishing a series of *King of the Royal Mounted* comic books with Zane Grey given credit as the comic books' author. Dell continued to publish the *King of the Royal Mounted* series of comic books until 1959. In 1936, a feature film titled *King of the Royal Mounted* was released which starred Robert Kent as RCMP Sgt. King and Rosalind Keith as Helen Lawton a.k.a. Helen Curtis. This was an inexpensively produced, second feature film and did not enjoy great success. A more successful twelve part serialized version of *King of the Royal Mounted* was produced and released by Republic Pictures in 1940. This series of short films starred Alan Lane as Sgt. Dave King, RCMP and featured Stanley Andrews as Tom Merritt, Robert Kelland as Cpl. Tom Merritt, Jr., and Lita Conway as Linda Merritt.

A radio series version of *King of the Royal Mounted* was first aired in 1943. An audition disk for this program has surfaced, as well as three episodes from the series with the titles "Constable Reardon's First Case," and "Village of the Dead," "and "Woman With No Face." None of the names of the actors who were heard on this series have, as of this date, been identified. In 1947, radio station WXYZ in Detroit, acknowledged that it did use the *King of the Royal Mounted* comic strip and comic books as a guide when they developed their *Challenge of the Yukon*, also known as Sergeant Preston of the Yukon, series for radio. Like Sgt. King, the main character on *The Challenge of the Yukon*, whose name was Sgt. Preston, was a Canadian Royal Mountie. Unlike Sgt. King, Sgt. Preston depended heavily upon the loyalty and strength of his dog, named "Yukon King." *Challenge of the Yukon* made its radio debut in 1938 and featured Jay Michaels, Paul Sutton and Brace Beemer (who was The Ranger on *The Lone Ranger* for many years) as Sgt. Preston. John Todd, who played

Tonto on *The Lone Ranger*, was heard as the Inspector on the series. Fran Striker, who was one of the creators of *The Lone Ranger* and *The Green Hornet* radio series, was the creator of *Challenge of the Yukon* as well. *Challenge of the Yukon* remained on the air for seventeen years until 1955, which just six years shy of the amount of time *King of the Royal Mounted* remained in print.

(NONE OF THE PERFORMERS ON THE *KING OF THE ROYAL MOUNTED* SERIES HAVE BEEN IDENTIFIED)

L

LI'L ABNER

Al Capp's *Li'l Abner*, which distributed by United Features Syndicate, was first seen in newspapers in 1934, and from the moment it appeared in print it was one of America's favorite comic strip features. The strip, which was its creator Al Capp's satiric comment on American life and politics, continued to delight readers until 1977. To many people, Al Capp's Li'l Abner is the greatest comic strip and comic book character of all time. Al Capp (1909–1979) was born in New Haven, Connecticut. He began drawing when he was a child of nine and lost his leg in a trolley accident and had to spend many months at home recuperating from the accident. At nineteen, Capp became the youngest professional syndicated cartoonist in the United States when he began drawing a comic strip he called *Colonel Gilfeather* for the Associated Press. He got tired of drawing the Gilfeather character, who he thought was too "staid," and began assisting cartoonist Ham Fisher drawing panels for Fisher's successful *Joe Palooka* comic strip. In 1934, Capp went to work for United Features Syndicate, drawing a new comic strip which centered around a young hillbilly man he called Abner Yokum and his family and friends who lived in a mountain town called Dogpatch. The strip caught on with Depression Era (the 1930s) Americans and within three years the comic strip, *Li'l Abner*, was being read and enjoyed by over fifteen million readers all across the United States. In addition to its entertainment values, Capp's comic strip also permanently affected several aspects of American culture. In the strip, Capp introduced a holiday he called "Sadie Hawkins Day" during which hillbilly girls could actually ask a boy to a dance, which simply wasn't done up until that time. It soon became "the thing" for American girls to do. In 1948, Capp's loveable, fast multiplying, fat, bowling-ball-shaped creatures, which he called "Schmoos," became national merchandising sensations and thousands of Schmoo dolls, games and books were sold. *Li'l Abner's* main character, Abner Yokum, was a hardy, muscular, fully grown man/child/hillbilly who was a tall dark, handsome and beefy, but somewhat simple mountain boy. Abner was a citizen of Dogpath, U.S.A., a mythical place somewhere in the Ozark Mountains. He was the unlikely son of two undersized hillbilly parents, Mammy and Pappy Yokum, and he was the paragon of virtue in a dark and often cynical world. Abner's girlfriend was the scantily clad, blonde beauty, Daisy Mae Scraggs, who was hopelessly in love with the bumbling, seldom amorous Abner. Li'l Abner had no visible usual means of support, but he sometimes worked as a "mattress tester." Abner occasionally found himself far from home, often in the company of an unscrupulous industrialist named General Bullmoose. Abner and General Bullmoose often seemed to be set adrift in the dreary, snowbound fictional country of Lower Slobbovia. Abner was also an avid fan of a comic strip that was a parody of Chester Gould's *Dick Tracy* strip which was called "Fearless Fosdick." Episodes of the *Fearless Fosdick* comic-within-a-comic often took over the *Li'l Abner* comic strip for weeks on end. In 1952, much to the delight of the comic strip's many fans, Abner married Daisy Mae, an event which captured national attention and even became the cover story of a *Life* magazine issue. Their only child, Honest Abe Yokum, was born in 1953, amidst much fanfare among the strip's readers. The enormous success of the *Li'l Abner* comic strip artist was unquestionably due to artist Al Capp's fine sense of humor and his ability to make even the most outrageous situations intelligently amusing. Capp's contributions to American culture as presented in *Li'l Abner* was impressive. Words like "druthers," and "irregardless," were first seen in *Li'l Abner* and Kickapoo Joy Juice, the world's most hideous woman, Lena the Hyena, and the incredible ever-multiplying fat bowling ball shaped white creatures, the Shmoos, became national sensations. *Li'l Abner's* first foray into comic books was in 1936, when he appeared as one of the features in the *Tip Top Comics*. He had a comic book series of his own from 1947 until 1955. By the time Al Capp died in 1979, *Li'l Abner* was a national institution and Capp himself was one of the nation's most celebrated and respected cartoonists. Capp had become familiar to millions of Americans because of his many appearances on TV talk shows where he had proved himself to be a master raconteur.

(Credit: Photofest)

Al Capps' enormously popular comic strip *Li'l Abner* was not a success as a regular radio series and was on the air for just one year, 1939–1940. The series starred actor John Hodiak in one of his first major roles. Hodiak later became a successful motion picture star.

In 1939, NBC's Chicago-based Red network presented a weekly radio series based on Al Capp's imaginative and successful comic strip, *Li'l Abner*. John Hodiak starred as Abner and featured in the cast were Hazel Dopheide as Mammy Yokum, Clarence Hartzell as Pappy Yokum, and Laurette Fillbrandt as Daisy Mae. The series, unfortunately, had none of the intelligence or humor of the comic strip, even though it featured many of the same episodes that had delighted readers in the comic strips and later in the comic book series. It was off-the-air after only one year. In 1940, a feature-length *Li'l Abner* film was released that starred Jeff York as Abner and featured Martha O'Driscoll as Daisy Mae, Mona Ray as Mammy Yokum and Johnnie Morris as Pappy Yokum. The comedy was relatively successful, but not the blockbuster its filmmakers had wished for. Four years later, an animated series of *Li'l Abner* cartoons were released by the Charles Mintz animation studios. *Li'l Abner* and his family and friends also became the main characters of a Broadway musical comedy that was based on Al Capp's comic strip. The musical, which was also called *Li'l Abner,* was written by Gene de Paulk and Johnny Mercer starred Peter Palmer as Abner, Edith Adams as Daisy Mae, Chaerlottle Rae and Mammy Yokum and Joe E. Marks as pappy Yokum. The Broadway show gave a respectable 693 performances on the Great White Way. A 1959 film adaptation of the Broadway musical, which also starred Peter Palmer as Abner, featured Leslie Parrish as Daisy Mae.

Li'l Abner Radio Series Performers

Fillbrandt, Laurette b. 1915 (Daisy Mae)

Laurette Fillbrandt was born in Zanesville, Ohio and decided early in life that she wanted to be an actress when she finished her schooling. After graduating from high school, Laurette auditioned for, and won, roles in several plays that subsequently toured the country. In the mid-1930s, Laurette became a staff actress at the NBC Blue network in Chicago. Her charming, sweet voice and her convincing and natural acting led to major roles on several NBC soap opera series including *The Affairs of Anthony, Bachelor's Children, Girl Alone, The Guiding Light, Dan Harding's Wife, Lone Journey, Midstream, The Woman in White, Silver Eagle, Mountie, A Tale of Today,* and *Today's Children,* among others. Laurette was also often featured on the full-hour dramatic anthology series, *The Chicago Theater of the Air* for several seasons. In 1939, Laurette was cast as Daisy Mae in the radio adaptation of Al Capp's successful comic strip *Li'l Abner,* which only remained on the air for one year. Laurette played Daisy Mae with all of the innocence and sweetness that the character required and she was indeed a perfect-sounding object of Abner's eventual ardent affection. In the 1940s, Miss Fillbrandt went to Hollywood, where she continued to perform on several radio programs including Carlton E. Morse's long-running *One Man's Family* serial drama playing the major role of Claudia Barbour in 1949. Laurette continued to remain active on radio until radio drama faded from the airwaves in the late 1950s-early 1960s, and then she retired from show business.

HODIAK, JOHN B. 1914 – D. 1955 (LI'L ABNER YOKUM)

Actor John Hodiak was the son of a Ukranian-born coal miner who immigrated to the United States at the turn of the century. John was born in Pittsburgh, Pennsylvania, but moved to Detroit, Michigan with his family when he was a boy. When he was a teenager, John was "bitten by the acting bug," while he was appearing in a Ukranian folk play at his church. He began to appear in all of the plays that were presented in his high school and auditioned for a college drama scholarship which he won. He decided not to go to college, however, believing that because he came from a family that spoke little English, he did not have the language skills he needed to succeed in college. While working as a full time manager at an automobile assembly plant in Detroit, he perfected his English in night school. On an impulse, he auditioned for an acting job at WXYZ radio station in Detroit and to his delight was hired to appear on *The Green Hornet* radio series. Encouraged, Hodiak went to Chicago, which was, in the 1930s, the center of radio drama broadcasting and easily obtained roles on such soap opera series as *Mary Marlin, Bachelor's Children,* and other Chicago-based shows. He did feel, however, that he was not making enough money acting on the radio to support himself sufficiently and he had almost decided to quit broadcasting and return to Detroit when he won the leading role on the radio adaptation of Al Capp's popular *Li'L Abner* comic strip. The show was not a hit, but John, who was a tall, good looking, muscular young man, attracted the attention of a Hollywood talent scout who attended one of the *Li'l Abner* broadcasts. The actor was offered a contract to appear in films, after he made a successful screen test. Hodiak was an immediate success as a film actor and was soon being seen playing leading roles in such films as *Lifeboat, Command Decision, Battleground, The Harvey Girls,* and *Dinner for a Soldier.* In 1954, Hodiak made his Broadway acting debut in the play *The Caine Mutiny* which won the critical acclaim of the New York drama critics. John Hodiak's life was cut tragically short when he suffered a heart attack and died at the age of forty-one in 1955.

LITTLE ORPHAN ANNIE

In 1924, when Harold Gray was working as an assistant to comic strip artist Sidney Smith who was drawing the popular *Gumps* comic strip, he went to Smith's editor, Captain Joseph Patterson, with an idea for a comic strip of his own that he called *Little Orphan Otto*. The strip was about a young orphaned boy who did the best he could to survive in the cruel, big city on his own. Patterson liked the idea, but suggested that the orphan should be a girl, not a boy. Gray agreed and thus the *Little Orphan Annie* comic strip was born. Harold Gray's first work as a professional cartoonist was in 1913. When the United States entered World War One in 1918, Gray enlisted in the Army and served as a bayonet instructor. It was when the war ended, that Gray was employed by the *Chicago Tribune* as a letterer for the popular *Gumps* strip and eventually he also assisted *The Gumps'* artist, Sidney Smith, with the drawing of the comic strip. The *Little Orphan Annie* title that Patterson suggested Gray use when the artist first offered his comic strip to the Chicago Tribune was not an original one. It had originally been used as the title of an 1885 poem by James Whitcomb Riley. Even Gray's little orphan character was not original. Annie was not the first self reliant orphan kid who survived many hardships for an appreciative audience of followers. This was a recurrent theme of many mid-to-late Victorian melodramas and novels. The story line of Gray's *Little Orphan Annie* comic strip was a simple rags-to-riches and back again tale with a lot of homespun philosophy as Annie conducted herself with determination, self-reliance, and spunk. The early panels of the *Little Orphan Annie* comic strip began in an orphanage, but within a few months, the little orphan girl had met a rich man named Oliver "Daddy" Warbucks, who was a self-made millionaire who took a liking to her and sympathetically offered her a life of comfort and ease. Annie soon became separated from Daddy Warbucks, through no fault of her own, and found herself trying to make her own way in the world once again accompanied by her constant companion, a large yellow dog named Sandy. Annie kept reconnecting with Daddy Warbucks over the years, only to lose and find him again and again. When she was surviving on her own, she had to fight various criminals, crooked

Harold Gray's *Little Orphan Annie* was one of America's most popular comic strips, and it was equally as successful as a children's radio adventure series. Beginning in 1930, Annie was on the air for an impressive thirteen years.

politicians, and other villains along the way. *Little Orphan Annie* was probably one of the most violent comic strip ever published. It was not physically violent, although it did have occasional physical violence in it, but it always contained an underlying threat of danger and harm that inevitably befell the hapless, altruistic Annie. Annie endured many hardships during the comic strips' long and successful run, including not seeing her adoptive father for months on end, living in run down slums, tracking down wicked Nazis during World War Two, helping the cops apprehend countless criminals, and being kidnapped and tortured many, many times. Through it all, Annie always remained hopeful that eventually things were sure to get better. By the end of the 1920s, *Little Orphan Annie* was one of the most popular comic strips in America, and its popularity continued throughout the 1930s and 1940s, and continues to be popular to this day. Gray experimented with several other comic strips including *Private Lives* and *Maw Green*, but they did not come even close *Little Orphan Annie's* enormous popularity. When Harold Gray died in 1968, he had been working on the comic strip, *Little Orphan Annie,* for over forty-five years.

In 1930, one year after it made its debut as a comic strip, *Little Orphan Annie* had become popular enough to inspire a fifteen-minute-a-day, five-day-a-week Chicago-based children's radio adventure series that was heard on NBC's Blue network. The radio show remained on the air for the next thirteen years and rivaled the Little Orphan Annie comic strip in popularity. The radio series starred child actress Shirley Bell, and then for a short time Janice Gilbert, as Annie, and featured Henry Saxe, Stanley Andrews, and Boris Aplon as Daddy Warbucks over the years, Brad Barker as Sandy the Dog (who only barked), Olan Soule, as Aha the Chinese cook, Allan Baruck as Annie young friend, Joe Corntassle, Jerry O'Mera and Henrietta Tedro as Mr. and Mrs. Silo, Annie's temporary foster parents, and Hoyt Allen, Alan Baruck, St. John Tyrell, and James Monks, among others. Pierre Andre, who was called "Uncle Andy," was the *Little Orphan Annie* shows announcer. Andre introduced the show's memorable theme song that began:

> WHO'S THAT LITTLE CHATTERBOX?
> THE ONE WITH PRETTY AUBURN LOCKS?
> WHO CAN IT BE?
> IT'S LITTLE ORPHAN ANNIE.
> SHE AND SANDY MAKE A PAIR.
> THEY NEVER SEEM TO HAVE A CARE.
> CUTE LITTLE SHE,
> IT'S LITTLE ORPHAN ANNIE.

Pierre Andre also told young listeners about all of the wonderful premiums and giveaway prizes they could receive be sending in a label from a jar of Ovaltine (the program's chocolate "health" drink sponsor), such as decoding badges, rings, and mug and treasure maps and books. The *Little Orphan Annie* radio show was directed for many years by Alan Wallace and written by Roland Martin, Ferrin N. Fraser, Day Keene, and Wally Norman.

In addition to the *Little Orphan Annie* daily comic strip and radio show, Annie was also the subject of a film produced by RKO in 1932, which featured Mitzi Green as Annie and Edgar Kennedy as Daddy Warbucks. Another *Little Orphan Annie* film was released by Paramount Pictures in 1938 and starred Ann Gillis as Annie. With other Tribune Syndicate comic characters, Annie was also featured in the *Super Comic* series from 1938 through 1949 and in her own comic book series from 1937 until 1948. In 1977, *Little Orphan Annie* was the main character in a Broadway musical that had a book by Thomas Meechan and music and lyrics by Charles Strouse and Martin Charnin, and was simply called *Annie*. The musical starred Andrea McArdle as Annie, and featured Reid Shelson as Daddy Warbucks and Dorothy Loudan as the wicked orphanage operator, Miss Hannigan. It ran on Broadway for over 2,000 performances, before closing in 1983. While the show was still playing on Broadway, a 1982 film based on the musical comedy was released. It starred Aileen Quinn as Annie, Albert Finney as Daddy Warbucks, and Carol Burnett as Miss Hannigan. A subsequent TV Special version of the musical comedy *Annie* was presented in 1999, with Alicia Morton playing Annie, Victor Garber playing Daddy Warbucks, and Kathy Bates playing Miss Hannigan.

LITTLE ORPHAN ANNIE RADIO SERIES PERFORMERS

ANDRE, PIERRE B. 1900 – D. 1962 (ANNOUNCER)

When radio was at the peak of its popularity in the 1920s and 1930s, few announcers had a more commanding and stirring voice than Pierre Andre. As Andre announced the popular *Little Orphan Annie* and *Captain Midnight* radio series to youngsters five afternoons a week in the 1930s, it was almost as if he dared them to listen to any other program, so convincingly urgent were his introductions and descriptions of previous events that were heard on those series. Pierre Andre began his radio announcing career in the 1920s hosting *The Midnight Flyer*, a big band remote program that was aired by KSTP in St. Paul, Minnesota. For many years thereafter, Andre was an announcer at WGN in Chicago, for the NBC Blue network. Among the celebrated radio shows that Andre announced from *Chicago*, in addition to *Little Orphan Annie* and *Captain Midnight*, were *The Romance of Helen Trent*, *Betty and Bob*, and *Backstage Wife*.

BELL, SHIRLEY B. 1921 (LITTLE ORPHAN ANNIE)

Shirley Bell, who was born in Chicago, Illinois, was only six years old when she made her professional radio acting debut on WGN in Chicago in 1927. When she was ten years old, Shirley was hired to play "Little Orphan Annie" on a radio series that was based on Harold Gray's popular comic strip. The radio series was sponsored by the chocolate "health" drink, Ovaltine, which due to the show's immense popularity became one of America's best selling beverages. Bell, who was originally paid $50 a week for her work on the series and eventually earned $150 a week due to the show's success, which was an excellent salary in those Great Depression years of the 1930s. The young actress played the Annie role for most of the entire nine years the program was aired, as well as being heard regularly on the *Arnold Grimm's Daughter* program. Bell retired from radio and show business when she left the *Little Orphan Annie* radio show in 1940. She eventually married a banker and lived the life of a suburban housewife until once again she stepped into the spotlight when Annie became popular again on Broadway, and as a subsequent film adaptation was released and she was interviewed as "the original Little Orphan Annie" on numerous TV shows. The only acting Shirley had done after she left *Little Orphan Annie* was as a dedicated volunteer reader of books that were recorded for the blind.

GILBERT, JANICE B. 1922 (LITTLE ORPHAN ANNIE)

Actress Janice Gilbert replaced Shirley Bell as Annie for a few months, shortly before the *Little Orphan Annie* series left the air in 1940. The young actress, who was in her teens at the time, subsequently worked on several Chicago-based radio programs after *Little Orphan Annie* was canceled including *Bachelor's Children, Doc Barclay's Daughters, Gasoline Alley* (as Nina Clock), *Her Honor, Nancy James, Hilltop House, The O'Neills,* and *The Sea Hound.* Gilbert was seen on television briefly in the TV version of *The O'Neills* in 1949, after which she apparently decided to retire from show business.

THE LONE RANGER

When people hear the phrase, "Radio's Golden Age," two programs, more than any others, usually come to mind; *The Shadow* and *The Lone Ranger.* Before it was a comic strip, a series of comic books, or adventure novels, *The Lone Ranger* was a radio series. In 1930, an ambitious and creative radio station owner, George W. Trendle, with other independent radio station owners, established a state-wide radio network in Michigan, with WXYZ in Detroit as the network's key station. Trendle became interested in developing a radio adventure series that would appeal to youngsters and contain action-filled episodes but exclude the violence and instruct and inspire young people in the virtues of fighting evil and also be appealing to adults. Trendle hired a writer who lived in Buffalo, New York, Fran Striker, who had submitted an idea for a radio show about pioneer days out West to him when WXYZ first advertised that it was looking for ideas for new radio programs for their network. Trendle liked Striker's writing but instructed him to create a hero for the new series that would be "serious, sober-minded and realistic," and be a good example for youngsters of the virtues of "good living and clean speech." Striker obliged and on January 30, 1933, the first episode of *The Lone Ranger* was aired. Striker's *Lone Ranger* character was a Texas Ranger and the circumstances of his background were revealed gradually as the series developed a following. Eventually everyone in America learned that the *Lone Ranger's* name was John Reid, and that he was the sole survivor of an ambush by a band of cut-throat outlaws led by a villain named Butch Cavindish. The ambush had left four of his fellow Texas Rangers dead, including his brother Captain Dan Reid. John Reid survived the attack and was found dying by a compassionate Native American, an Indian named Tonto, who nursed him back to health. Fully recovered, Reid decides to dedicate his life to fighting evil-doers and donning a mask and toting two six shooters, he assumes the identity of "The Lone Ranger," in order to keep his true identity a secret. Because of the mask, many people assume that he and his Indian companion, Tonto, are outlaws. But by the end of each episode of *The Lone Ranger* program listeners knew the truth and his reputation as crime-fighter in the Old West, steadily grows top legendary status. It was one year after *The Lone Ranger,* was first heard on WXYZ, that Trendle joined forces with the three other successful, independent radio stations, WGN in Chicago, WOR in New York City, and WLW in Cincinnati, Ohio, and the four radio stations formed a national network they called the Mutual Broadcasting System. *The Lone Ranger* became the new network's first major national attraction and the series was sold in syndication to other stations in the United States, including affiliates of the powerful CBS and NBC networks. In less than one year after it made its radio debut, *The Lone Ranger* became one of the most listened-to programs in America. The first actor to play the part of the Lone Ranger was George Stenius. Stenius played The Ranger for four months and was replaced by Jack Deeds, who played the role for just one performance. The role was then taken over by the show's director, James Jewell, for a while, and then by first of two successful actors who played the Ranger role the rest of the time the program was aired. The first actor's name was Earle Graser, who played the role from May 16, 1933 until April, 1941, when he died in an automobile accident. The last actor to play *The Lone Ranger* on radio beginning in 1941 was Brace Beemer, whose voice sounded

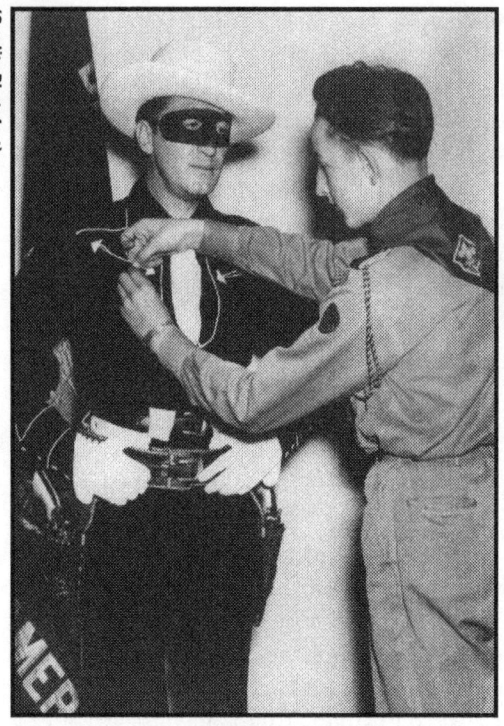

(Credit: Photofest)

Actor Brace Beemer played the role of *The Lone Ranger* on radio for 2,958 episodes, broadcast between 1941 until 1954. Beemer became well known for making numerous public appearances in his *Lone Ranger* costume for a variety of charities. He is seen here with a member of the Boy Scouts, receiving an award for his generous support of that organization.

amazingly like Graser's. Beemer had been the program's announcer for many years and it is Beemer's voice that is probably best remembered by listeners in the role. He played The Ranger part until 1954, when the program finally left the air. A staff actor at WXYZ, John Todd, played the role of Tonto the entire time the series was on the air and other actors who played various roles on the program over the years were Paul Hughes, and Ernie Winstanley, Dick Beals, and James Lipton, who played the Ranger's nephew who joined his uncle and Tonto for many of their adventures, Dan Reid, and John Hodiak, Rollon Parker, Ted Johnstone, Bob Maxwell, Jack Petruzzi, Elaine Alpert, Fred Rito, Bertha Forman, Ruth Dean Rickaby, Bill Saunders, Harry Golder, Beatice Leibee, Frank Russell, Herbert Mayall, Mel Palmer, and Amos Jacobs (who later became better known as Danny Thomas). The program's memorable opening, which was heard on both the radio and subsequent television series, began with the sound of hoof beats and the Lone Ranger calling out, "Hi-yo, Silver!" This was followed by the sound of gunshots and the show's announcer (Harold True, Brace Beemer, Harry Golder, Charles Woods, Bob Hite or Fred Foy) would say, "A fiery horse with the speed of light, a cloud of dust and a hearty hi-yo Silver! The Lone Ranger!" The was followed by the program's theme music, Rossini's "William Tell Overture," which would swell, and then the announcer would state, "With his faithful Indian companion, Tonto, the daring and resourceful masked rider of the plains led the fight for law and order in the early western United States. Nowhere in the pages of history can one find a greater champion of justice. Return with us now to those thrilling days of yesteryear. From out of the past come the thundering hoof beats of the great horse Silver. The Lone Ranger rides again!" The Ranger's voice would then call out, "Come on, Silver! Let's go, big fellow! Hi-yo Silver! Away!"

The unparalleled success of *The Lone Ranger* radio series led to a popular newspaper comic strip version of the series that began to appear in newspapers

"Hi-yo, Silver!" was *The Lone Ranger's* familiar call to his "great white horse," "Silver," on the popular radio series, as well as in many comic books and a successful newspaper comic strip.

throughout the country in September, 1938 and continued to be published until December, 1971. The strip was written by Fran Striker, the man who had created the radio series for WXYZ and wrote many of the show's scripts. The comic strip was originally drawn by artist Ed Kressy. Kressy was replaced in 1939 by Charles Flanders, who stayed with the newspaper strip until 1971

The Lone Ranger radio program offered listeners many premiums that they could send away for by mailing a label or box top from a sponsor's product. Above are just a few of the many items that were offered to fans of the series.

when its thirty-two year run ended. (For Flanders biography see *King of the Royal Mounted*). A long running comic book series published first by Dell, and then Gold Key Comics, as well as other comic books that featured Tonto and the Lone Ranger's horse, Silver, as the main characters, followed. Three movie serials, several feature films, and a popular television series, as well as numerous other *Lone Ranger* items such as lunch boxes, coloring books, gum cards, and many other products flooded the market over the years.

The Lone Ranger first appeared in films in 1938 when Republic Pictures released a fifteen chapter serial called *The Lone Ranger* that starred actor Lee Powell as The Lone Ranger and Native American Chief Thundercloud as Tonto. Republic followed the series with another serial, also seen in fifteen chapters called *The Lone Ranger Rides Again,* that starred Bob Livingstone as The Ranger and Chief Thundercloud as Tonto. In 1956, a technicolor, feature length film simply called *The Lone Ranger,* which starred Clayton Moore as the Ranger and Jay Silverheels as Tonto, was released. This was based on the popular *Lone Ranger* television series, which made its TV debut in 1949 and starred Moore and Silverheels and was on the air for 221 episodes and aired for five years. In 1958, a second feature film, *The Lone Ranger in the Lost City of Gold,* with Moore and Silverheels also in the cast, was released. The last *Lone Ranger* film, to date, which was called *The Legend of the Lone Ranger* was released in 1981. It was a dreary, over-produced, badly acted affair that starred a good looking but untalented newcomer named Klinton Spilbury as The Ranger, and Native American Michael Horse as Tonto.

The Lone Ranger radio series performers

Beemer, Brace b. 1902 – d. 1967 (The Lone Ranger)
Although he was not the first actor to portray "the masked rider of the plains," *The Lone Ranger,* on radio, Brace Beemer played the role longer than anyone else and is certainly the actor who is best remembered in the role. Beemer, who was born in Mt. Carmel, Illinois, began his radio career in Indianapolis in 1922 after a stint in the U. S. Army during World War One, serving with the famed Rainbow Division in France. Wounded in action, Beemer, who was only in his early teens at the time because he had lied about his age when he enlisted, was awarded a Purple Heart for having suffered injuries in battle. In 1932, after working at various odd jobs, he joined the staff at WXYZ in Detroit, Michigan as a staff announcer. One of his first assignments at WXYZ was as the announcer/narrator of the station's popular *Challenge of the Yukon* series. In 1941, when the actor playing the role of the Ranger, Earl Graser, died in an automobile accident, Beemer, whose voice sounded like Graser's, was recruited to play the Ranger role on the popular series. Beemer played *The Lone Ranger* from 1941 until the last episode of the series aired in 1954 and 2,958 episodes of the popular series had been aired. Beemer took his assignment of the heroic *Lone Ranger* very seriously, believing he had a responsibility to set a good example for the millions of young people who listened to the series faithfully. When he wasn't playing *The Lone Ranger* on radio, he donned his *Lone Ranger* costume and mask and visited hospitals, orphanages and retirement homes, and during World War Two, he visited hundreds of military bases giving the troops a boost in any way he could. Beemer made numerous guest starring appearances on other hit radio shows in the 1940s and 1950s, including *The Jack Benny Show, The Quiz Kids* and *Duffy's Tavern.* After *The Lone Ranger's* final broadcast on September 3, 1954, Brace Beemer retired bur he continued to make pubic appearances throughout the country as *The Lone Ranger* character he had played for so many years. The actor died in March, 1965 after suffering a heart attack at his ranch, which was located near Detroit and where he raised thoroughbred horses for many years.

Graser, Earl b. 1909 – d. 1941 (The Lone Ranger)
Actor Earl Graser, who had a deep, resonant baritone voice, played the role of *The Lone Ranger* on the popular radio program and was the first performer to be undeniably identified with that role. After he graduated from Wayne University, Graser, who had already decided that he wanted to be an actor after playing major roles in several school plays, auditioned for a job as a staff announcer at WXYZ in Detroit. His excellent diction and wonderful voice

impressed the station's owner, George W. Trendle, who immediately hired him to replace the usually inebriated actor who was, at the time, playing the role of *The Lone Ranger* on WXYZ's successful adventure series. With Graser in the role of the Ranger, the program became even more popular than it already was. Graser's tenure in the role ended suddenly, however, when he tragically killed in an automobile accident in 1941 on his way to a broadcast. Graser was replaced by a staff announcer at WXYZ, Brace Beemer, whose voice sounded remarkably like Earl Graser's voice. Many listeners were totally unaware that another actor was playing the part of *The Lone Ranger*, when Beemer took over the role.

TODD, JOHN B. 1873 – D. 1957 (TONTO)

The actor who played the part of The Lone Ranger's "faithful Indian companion, Tonto, the entire time the series was aired from 1933 until its final broadcast in 1954, was John Todd. Todd was sixty years old when he first stepped in front of a microphone to read the part of Tonto and he was almost eighty when the series ended. Before he was assigned the role of Tonto on *The Lone Ranger*, Todd had been a member of a company of actors employed by WXYZ's director, James Jewell, to act on that stations' roster of radio dramas. Todd had been a stage actor before beginning his career on radio in the early 1930s, and he had appeared in hundreds of stage plays from light comedies to Shakespearean tragedies. Once he began playing Tonto, however, his distinctive voice became so identified with that role that he was infrequently heard playing any other part. Because he was a relatively stout man and much older than Tonto was supposed to be, Todd rarely made personal appearances like his co-star, Brace Beemer, who actually looked the way *The Lone Ranger* was supposed to look…tall, muscular, and handsome. Todd retired shortly after *The Lone Ranger* left the air and died three years later in 1957 at the age of eighty-four.

M

MAJOR HOOPLE
(A.K.A. OUR BOARDING HOUSE)

In 1921, cartoonist Gene Aherne's daily comic strip *Our Boarding House* made its first appearance in the Newspaper Enterprise Association's affiliated publications. The comic strip became one of America's most popular newspaper panel strips after only a few short months in print. Artist Gene Aherne (1895–1960) had received his art training at the famous Chicago Art Institute and began his career as a professional artist in 1910, drawing such comic strips as *Taking Her to the Ball Game*, *Featherhead Fritz*, *Dream Dope*, and *Squirrel Food*, all of which were very well received by the public and made Aherne well known to the public. In the *Squirrel Food* comic strip, Aherne introduced his very amusing Nutt brother characters, Ches

When Gene Aherne's popular *Our Boarding House* comic strip, which was first published in 1921, finally arrived on radio in 1942, the series was retitled *Major Hoople*. It was named after the comic strips main character, Major Amos Hoople, who was an amusing windbag and sponge, who lived in his wife's boarding house. As far as anyone could tell, had never worked a day in his life.

(Credit: Author's collection. © Whitman/Big Little Books.)

and Wal, to the American public and the brothers soon had the country laughing at their daily comic panel antics. It was in 1923 that Aherne introduced his *Our Boarding House* comic strip to the public and overnight, everyone was talking about a hilarious new comic strip character named "Major Hoople," who was an outrageous windbag who was so totally full of himself that no one else even seemed to exist. Aherne continued to draw the *Our Boarding House* strip until 1936, when he sold the rights to *Our Boarding House* and began drawing another strip he called Room and Board. Aherne continued to draw his *Room and Board* strip until 1960, when he died of a heart attack. The *Our Boarding House* strip was subsequently drawn by artist Bill Freyse, until 1981. By the time it ended its long and successful run *Our Boarding House* was the longest running continuous comic strip ever published.

The *Our Boarding House* comic strip was almost entirely set in Martha Hoople's seedy boarding house establishment where Martha lived with her lazy, windbag of a husband, Major Amos B. Hoople. The very funny Major Hoople character made his first appearance in *Our Boarding House* four months after the strip was first published. Readers learned that Amos Hoople had returned home after a ten year absence from Martha Hoople's life, the minute he heard that she had a business and a place where he could live and sponge off of her. The Major quickly became the main character in the strip and to many readers the *Our Boarding House* comic strip became known as "Major Hoople." In the strip, the Major bragged a lot about his questionable accomplishments and Martha scowled a lot as she ran her boarding house like a sergeant major, letting her husband get away with very little, but never quite being able to get herself to kick him out of the establishment. Martha's boarders included such colorful characters as an amusing trio called Buster, Clyde and Mack, who came and went during the comic strips long tenure. Martha bearly endured the Major who was a bore of a man with a large bulbous nose, a huge belly, a scraggly mustache and usually wore a pretentious looking Egyptian fez. He often used archaic expressions like "egad," and "drat" and often mouthed such non-words as "fap," "awp," and "kaff," which were soon being used by people all across the country. The Major was always making pretentious discourses about his supposedly "astonishing experiences," which nobody, especially Martha, ever believed had actually taken place. Occasionally, the Major's nephew, Alvin, who lived with the couple, made believe that he was listening to him.

Because of *Our Boarding House's* enormous popularity, it was also published as several Big Little books in the 1930s, and as a comic book series. It was also adapted to radio in 1942 as a situation comedy series which was heard on the NBC Blue network. The series, which was called *Major Hoople*, and not *Our Boarding House, i*n order to capitalize on the popularity of the Major Hoople character, starred veteran character actor Arthur Q. Bryan, who later became very well known as the voice of the cartoon character Elmer Fudd, as the Major. Comedienne Patsy Moran co-starred with Bryan as Martha Hoople and Franklin Bresee, and then Conrad Binyon, played Little Alvin. The

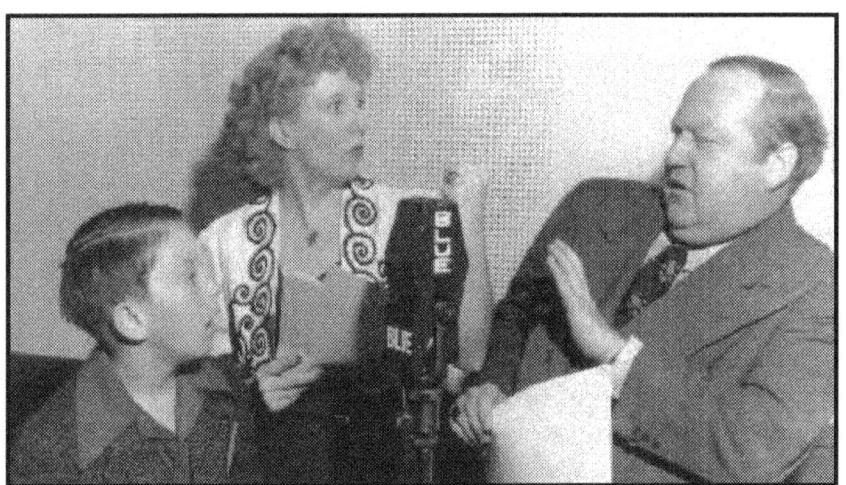

On the *Major Hoople* radio series, Conrad Binyon played the role of Little Alvin, Patsy Moran played Martha Hoople and Arthur Q. Bryan played Major Amos Hoople.

versatile Mel Blanc played a boarder named Mr. Tweedy on the series. The program, which was written by Phil Leslie, began each episode with the announcer saying, "He's not a sergeant...he's not a lieutenant...he's not a captain....he's a Major! Yes, ladies and gentlemen, it's *Major Hoople*! From out of the comic strip and into your homes, we bring you that overstuffed philosopher...Major Amos Hoople! His ever-loving, but not-too-trusting wife, Martha...his precocious nephew, Little Alvin...and his star boarder and number one complainer, Tiffany Twiggs!" Even though there were several very amusing episodes aired, and the series closely adhered to the basic premise of the popular comic strip, the radio program failed to attract an audience and was canceled before it completed two full years on the air.

Major Hoople Radio Series Performers

Binyon, Conrad b. 1931 (Little Alvin)

In the late 1930s into the 19450s, Conrad Binyon was one of the most active child performers in show business. Conrad literally grew up working in films and on radio and made his first professional appearance in a film when he was six months old as a baby being wheeled by his mother in a carriage. Before he was ten years old, Conrad had major roles on such popular radio programs as *One Man's Family* (on which he played the role of Hank for twelve years), *Mayor of the Town*, the long running series that starred Lionel Barrymore and Agnes Moorehead, playing the role of the mayor's ward, Butch Roscoe for six years, and *The Life of Riley*, which starred William Bendix, as

Riley's son, Junior. Binyon, who had no formal training as an actor, after being coached by his parents, auditioned for various radio shows when he was still a toddler. He was natural in front of the microphone and because he couldn't read, he had to memorize all of the lines he had to say, which he did with little difficulty. Binyon claims that he knew, even as a youngster, that he had to speak clearly enough to be heard by the engineers in the control booth and that he actually directed his performances to them, never thinking about the millions of people who might be listening to him in their homes. Conrad enjoyed making people laugh and the engineers always encouraged him by laughing louder than anyone else in the studio audience at everything he said. In the late 1930s, the young actor had major roles on three radio series that were based on popular comic strips; *The Buster Brown Gang, The Nebbs,* and *Major Hoople.* On *Major Hoople,* Conrad played Hoople's nephew, Little Alvin.

In addition to his very active career as a radio actor, Binyon was also active in films. As a very young child, he was one of the children in the very famous *Our Gang* film comedies, and he had featured roles in such classic films as *The Glass Key* (1942), *The Boy from Stalingrad* (1943), *The Human Comedy* (1943), *Since You Went Away* (1944), *And Now Tomorrow* (1944) *The Courage of Lassie* (1946), and *My Blue Heaven* (1950), which starred such film personalities as Alan Ladd, Mickey Rooney, Claudette Colbert, Cary Grant, Joseph Cotton, and Elizabeth Taylor.

From the time he was little boy, Conrad was always interested in aviation and when he was seventeen years old, he got his pilot's license. In the 1950s, Binyon joined the Air National Guard and when his National Guard unit was called up for active service during the Korean conflict in the 1950s, Binyon left his acting career behind him and became a combat aviator. Conrad, who later admitted that he loved flying much more than he did acting, remained in the Air Force for the next twenty years and never again basked in the show business spotlight.

BLANC, MEL (SEE *SAD SACK* FOR BIOGRAPHY OF MEL BLANC)

BRYAN, ARTHUR Q. B. 1899 – D. 1959 (MAJOR HOOPLE)
Actor Arthur Q. Bryan was born in Brooklyn, New York and began his show business career as a tenor singing in a barbershop quartet that toured the vaudeville circuit and first worked on radio in 1929. After playing small parts in films and on various radio shows, Bryan got his first big break as an actor when he was cast as Fibber McGee's nemesis, Doc Gamble, on the popular *Fibber McGee and Molly* radio program which starred Jim and Marian Jordan as Fibber and Molly. Bryan was also heard on the *Billy Burke Show, Blondie* (as

Blondie and Dagwood Bumstead's neighbor, Fuddle, whose lateral lisp sounded just like the one his Elmer Fudd character had in numerous animated cartoons had), *The Fitch Bandwagon* (as "Waymond Wadcliffe, who also sounded like Elmer Fudd), *Forever Ernest*, *The Great Gildersleeve* (as Floyd the Barber), and as the title character on the *Major Hoople* series, which was a radio version of the popular Gene Aherne comic strip, *Our Boarding House*. Bryan never played very large roles in films, although he did provide the voice for many highly successful film cartoons and short subjects. He was seen in *Day at the Zoo* (1939), *These Glamour Girls* (1939), *The Road to Singapore* (1940), *Larceny, Inc.* (1941), *National Barn Dance* (1943), *Stage Door Canteen* (1944, once again providing the voice of Elmer Fudd), *Idea Girl* (1946), *The Road to Rio* (1947), and *Samson and Delilah* (1949, among others. He fared much better as an on camera actor on television and had good supporting roles on episodes of such TV shows as *I Love Lucy*, *The Spike Jones Show*, *Jane Wyman Presents the Fireside Theater*, and *The Screen Directors' Playhouse*. In poor health for many years due to heart disease, Arthur Q. Bryan died at the age of sixty in 1959.

MORAN, PATSY B. 1903 – D. 1968 (MARTHA HOOPLE)

Although comedienne Patsy Moran, who was a native New Yorker, had the leading female roles on two radio adaptations of popular comic strips, *Major Hoople* (as Martha Hoople) and *The Sad Sack* (as Mrs. Flanagan), the actress labored for many years playing relatively small roles in mainly second feature films. Among the films she appeared in were *The Block-Heads* (1938), *The Cowboy From Sundown* (1940), *The Bank Dick* (1940, with W. C. Fields), *Baby Face Morgan* (1942), *The Guerins from Brooklyn* (1942), *Slightly Dangerous* (1943), *The Lady Takes a Chance* (1943), *Mr. Muggs Steps Out* (1943), *Meet the People* (1944), *The Docks of New York* (1945), *Betty Co-Ed* (1946), *The Corpse Came C.O.D.* (1947), *Billie Gets Her Man* (1948), *Bride for Sale* (1949, *Two Knights from Brooklyn* (1949), and *Sweethearts on Parade* (1950), to name just a few. Miss Moran also appeared on one very funny episode of the *I Love Lucy* show in the early 1950s, "Bonus Bucks," playing a hilarious Laundry Worker.

MANDRAKE THE MAGICIAN

Mandrake the Magician was one of the first comic strip super heroes to wear a unique costume. Unlike *Superman* and *Batman*, Mandrake did not wear tights, he wore a sophisticated tuxedo, a top hat, and, like those other superheros, a cape. *Mandrake the Magician* was created by a nineteen year old writer named Lee Falk in 1924. Lee Falk (1912–1999) was born in Missouri in 1912. After

Lee Falk's *Mandrake the Magician* comic strip, which was first seen in print in 1933, was heard on radio in 1940, but it did not remain on radio long. The series was canceled in 1942, just two years after its radio debut.

graduating from the University of Illinois, Falk went to work as a copywriter for a St. Louis advertising agency and then became a producer and writer for a St. Louis radio station. He had been trying to sell his idea for a comic strip he called *Mandrake the Magician* for ten years, but he had met with little success until he enlisted the talents of artist Phil Davis (1906–1964) who improved Falk's original drawings for the strip. Phil Davis was also born in St. Louis, Missouri, had worked as a commercial artist for the local telephone company in that city when he graduated from Washington University Art School. Davis left the telephone company and went to work for The St. Louis Dispatch as its Advertising Director and also began to draw illustrations and covers for various magazines. Davis met Lee Falk in 1933 and the two men began to work on Falks' *Mandrake the Magician* comic strip together. King Features Syndicate bought the rights to distribute the comic strip nationally and it became immediately popular with the public.

In the strip, *Mandrake the Magician* had obtained special powers when he studied in Tibet as a boy. One of his teachers was a man named Luciphor, who later used his special powers for evil purposes and used the name of "Cobra." for himself. Cobra appeared as a recurring villain in the *Mandrake the Magician* comic strips over the years. With his slicked down, black hair, his mustache and his luminescent black tuxedo and top hat and cape, Mandrake was the very picture of urban sophistication and his amazing ability to use the magic he had learned in the Orient to apprehend criminals was truly extraordinary. With his African friend, Lothar, who was, when the comic strip first surfaced

Mandrake's valet and bodyguard, but became his partner as the strip continued, Mandrake solved many mysteries and apprehended countless numbers of criminals over the years. Other running characters who appeared in the comic strip were Mandrake's troublesome sister, Lenore, his evil brother, Derek, his elderly master teacher, Theron, and Mandrake's girlfriend, the exotic Princess Narda of Cockaigne, who preferred Mandrake's company to remaining in her tiny European kingdom. In 1998, Mandrake and Narda were finally married much to the delight of the strips many loyal fans. The success of the *Mandrake the Magician* comic strip encouraged Lee Falk to develop another comic strip, which became equally as popular as *Mandrake the Magician* that was called *The Phantom,* and was drawn by artists Ray Moore, Wilson McCoy, and Sy Barry. Falk also wrote several stage plays the most successful being "Eris," which was produced in Paris in 1968. In 1968, Falk began to write a series of *Phantom* novels which were published by Avon books. Lee Falk continued to write the story lines for the *Mandrake the Magician* and *Phantom* comic strips until he was well into his eighties. Falk died in 1999 at the age of eighty-eight. During World War Two, Phil Davis was drafted into the United States Army and his wartime assignment was to edit and illustrate the instrumental manual for the A-25 bomber. After the war, he resumed drawing the *Mandrake the Magician* comic strip with the help of his wife, Martha, who he had met during his Army days. They continued to work on the *Mandrake the Magician* comic strip together until Davis died at the age of fifty-eight in 1964.

Mandrake the Magician also enjoyed limited success as a comic book series as well as a comic strip and was featured with *Barney Baxter* and *Secret Agent X-9* in Magic Comics special editions. The character also appeared in Dell and Harvey comic books in the 1930s and 1940s and was published as a Big Little book as well. *Mandrake the Magician* was also seen in a forgettable movie serial that starred actor Warren Hull as Mandrake and Al Kikume as Lothar. In the 1980s, Mandrake was also one of the animated cartoon characters seen in the *Defenders of the Earth* TV series on which he alternated episodes with *Flash Gordon* and *The Phantom*.

In the 1940s, *Mandrake the Magician* was on radio as a fifteen-minute-a-day, five-days-a-week children's adventure series on the Mutual Broadcasting System's network of stations. Veteran radio actor Raymond Edward Johnson starred as Mandrake, African/American actor Juano Hernandez played Lothar, and Francesca Lenni played Princess Narda on the series, which ended its radio run on February 6, 1942. The only episode of this series that seems to have survived is the audition recording of the program, which to this author sounded rather stilted and just a bit "over-the-top."

Mandrake the Magician Radio Series Performers

Hernandedz, Juano (Lothar. See *Jungle Jim* for Biography)

Johnson, Raymond Edward b. 1914 – d. 2001 (Mandrake the Magician)

Veteran radio actor Raymond Edward Johnson, who is perhaps best known as Host Raymond on Himan Brown's *Inner Sanctum Mysteries* radio program, played the suave and sophisticated *Mandrake the Magician* on the radio version of Gene Aherne's popular comic strip.

There were few busier actors on radio in the 1930s and 1940s than Raymond Edward Johnson. Johnson's formidable list of radio credits includes most of the programs that were aired during those "golden age" years of radio. Born in Kenosha, Wisconsin, Raymond Johnson began his radio acting career in the 1930s in Chicago. The many programs on which he was featured over the years included the soap operas *Bachelor's Children, Brave Tomorrow, Girl Alone, The Goldbergs, I Love Linda Dale, Joyce Jordan, Girl Intern, Kate Hopkins, Angel of Mercy, Myrt and Marge, Of Human Bondage, Stella Dallas, The Story of Mary Marlin, A Tale of Today, There Was a Woman, Today's Children, Valiant Lady, Welcome Valley,* and *Your Family and Mine.* He was also heard on the prime time programs *Cavalcade of America, Curtain Time, Dimension X, The First Nighter, Everyman's Theater, Grand Hotel, The Philip Morris Playhouse,* and Fletcher Markle's *Studio One.* The mystery and adventure programs on which Johnson was featured included *Clock and Dagger, Crime Fighter, Famous Jury Trials, Gangbusters, Lights Out, Nick Carter, Master Detective,* and *Roger Kilgore, Public Defender.* He was also heard on the children's shows Tennessee Jed and Young Hickory and also played *Mandrake the Magician* on the adaptation of Lee Falk's popular comic strip and played the title role on the *Don Winslow of the Navy* radio program. Johnson is probably best remembered by radio listeners as "Raymond," the creepy host of Himan Brown's eerie series *Inner Sanctum Mysteries.*

In addition to his work on radio, Raymond Edward Johnson was also featured in the Broadway play *The Patriot* in 1943 and was seen in the films *Mr. Bell* (1947), and *Knock on Any Door* (1949). He was also heard as the narrator of the TV series *Night of the Auk.* Mr. Johnson died at the age of ninety-three after a long battle with multiple sclerosis, which was first diagnosed when he was in his early forties.

Mark Trail

An outdoorsman and conservationist named "Mark Trail" has been the main character in a popular comic strip for over sixty years. Created by artist Ed Dodd in 1946, Mark has taught people how to preserve our natural resources such as our forests, waterways, and wildlife, in over 75 newspapers that have been read by at least 23 million people all over the world. Ed Dodd studied engineering technology in Georgia, but decided while in college that he wanted to be a professional artist. He studied Art at the celebrated Art Students League and went to work for a while as a commercial illustrator for magazine short stories. He saved his money diligently and his love of the out-of-doors and nature in general led him to buy a small ranch in Wyoming in 1926. In order to pay his bills, Dodd went to work as a guide for the National Parks Administration. In 1930, Dodd started drawing nature illustrations for a series of illustrations he called "Back Home Again," which was published in 1945 by United Features Syndicate. In 1946, he launched a comic strip that featured a pipe smoking man who loved nature. The strip became popular with people all across America. Dodd continued to draw the daily and Sunday Funnies comic strip series he called *Mark Trail,* named for the strips' hero,

Outdoors man and conservationist Mark Trail was a major crusader in the fight to save the natural environmental resources of America in a popular, long-running comic strip, created by artist Ed Dodd in 1946.

until 1978 when, at the age of sixty-seven, he turned the strip over to his assistant, Jack Elrod. Dodd died at the age of eighty-nine in 1991.

In Dodd's *Mark Trail* comic strip, Trail is a forever-thirty-two year old photojournalist who works for the fictional "Woods and Wildlife" magazine. Mark loves the out-of-doors and spends most of his non-working hours hunting, fishing and simply enjoying the nature around him. He is usually busy working to preserve the nation's dwindling wetlands and fighting people who want to exploit our environment for personal profit. When Mark is not fighting greedy businessmen, he is usually at his home in the wilderness at the Lake Forest Game Preserve where he lived with his wife, Cherry, and his faithful dog, Andy, a large St. Bernard who has rescued Mark on many of his missions to save the environment. Besides Mark, Cherry and Andy, other characters who appear regular in the Mark Trail comic strips are Doc Davis, Cherry's father who is also an active outdoorsman, Johnny Malotte, Mark's friend and fellow adventurer and nature lover, and Rusty, who is Mark and Cherry's adopted son who is a kid with a heart of gold who sometimes gets into jams that Mark has to rescue him from. In recent years, *Mark Trail's* full color Sunday comic have focused on weather safety issues, including flash floods, tornados, and hurricanes and have been credited with alerting millions of people about the dangers of these natural disasters. In 1988, Jack Elrod, who was drawing the *Mark Trail* comic strip at the time, was honored by President Ronald Reagan for his efforts to develop more pride in America. Mark Trail is currently the spokesman for the National Oceanic and Atmospheric Administration (NOAA), and is heard as the voice of the National Weather Service and NOAA Weather Service.

In 1950, Ed Dodd's comic strip *Mark Trail* took to the airwaves as the main character on a radio series that was heard on the Mutual Broadcasting System's network. The *Mark Trail* radio series was an exciting adventure program which was informative as well and was mainly directed at the younger members of the household. On the radio series, Mark was a forest ranger who roamed the wilderness to track down bad guys while teaching his pals Scotty and Cherry, who was not his wife on the radio series, about nature. Three actors played *Mark Trail* during the years the series was aired; Matt Crowley, John Larkin and Staats Cotsworth. Ben Cooper, and then Ronald Liss, played Scotty and Joyce Gordon played Cherry. Jackson Beck and Glenn Riggs were the show's announcers. The series was directed by Drexel Hoffman and written by Albert Alley, Palmer Thompson, Edward Hoffman and Gilbert Brown. The program's opening was like a litany for conservationists and read:

ANNOUNCER:	KELLOGGS PEP, THE BUILD-UP WHEAT CEREAL WITH A PRIZE IN EVERY PACKAGE, INVITES YOU TO SHARE ANOTHER THRILLING ADVENTURE WITH MARK TRAIL.
SOUND:	*BURNING FOREST*
ANNOUNCER:	BATTLING THE RAGING ELEMENTS!
SOUND:	*WOLF HOWL*
ANNOUNCER:	FIGHTING THE SAVAGE WILDERNESS!
SOUND:	*HORSE HOOF BEATS*
ANNOUNCER:	STRIKING AT THE ENEMIES OF MAN AND NATURE!
MUSIC:	*STING*
ANNOUNCER:	ONE MAN'S NAME RESOUNDS FROM SNOW-CAPPED MOUNTAINS DOWN ACROSS THE SUN-BAKED PLAINS. MARK TRAIL!
MUSIC:	*STING*
ANNOUNCER:	GUARDIAN OF THE FORESTS!
MUSIC:	*STING*
ANNOUNCER:	PROTECTOR OF WILDLIFE!
MUSIC:	*STING*
ANNOUNCER:	CHAMPION OF MAN AND NATURE!
MUSIC:	*STING*
ANNOUNCER:	MARK TRAIL!

The *Mark Trail* radio series remained on the the air, in one format or another, until the early 1960s.

Mark Trail Radio Series Performers

Cotsworth, Staats b. 1908 – d. 1979 (Mark Trail)

Actor Staats Cotsworth, who played *Casey, Crime Photographer* on radio, was the third and final actor to play Mark Trail on the *Mark Trail* radio program, which ended its run in the early 1960s. The role was previously played by Matt Crowley and John Larkin.

Probably best remembered for playing *Casey on the Casey, Crime Photographer* radio series, which was on the air from 1945 until 1950, actor Staats Cotsworth, in addition to being heard as Casey, as well as on hundreds of radio programs during Radio's Golden Age, also had a distinguished career as a stage actor. Born in Oak Park, Illinois, after he graduated from college Cotsworth went to New York City to become an actor and he was soon appearing in repertory company productions of Shakespeare's plays *Macbeth*, *As You Like It* and *Othello* on Broadway. He subsequently appeared in Broadway productions of such plays as *Damaged Goods* (1937), *Shop-Over* (1938), *Madame Capet* (1940), *Boudier* (1941), *Pictures in the Hallway* (1956), *Inherit the Wind* (1957), *Advise and Consent* (1961), *The Right Honorable Gentleman* (1966), *Weekend* (1968), *A Patriot for Me* (1967), and *Lost in the Stars* (1972). As was the case with most Broadway actors, stage roles only offered temporary employment and therefore Cotsworth supplemented his income by working on various radio programs. In addition to his regular running role on *Casey, Crime Photographer*, he was featured on an impressive number of radio shows throughout the 1930s, 1940s and 1950s, including *Lorenzo Jones* (1943 – 1945), *Front Page Farrell* (1945 – 1954), and *Stella Dallas, Mr. and Mrs. North, When a Girl Marries, Marriage for Two, The Cavalcade of America, Amanda of Honeymoon Hill, The Right to Happiness, The Second Mrs. Burton, Big Sister*, and many, many others. Because of his pleasant, compassionate and, masculine sounding voice, which had just a trace of humor in it, Cotsworth replaced actor Matt Crowley, who originated the role on radio, as outdoorsman *Mark Trail* on the radio adaptation of Ed Dodd's popular comic strip character. After radio dramas disappeared from network radio in the late 1950s – early 1960s,

Cotsworth began to appear on several television series such as *The Edge of Night* (1962), *As the World Turns* (1967–1968), *The Armstrong Circle Theater, Studio One, The Hallmark Hall of Fame, Robert Montgomery Presents, The Kraft Television Theater, The Goodyear Theater, The General Electric Theater, The Defenders, The Nurses, East Side, West Side, Dr. Kildare,* and *Bonanza*. Staats Cotsworth died at the age of seventy-one in 1979.

CROWLEY, MATT (SEE *JUNGLE JIM* FOR BIOGRAPHY)

LARKIN, JOHN (SEE *BUCK ROGERS IN THE 25TH CENTURY* FOR BIOGRAPHY)

LISS, RONALD (SEE *BUCK ROGERS IN THE 25TH CENTURY* FOR BIOGRAPHY)

MICKEY MOUSE ON THE AIR

In 1937, Walt Disney brought his wonderful assortment of cartoon characters to radio on a variety show for children that was called *The Mickey Mouse Theater of the Air*. The radio series featured the voices which were heard in Disney's animated cartoon films The radio show characters sang songs, acted in brief comedy sketches, and were interviewed by Mr. Disney. Clarence Nash was the voice of Donald Duck, Stuart Buchanan was Goofey, Thelma Borgman was Minnie Mouse, and Florence Gill was Clarabelle Cow, to name just a few. Walt Disney himself provided the voice of Mickey Mouse on the program, which was mainly one long promotional broadcast for Walt Disney's films and various cartoon inspired by-products. Written By Bill Deming, the short-lived radio series was heard on the NBC network and was on the air for less than one year, in spite of the popularity of Disney's films. It seems people preferred to see, as well as hear, Mickey, Minnie, Donald and the others.

In addition to Disney's numerous animated, short subject cartoons and his feature length films such as *Snow White and the Seven Dwarfs, Bambi, Pinocchio,* and *Dumbo,* Disneys. Characters also appeared in numerous children's books and comics and Mickey Mouse and Donald Duck had daily comic strips of their own published in newspapers throughout the country. The Mickey Mouse and Donald Duck comic books are still being published today and some of the earliest issues of these comics are among the most popular collector's items in then market selling for thousands of dollars for one issue. Among the cartoonist who have drawn Disney character comic books and comic strips over the years are Carl Buettner, Carl Barks, Pete Alvarado, Fred Quimby, Jesse Marsh, Walt Kelly, Al Taliaferro, Don Rosa, Marco Rota, William Van Horn, and Freddy Milton, among others.

My Friend Irma

The formula for the success of the CBS situation comedy series *My Friend Irma,* which made its radio debut in 1947 and remained on the air for the next seven years, was simple. Take two big city secretaries, one a sharp, witty and attractive brunette and the other a naive, gorgeous "dumb blonde," make them roommates, and surround them with a whole bunch of zany, amusing characters and wait for the laughs to come. *My Friend Irma* was a success from the first time it was heard over the airwaves and for a while, it was America's most popular radio program. The success of the show was in no small part due to the excellent casting of the program's principle characters by producer/director Cy Howard, and the writing talent of veteran comedy show writers Parke Levy, Stanley Adams, Jack Denton, and Roland MacLane. *My Friend Irma's* delightful cast included some of the most experienced performers on the air. Actress Marie Wilson, who had played similar attractive-but-not-very-bright blonde beauties in films and on several radio and stage shows such as *Ken Murray's Blackouts* for many years, was cast as Irma Peterson. Cathy Lewis, whose wry, intelligent and appealing sounding voice had been heard on

(Credit: Photofest)

Marie Wilson and Cathy Lewis, who played roommates Irma Peterson and Jane Stacy on the popular *My Friend Irma* radio series, are seen above looking over their scripts before a broadcast with actor John Brown, who played Irma's boyfriend, Al, on the show.

hundreds of radio programs over the years, was cast as Irma's long-suffering roommate, Jane Stacy. Other veteran performers who had regular roles on the series were; the very talented and popular character actor, Hans Conried, who played a fellow roomer at the boarding house where Irma and Jane lived, a mad-Russian named Professor Kropotkin; Gloria Gordon, who played the elderly Irish vamp who ran the boarding house and had an unrequited crush on Professor Kropotkin, Mrs. O'Reilly; Alan Reed, whose familiar voice was heard on a countless number of radio shows, played Irma's exasperated boss, Mr. Clyde; frequent radio funnyman John Brown played Irma's fast-talking conman boyfriend, Al; motion picture leading man Leif Erickson played Jane's rich boyfriend/boss, Richard Rhinelander; and Myra Marsh played Richard's snobbish, overbearing mother, Mrs. Rhinelander. *My Friend Irma's* popularity never diminished during the years it was aired and it eventually became a popular TV series and spun-off two popular feature films that starred Miss Wilson and introduced the comedy team of Dean Martin and Jerry Lewis to the movie-going public.

In 1950, three years after its first radio broadcast, Marvel comics bought the rights to publish *My Friend Irma* as a series of comic books. The talented cartoonist Dan DeCarlo (See Archie Andrews for DeCarlo's biography) was hired by Marvel to draw the *My Friend Irma* comic books. DeCarlo's renderings of Irma captured her dim witted free-spirit and her shapely good looks just as listeners imagined her to look, and his amusing drawings of the other characters in the comic books adaptation

The very successful situation comedy series, *My Friend Irma* was first heard on radio in 1947 and remained on the air until 1954. In 1950, because of the radio show's popularity, a comic book was released which remained in print until 1953, one year after the radio series had been canceled.

of the popular radio show, represented the voices that listeners heard on the radio series to perfection. "I love girls," DeCarlo once told a Washington Post reporter who was interviewing him when he was drawing the *Betty and Veronica* spin-off of the *Archie Andrews'* comic books. "I used to go to the high school to see what the girls were wearing, and draw that." The *My Friend Irma* comic books were among Marvel's best selling comic books and the series ran from issue #3, which was published in June, 1950, through issue #48, which was released in February, 1955, one year after the popular radio program left the air.

MY FRIEND IRMA RADIO SERIES PERFORMERS

BROWN, JOHN B. 1904 – D. 1957 (AL)

Actor John Brown, who was born in Hull, Yorkshire, England, immigrated to the United States with his parents when he was a boy. He first appeared on the vaudeville stage when he was in his teens and when he was in his twenties, he auditioned for and won a role on the popular *Eddie Canter* radio program. One of radio's busiest and most talented comedians, Brown estimated that he was heard on over 10,000 broadcasts one year in the 1940s. Among the many radio programs that Brown was featured on in the 1930s, 1940s and 1950s were *The Adventures of Ozzie and Harriet* (as Thornberry, or "Thorny," Ozzie and Harriet's neighbor), *The Amazing Mr. Smith*, *Beulah*, *The Charlotte Greenwood Show*, *The Danny Kaye Show*, *The Fred Allen Show*, *The Life of Riley* (as Digger O'Dell, the Friendly Undertaker), *Lorenzo Jones*, *Maisie*, *Mystery in the Air*, *The Saint*, *A Day in the Life of Dennis Day*, *Duffy's Tavern*, *A Date With Judy*, and the *The Edgar Bergen/Charlie McCarthy Show*, to name just a few. In 1952, he also appeared on an episode of the popular *I Love Lucy* TV series. Somehow, Brown even found time to appear in several motion pictures in the 1940s and 1950s, including *Casanova Brown* (1944), *A Horn Blows at Midnight* (1945), *The Life of Riley* (1945, as Digger O'Dell), *Strangers on a Train* (1951), *The Day the Earth Stood Still* (1951), *Hans Christian* (1952), *The Wild One* (1953) and *Crazylegs* (1953), and others.

CONRIED, HANS B. 1915 – D. 1982 (PROFESSOR KROPOTKIN)

A talented and versatile character actor, Hans Conried was equally as busy on radio, on the stage, in films, and on television. Conried originally wanted to be a Shakespearean actor and begin his career on the stage after graduating from Columbia University in New York. When he was in his early twenties he became one of the company of players with Orson Welles' *Mercury Theater* and was seen in many of that company's early productions. In the late 1930s, he was heard on Welles' *Mercury Theater of the Air* dramatic anthology radio series, and this led to various roles on such radio programs as Arch Oboler's *Lights Out* and *The First Nighter*, and then on a wide variety of shows which were broadcast from Hollywood including *Suspense, The Adventures of Sam Spade, Burns and Allen, The Mel Blanc Show, Escape, One Man's Family, The Lux Radio Theater, The Screen Director's Playhouse, Hollywood Hotel,* on which he often used his perfect stage diction and talent to speak in any dialect and sound convincingly foreign, to advantage. Conried is probably best remembered on radio, however, for playing Professor Kropotkin on the very popular *My Friend Irma* radio series, Oliver Honeywell on *The Great Gildersleeve,* Mr. Honeywell on *The Judy Canova Show,* and Uncle Baxter on *The Life of Riley.* In addition to his work on radio, Conried was also a busy character actor in films. After his film debut in *Dramatic School* in 1938, Conried appeared in well over one hundred films over the years including *On Borrowed Time* (1939), *Maisie Was a Lady* (1941), *Underground* (1941), *The Gay Falcon* (1941), *Joan of Paris* (1942), *Hitler's Children* (1943), *Mrs. Parkington* (1944), *The Barkley's of Broadway* (1944), *My Friend Irma* (1949, playing his radio role of Professor Kropotkin on film), *I'll See You in my Dreams* (1951), *Peter Pan* (1953, as the voice of Captain Hook/Mr. Darling), *5,000 Fingers of Dr. T* (1953), *The Big Beat* (1958), and *My Six Lovers* (1963), among others. During World War Two, the actor was often cast as a Nazi officer in films. Hans Conreid was equally as busy as an actor on television. His most memorable role on television was as Danny Thomas' Uncle Tonoose on the *Make Room for Daddy* TV series from 1956 until 1971. He was also featured on such TV shows as *I Love Lucy, The United States Steel Hour, Four Star Playhouse, The Real McCoys, Maverick, The Donna Reed Show, Adventures in Paradise, Mister Ed, Dr. Kildare, Burke's Law, Ben Casey, Lost in Space, The Beverly Hillbillies, Laverne and Shirley, The Love Boat, Fantasy Island,* and others. In the 1960s and 1970s, in addition to numerous tours in various stage plays, Conried was also featured on Broadway in *Can Can* (1963–1965), *Tall Story* (1969), *70 Girls, 70* (1971), *Irene* (1973–1974), and *Something Old, Something New* (1977).

LEWIS, CATHY B. 1918 – D. 1968 (JANE STACY)

Actress Cathy Lewis was born in Spokane, Washington. She began her career as a band singer singing with the Herbie Kaye, Ted Weems, and Glen Gray orchestras. In the 1930s, Cathy decided that she wanted to become an actress and her persistence won her roles in touring and repertory company stage productions of such plays as *Winterset, Bitter Sweet, The Man Who Came to Dinner* and *Stage Door.* But it was as a radio actress that Cathy enjoyed her greatest success. In the mid 1930s, Cathy went to Chicago, which, at the time, was the center of radio drama production and she was soon being heard on most of the soap operas that were broadcast from that city. She was also frequently featured on Arch Oboler's eerie, late night *Lights Out* series and was heard as a supporting player on the popular *First Nighter* series. In the early

1940s, Miss Lewis moved to Hollywood and before long she was being heard on most of the radio programs that originated in that city as well, including *The Eddie Bracken Show, Sam Spade, Detective, The Great Gildersleeve, The Drene Show, Whispering Streets, I Love a Mystery, One Man's Family* and on many occasions, she was featured on the popular and long running *Suspense* series, as leading lady to many of Hollywood's most successful film actors. Cathy also starred on a weekly series of original drama, On Stage, which co-starred her husband, Elliott Lewis, heard on the CBS network. It was, however, as Jane Stacy on the very successful situation comedy series *My Friend Irma*, and later on the subsequent television series of that show, that Cathy Lewis is perhaps best remembered. In the late 1950s, Cathy was also featured as the sister of the maid Hazel's (played by Shirley Booth) boss on the very popular TV situation comedy series *Hazel*. Shortly before she died, after a long battle with cancer, Cathy was seen on an episode of the TV series *F Troop* playing an aging Native American chief's daughter.

WILSON, MARIE B. 1916 – D. 1972 (IRMA PETERSON)

When she was fifteen years old in 1931, pretty, blonde and shapely Marie Wilson, who was born Katherine Elizabeth White, took a bus to Hollywood from her birthplace in Anaheim, California, determined to break into the Movies. The ambitious young girl entered the "Miss Pacific Fleet" contest and won the title and a contract to appear in a film. Her first film role of any consequence was playing a dumb blonde in the film *Satan Meets a Lady* in 1936 and she was so good in the role, she found herself typecast in all of her future films which included, among others, the critically acclaimed comedy *Boy Meets Girl* (1940) and *Mr. Hobbs Takes a Vacation* (1962). After a long run in *Ken Murray's Blackouts* variety stage show, radio director/producer Cy Howard cast Marie as Irma, another dumb blonde, on a new radio situation comedy series that he was producing called *My Friend Irma*. The series, and Marie, were an immediate hit with the public and Marie played the role on radio from 1947 until 1954, repeating the role in two *My Friend Irma* films, one with the comedy team of Dean Martin and Jerry Lewis making their film debut. She also played Irma in a TV version of the series which proved to be less successful than the radio show had been. Before she died at the premature age of fifty-six in 1972, Marie Wilson also provided the voice of the cartoon character Penny on the *Where's Huddles* animated TV series.

N

THE NEBBS

In the 1920s and 1930s, comic strips about family life were very popular with the public. *The Gumps, Gasoline Alley, Blondie* and others were enormously popular. Writer Sol Hess' comic strip *The Nebbs* was one comic that certainly capitalized on the popularity of this type of strip and it managed to remain in print for over twenty years, even though *The Nebbs* was never as popular as the comic strips mentioned above. *The Nebbs*, like those other strips, however, had

Sol Hess' comic strip *The Nebbs*, which made its debut in 1922, became a situation comedy series on radio in 1945. The series did not even remain on the air for one full season.

a short run as a radio show in 1945, as well as appearing in a Big Little book. *The Nebb's* artist, Sol Hess (1872–1941) was born on a farm in rural Illinois but moved to Chicago with his parents when he was a boy. When his father died, Hess went to work for a jewelry company traveling around the country as a salesman. Always interested in writing, Hess turned his writing hobby into a career when an artist-friend of his, Sidney Smith, who had created the popular *Gumps* comic strip, asked him to write dialogue for his successful comic strip. In 1922, Hess created his own comic strip, *The Nebbs,* and hired artist Wallace A. Carlson to do the art work. The comic strip clicked with the public and Hess quit the jewelry business to settle down to a full time career as a comic strip writer.

The Nebbs family consisted of a plump, motherly looking woman named Fanny, her balding, dark-haired, mustached husband, Rudy, their son, Junior, who looked like a miniature version of his father, without the mustache, and their little yellow dog. The family were often seen entertaining friends and family at home or at outdoor picnics when something would go wrong such as Fanny dropping the turkey on the floor or an invasion of ants carried away the food. When Rudy was doing something around the house, a catastrophe was bound to occur. In one of the daily strips, the entire storage he was constructing collapsed just when he thought it was completed. American families apparently identified with Rudy's and Fanny's household ineptitude and the folksy, familiar strip remained a popular newspaper feature for many years. *The Nebbs* appealed to readers who wanted to see people who they felt were like them, hardly perfect, or who they somehow wished they were like because they were able to shrug off the everyday annoyances of family life.

In 1945, the short-lived radio program based on Hess' *Nebbs* comic strip surfaced. The radio series featured veteran Hollywood character actor Gene Lockhart and his wife, Kathleen, as Rudy and Fanny Nebbs, and juvenile actor Conrad Binyon as their son, Junior. Other actors who were heard regular on the program were Billy Roy, Francis "Dink" Trout, Dick Ryan and Ruth Perrott. The show's announcer was Tommy Dixon. The scripts for this series, although somewhat amusing, were more like a not-particularly funny situation comedy version of the popular *One Man's Family* radio series, which, like *The Nebbs,* centered around the comings and goings of one family. *One Man's Family,* however, got the listening audience involved with the family's problems and the Barbour family on that series was a large, complex and diverse group of people, whereas the Nebbs family and their everyday problems whereas the Nebbs family were just three rather uncomplicated people whose problems were mundane compared o the Barbours. *The Nebbs* radio series also lacked the warmth and appeal, and certainly had none of the good writing that listeners could hear on Carlton E. Morse's *One Man's Family* radio program, which was the primary reason for the programs long-running success.

THE NEBBS RADIO SERIES PERFORMERS

BINYON, CONRAD (JUNIOR. SEE *MAJOR HOOPLE* FOR BIOGRAPHY)

LOCKHART, GENE B. 1891 – D. 1957 (RUDY NEBBS)
Although he appeared in hundreds of films and on numerous television series, character actor Gene Lockhart had a regular role on only one radio series, *The Nebbs.* Lockhart played Rudy Nebbs, a somewhat inept but loving

 Radio's Golden Age

father and husband on the radio adaptation of Sol Hess' *The Nebbs* comic strip. The actor, who was born in London, Ontario, Canada, had one of the most familiar faces in films, usually playing middle aged men with questionable agendas, and he had important roles in such movies as *Smilin' Through* (a 1922 silent film, which was his film debut) and *By Your Leave* (1934), *Crime and Punishment* (1935), *Make Way For Tomorrow* (1937), *Algiers* (1938), *Blondie* (1938), *A Christmas Carol* (1938), *The Story of Alexander Graham Bell* (1939), *His Gal Friday* (1940), *South of Pago Pago* (1940), *Meet John Doe* (1941), *Going My Way* (1944), *Leave Her to Heaven* (1945), *Sea Wolf* (1945), *The Miracle of 34th Street* (1947), *Joan of Arc* (1948), *Madame Bovary* (1949), *Carousel* (1956), *The Man in the Gray Flannel Suit* (1956), and *Jeanne Eagles* (1957). On television, Gene Lockhart was seen on such series as *Lights Out, The Lux Video Theater, Family Theater, The Ford Theater. Dander, Crossroad,* and *Climax,* among others. Lockart was married to character actress Kathleen Lockhart who costarred with him on *The Nebbs* radio series. The couple had a daughter, June, who was also an actress and was the star of the popular *Lassie* and *Lost in Space* TV series.

LOCKHART, KATHLEEN B. 1894 – D. 1978 (FANNY NEBBS)
Like her husband, Gene Lockhart, Kathleen Lockhart was a popular character actor in films. Mrs. Lockhart was born in Southsea, Hampshire, England, but immigrated to the United States after having a successful acting career in England to work on the Broadway stage. In 1930, the actress appeared on Broadway in the play *The Little Father of the Wilderness* and in the mid-1930s, she went to Hollywood and appeared in the film *Brides Are Like That* in 1936. Thereafter the actress remained in Hollywood, except for a brief return to Broadway in 1945 to appear in the play *Happily Ever After,* and was seen in numerous films, usually playing mothers and matrons in such movies as *The Devil is a Sissy* (1936), *Career Woman* (1936), *Men Are Such Fools* (1938), *Blondie* (1938), *A Christmas Carol* (1938), *What a Life* (1939), *Love Crazy* (1941), *Mission to Moscow* (1943), *Two Years Before the Mast* (1946), *Lady in the Lake* (1947), *Gentlemen's Agreement* (1947), *Plymouth Adventure* (1952), and *The Glenn Miller Story* (1953). Mrs.Lockhart came out of retirement to appear in the film *The Purple Gang* in 1960.

P

POPEYE THE SAILOR

Before artist Elzie Crisler Segar (1894–1938) created the very successful *Popeye the Sailor* comic strip character and became a legend in the world of cartooning, he was a projectionist in a motion picture theater in Chicago.

There were no less than three unsuccessful attempts to adapt Elzie Segar's very successful *Popeye the Sailor* comic strip character to radio. All three attempts failed after less than one full season on the air.

Segar became fascinated with the film comedies of Charlot and he began to draw cartoon characters based on the actors he saw in that director's film comedies. When he tried to sell his comic strip ideas to the local Chicago newspapers, he met with little success. In 1910, Segar met Richard Felton Outcault, the creator of *The Yellow Kid* comic strip which is said to have been one of the first comic strips ever published. Outcault liked Segars's comic strip ideas and introduced him to his editors at the *Chicago Herald*. Also suitably impressed with Segar's artistic talents, the editors asked Segar to create a new strip for them. The editors liked his first submission, *Charlie Chaplin Comedy Capers*, and agreed to publish the comic strip in The Herald. The strip met with only moderate success, but Segar soon came up with an idea for a new comic strip he called *Looping the Loop*, which was published in *The Chicago Sun* and met with moderate success. By 1919, Segar's comic strips attracted the attention of the King Features Syndicate and Segar was asked to create a new comic strip for them which he called *The Five Fifteen*. Within a few months, the title of the strip was changed to *The Thimble Theater*, and the strip soon became his most successful comic strip effort. *The Thimble Theater* had a character in it who was a pencil-thin lady named Olive Oyle, who soon became the main characters in the comic strip along with her brother, Castor Oyle and Castor's friend, Ham Gravy. By 1929, ten years after *The Thimble Theater* had first been introduced to the American public, it was one of the most popular comic strips in the country. That year, a new character named "Popeye the Sailor," made his first appearance in the strip and became an immediate favorite of fans of the comic strip. One year after Popeye was introduced in the strip, *The Thimble Theater* was the most popular comic strip in the United States. Elzie Segar died in 1938, and when he died, he was one of the most famous cartoonists in the world.

Popeye the Sailor's rise to fame began when the characters Castor Oyle and Ham Gravy embarked on an adventure that involved overseas travel in the January 17, 1929 *Thimble Theater* comic strip. While Castor and Ham were on the dock arranging for their transportation to a foreign port of call, they met a one-eyed sailor who had an anchor tattooed on one of his oversized arms. "Hey there," Castor called out to the sailor, "Are you a sailor?" "Ja think I'm a cowboy" the one eyed sailor shot back, his one glaring eye at the two men. From then on, Popeye was a regular member of the *Thimble Theater* cast and one year later he was the "theater's" star attraction and had replaced Ham Gravy as Olive Oyle's sweetheart. Other new characters that began to appear in the strip after Popeye joined the cast were a shiftless, hamburger-loving dolt named Wimpy, a foundling baby who Popeye and Olive adopted and called "Swee'pea," and a big brute of a fellow named Bluto, who became Popeye's nemesis and a main rival for Olive Oyle's affections. As the Popeye character's popularity increased, the strip became known to most people as "Popeye," although it retained the *Thimble Theater* title. When Elzie Segar died in 1938 at the height of the *Popeye* comic strips' popularity, it was taken over by an artist named Charles H. "Doc" Winner, and then by Bela Zaboly, and then Forrest "Bud" Sagendorf, who drew the strip until1958. All three artists painstakingly copied Elzie Segar's style of cartooning so that most people never knew the original artist was no longer drawing the comic strip. *Popeye the Sailor* comic books began to surface in the 1940s and were mainly draw by Bud Sagendorf for Dell, and then Gold Key, comics. These comic books continued to be published until 1984. Sagendorf continued to draw *Popeye/The Thimble Theater* comic strip until he died in 1994 and the strip was taken over by artist Bobby London, who draws it to this day.

The success of the *Popeye the Sailor/Thimble Theater* comics led to many by-products including numerous animated film cartoons. The first *Popeye* cartoon film that was released was *Betty Boop Meets Popeye the Sailor* in 1933. Numerous cartoons made by the Max Fleischer Studio followed from 1933 to 1942. Popeye also appeared in a 1933 short subject film called *I Yam What I Yam*. In 1942, Fleischer's animation studio was absorbed by Paramount Pictures and several *Popeye* cartoons were later released by Famous Films and continued to be produced until 1957. In 1980, Popeye became the major character in a feature length film musical comedy called *Popeye* that starred Robin Williams as Popeye, Shelly Duval as Olive Oyle, Paul Smith as Bluto, and Ray Walston as Popeye's father, Poopdeck Pappy. The film had a somewhat "dark" and menacing feel to it, but was a brilliant effort nonetheless. It was imaginatively produced and it is actually quite faithful to Elzie Segar's original *Thimble Theater* concept.

There were no less than three unsuccessful attempts to bring *Popeye the Sailor* into American homes as a radio series. The first attempt was in 1935. This radio program was sponsored by Wheatena hot cereal. The first broadcast of this fifteen minute, three-days-a-week series was heard on Sept, 10, 1935 and its last broadcast was aired on March 28, 1936. In all, eighty-seven episodes were aired on the NBC Red network on Tues, Thursday and Saturday nights at 7:15 pm. NBC reportedly paid King Features Syndicate $1,200 a week for the rights to air *Popeye,* which was a princely sum of money for those Depression Era days. Veteran Broadway character comedian Detmar "Det" Poppen played Popeye on this radio series, Olive LaMoy played Olive Oyle, Charles Lawrence played Wimpy, and child actor Jimmy Donnelly played a non-Segar character named Matey, the Newsboy. A second attempt to present *Popeye* on radio was made by CBS with a series that was aired from August 31, 1936 until February 26, 1937. This series was also sponsored by Wheatena and basically had the same cast as the original radio series, with the exception of Det Poppen, who had been replaced by an actor named Floyd Buckey as Popeye. This second series also failed to capture an audience and was canceled after only six months on the air. The third and last attempt to make *Popeye* a successful radio series was also presented on the CBS network and featured several new actors in the cast including Miriam Wolfe, who played the hideous Sea Hag character, and also, on occasion, played the role of Olive Oyle on the series, Mae Questal, also played Olive, and Everett Sloane, Jean Kay, and Don Costillo, and others were in the supporting cast. This last *Popeye* radio series, which was sponsored by Popsicle iced bars, was heard from May 1, 1938 until July 29, 1938, and once again, it was canceled because it failed to attract a sizeable enough audience to keep it in the air.

Popeye the Sailor Radio Series Performers

Poppen, Detmar "Det" b. circa 1886 – d. 1946 (Popeye the Sailor)

From 1906 until 1943, musical operetta comedian/actor Detmar "Det" Poppen, who was a descendent of a famous Dutch theatrical family, was one of Broadway's leading performers. In 1906, Det Poppen made his Broadway debut in a production of the operetta *The Student King*, and from 1916 until 1944 he appeared in Broadway productions of such celebrated operettas as *Pom Pom* (1916), *The Chocolate Soldier* (1921), *Lady in Ermine* (1922), *Princess Ida* (1925), *Dearest Enemy* (1925), *The Three Muskateers* (1928), *Sweethearts* (1929), *Mle. Moiste* (1929), *The Fortune Teller* (1929), *The Chocolate Soldier* (revival, 1931) *Chimes of Normandy* (1931), *Naughty Marietta* (1931), *The Firefly* (1931), *Bohemian Girl* (1933), *The Chocolate Soldier* (another revival, in 1934), *Lady Precious Stream* (1936), and *The Student Prince* (a revival, 1943). In the 1930s, Peppen also appeared in several films including *Tomalio* (1933), *The Flame Song* (1934), *The Officer's Mess* (1935), and the short subject *Leon Navara and His Orchestra*. In 1936, Poppen was cast as *Popeye the Sailor* in the first adaptation of Elzie Segar's popular comic strip character that was presented on radio. The role was Poppen's first and only known attempt to star on a radio program and the actor had no further radio program credits, as far as this author could determine. Poppen, who had a deep and husky, very funny vocal quality, according to people who saw him perform many times on the Broadway, stage, apparently was unable to project his formidable comic presence in the non-visual medium of radio and was judged to be inadequate in the Popeye role on the radio series.

Wolfe, Miriam b. 1922 – d. 2001 (Sea Hag and Olive Oyle)

Actress Miriam Wolfe was one of radio's most versatile performers. Her amazing vocal talents as an actress allowed her to convincingly produce any dialect of any age that was needed for a part. Miriam was born in Brooklyn, New York and made her professional radio acting debut reading poems and stories on WGBS in New York when she was four years old. When she was still in her early teens, Miss Wolfe played the ancient witch-narrator, Old Nancy, on the eerie *Witch's Tale* radio series, taking over the role from an elderly actress named Adelaide Fitz-Allen. She played Old Nancy for five years on the series. In 1933, while she was playing Old Nancy, the actress joined the regular cast of performers on Nila Mack's children's fairy tale anthology series, *Let's Pretend* and remained on this show until the 1950s when she was a mature actress. On *Let's Pretend*, Miriam became known for playing witches, wicked and wise queens, good and bad mothers and stepmothers, fairies and sprites, and many other roles requiring a more mature voice. Miss Wolfe was also actively heard on Fletcher Markle's *Studio One* and *Ford Theater* programs, acting in the supporting casts, and on rare occasions playing the leading female role, on every hour-long drama that was broadcast during the two years these series were aired from 1947 until 1949. She was also heard on such programs as *The American School of the Air, Mystery Hall, Casey, Crime Photographer, Suspense,* and a host of soap operas. On the *Popeye the Sailor* radio series, Miss Wolfe played the screeching, hideous Sea Hag character, as well as the show's heroine, Olive Oyl. She was also a regular on the *Rayburn and Finch Comedy Hour* program. On television, Miss Wolfe played the Virgin Mary on Fletcher Markle's *Studio One* TV production of "The Nativity." In the late 1950s, Miriam moved to Canada with her Canadian born husband and became an active performer on the Canadian Broadcasting Company. She played all of the roles on the children's series *Miss Switch* on CBC and was featured on many CBC commercials, comedy hours, and dramas.

R

RED RYDER

Before he created his popular *Red Ryder* comic strip hero in 1938, artist Fred Harmon was drawing a similar Western character he called "Bronc Peeler," that he had created in 1935. *Bronc Peeler,* however, did not meet with the public's approval, and Harmon revised his thinking and came up with another cowboy comic strip character who was called *Red Ryder.* Fred Harmon (1902–1982) began his career as a staff artist for *The Star* magazine in 1920. In 1921, Harmon went to work for the Kansas City Film Ad company and then joined the Walt Disney company and Ub Iwerks. Discouraged with the direction in which his career was going, Harmon left the commercial Art field and went to work at various other odd jobs in California, Minnesota, and Iowa for the next several years. In the 1930s, Harmon decided to draw again and it was then that he created his first two comic strips *Bronc Peeler* and *King of the Royal Mounted.* In 1938, when Harmon created his *Red Ryder Western* adventure strip, he finally achieved the success as an artist he had hoped for. Red Ryder became one of the most read Western comic strip characters in America and its popularity led to film adaptations and even a successful radio program. *Red Ryder* actually owed its success to a master promoter named Stephen Slesinger, who not only convinced Harmon to give his cowboy hero a "snappier name" than "Bronc Peeler," but was also able to sell Harmon's new cowboy character, *Red Ryder,* to Newspaper Enterprise Associates. This company had the wherewithal to promote the new comic strip and convince the American public to read through a clever advertising campaign. In the early *Red Ryder* comic strips, Red had a girlfriend named Betty Wilder and he also had an arch-enemy named Ace Harmon, as well as a young Native American boy companion and ward who was called "Little Beaver." Red also had a beloved horse named "Thunder." Slesinger knew a cowboy hero had to surround himself with equally as appealing characters as himself, a fact he had learned from the enormous success of cowboy heroes like *The Lone Ranger,* which was popular at the time *Red Ryder* was created. Like the *Lone Ranger, Red Ryder* was great champion of the underdog and fought for justice in the Old West, engaging in constant battles with the bad guys to keep from succeeding in their wicked ways. Red tracked down outlaws, helped those in need, saved damsels in distress, and always triumphed. In addition to the *Red Ryder* comic strip which received nationwide distribution, *Red Ryder* was also published as a comic book series by Dell in 1939. In his first comic book appearance in *Crackerjack Funnies* issue #9, Red was featured with other familiar comic strip characters, *Dan Dunn, Don Winslow of the Navy* and *Apple Mary*. Red had already been seen as the hero in a Big Little Book which was published by the Whitman company as well, shortly after his comic strip debut. *Red Ryder* became the only feature in a comic book series of his own published by Dell beginning in September, 1940 and the comic book series remained in print for the next seventeen years. Even Red's companion, Littler Beaver, had a comic book series of his own beginning in the early 1950s. *Red Ryder's* prestige certainly increased, especially as far as young boys were concerned, when he became the spokesman for Daisy Air Rifles. Ads for Daisy air rifles were published on the back covers of every *Red Ryder* comic book and every boy in America was soon dreaming about having his very own Daisy air gun. The Red Ryder/Daisy air rifle connection resulted from a mutually lucrative financial arrangement Slesinger had made between Harmon and the Daisy company when the *Red Ryder* comics were out for just one year, and the deal proved to be most rewarding for everyone concerned. Harman retained control of the *Red Ryder* comic strip and drew many of the Dell comic books until 1962, when he decided to retire. His assistant, Bob McLeod, took over the *Red Ryder* comic strip, which finally ended its long and successful run as a newspaper feature in 1964. The comic books still continue to be published with various artists doing the drawing to this day.

Two years after Red Ryder and his young Native American companion, Little Beaver, first appeared in print in 1938, they became the main characters in a twelve-part 1940 movie serial that starred Don Barry and Tommy Cook as Red and Little Beaver. The characters then appeared in a twenty-three part serial from 1944 through 19047, with "Wild Bill" Elliott, and then Allan Lane, as Red, and Robby Blake (Robert Blake) as Little Beaver. In the early 1950s, Red Ryder was the main character in a feature length film that was released by Eagle-Lion Pictures and starred Red Bannon as Red. In the late 1950s, and unsuccessful pilot for a TV series was filmed which also starred Bannon but failed to become a regular series on TV.

The radio version of *Red Ryder*, which was called *The Adventures of Red Ryder*, was first broadcast in 1942 on the Mutual Broadcasting System's network of stations. Radio actor Reed Hadley, who had a deep, rich, heroic-sounding voice was the original Red on this series and he was followed by Carlton KaDell and finally by Brooke Temple, in the role. Tommy Cook, who had played the Little Beaver role in films was heard as Little Beaver on the radio series, and Cook was followed in that role by Henry Blair. Actress Mercedes

Cambridge, who was a frequent performer on the series in the early 1940s, played the Little Beaver character on occasion, when Cook was indisposed. Also heard on the program regularly were Arthur Q. Bryan and Horace Murphy in the supporting cast, and announcers Art Gilmore and Ben Alexander. The series, which remained on the air from 1942 until 1949, always began with the announcer saying, "From out of the West comes America's famous fighting cowboy....Red Ryder!" The Red Ryder program was written by Albert Van Antwerp and produced and directed by Paul Franklin. The setting of the *Adventures of Red Ryder* program was the fictional Painted Valley, where Red lived with his partner, Buckskin, his ward Little Beaver, and his aunt who he called, "The Duchess."

Some of the more intriguing titles of various episodes heard on the *Red Ryder* radio series were "Trouble on the Shogono Trail," "Hot Lead in Scorpion Gulch," "Trouble at Iron Horse Junction," "Trouble in Devil's Hole," "Devil's Circus," "The Law Comes to Stovepipe," "Flame of Hate," "Tornado on the Trail," and "Happy Birthday, Red Ryder."

RED RYDER RADIO SERIES PERFORMERS

HADLEY, REED B. 1911 – D. 1974 (RED RYDER)

Even though he possessed one of the best voices in Hollywood, Reed Hadley is better known for his work in films and on television than for anything he did on radio. Hadley's only major radio role was as the first actor to play the role of Western hero *Red Ryder*, when that popular comic strip and comic book series was first presented on radio in 1942. The six foot four inch, dark haired, reed-thin actor is mainly known for playing villain roles in films. Reed Hadley, who was born in Petrolia, Texas, entered radio as an announcer soon after he finished his schooling

Actor Reed Hadley, one of Hollywood's busiest supporting players and voice-over actors, appearing in hundreds of films and television programs, was only featured on only one radio series of any consequence, the Western series *Red Ryder*. Hadley played the title role on the program for four years until 1947, when Carlton KaDell and Brooke Temple took over the role for two years.

Radio's Golden Age 155

and then went to Hollywood where he was soon appearing in a countless number of films including *Calling Dr. Kildare* (1939), *I Take This Woman* (1940), *The Bank Dick* (1940), *The Adventures of Captain Marvel* (1941), *Ziegfeld Girl* (1941), *The Mystery of Marie Roget* (1942), *I Married a Witch* (1942), *Now Voyager* (1942), *Pin-Up Girl* (1944), *Diamond Horseshow* (1945), *A Bell for Adano* (1945), *13 Rue Madeleine* (1947), *Captain From Castille* (1947), *The Iron Curtain* (1948), *I Shot Jesse James* (1949), *Riders of the Range* (1950), *Little Big Horn* (1951), *The Woman They Almost Lynched* (1953), *Young Dillinger* (1965), and *Brain of Blood* (1972), and many others. Hadley also played Zorro in the Republic Pictures serial Zorro's *Fighting Legion*. On television, Hadley was one of the major characters on the *Racket Squad* and *Public Defender* series and he was also seen on such TV series as *Cavalcade of America, Restless Gun, Wagon Train, Bat Basterson, Rawhide, The Texan, Sea Hunt, Perry Mason, Hondo, Green Acres,* and many others. Some of the most memorable performances he gave was as a Narrator for films such as *The House on 92nd Street,* in which his deep, rich, baritone voice was certainly used to advantage.

KaDell, Carlton b. 1906 – d. 1975 (Actor/Announcer Red Ryder)

Carlton KaDell's radio career spanned a forty year period. Born in Danville, Illinois, KaDell's father owned a chain of motion picture theaters, so his introduction to show business came naturally. When he was a young man, KaDell enrolled in speech improvement classes determined to pursue a career as an actor. Because he had a well trained, excellent baritone voice, KaDell soon found work on radio, not only as an actor, but also as an announcer. His voice was heard on such popular Golden Age of Radio programs as *Amos and Andy, Kitty Keene, Masquerade, The Mayor of the Town, The Dorothy Lamour Show, The Jack Carson Show, The Edgar Bergen/Charlie McCarthy Show,* and *Big Town*. Among the radio series on which KaDell worked as an actor were *Backstage Wife, Jonathan Kegg, Kitty Keene, The Right to Happiness, The Road of Life, The Romance of Helen Trent, Wings of Destiny,* and as the title character and as an announcer on *The Adventures of Red Ryder* radio series, which was adapted from the popular comic strip and comic book series. When radio's hey-day ended, KaDell left Hollywood and went to Chicago, where he was heard on the *Classical Kaleidoscope* program on KEFM for many years. The program had a large and loyal listening audience and KaDell continued to be heard on the program until the day he died in 1975.

THE ROY ROGERS SHOW

The popular motion picture cowboy star, Roy Rogers, had a successful radio program on the air for many years which was appropriately called *The Roy Rogers Show*. Roy's radio series was first aired in 1944, after Roy had become one of the silver screens most successful cowboy actors. The radio show featured cowboy songs, sung by Roy and others, and a weekly Western adventure story. The Sons of the Pioneer singing group also joined Roy at the microphone and in 1948, Roy's film co-star, Dale Evans, who became his wife, also became a regular on the series. For most of the years it was aired, *The Roy Rogers Show* was heard on Sunday nights. Comedy sketches and the adventure stories that were heard on the program featured character actors Pat Brady and George "Gabby Hayes, who also appeared with Roy in many of his films.

The King of the Cowboys, Roy Rogers, was a major Western film star when his radio series, a series of comic books and a daily comic strip surfaced.

At the height of his popularity, Roy became the hero of a very successful series of comic books which were published by Dell from the late 1940s into the mid 1950s. In the *Roy Rogers* comic books, Roy was a cowboy, who, like the *Lone Ranger* and *Red Ryder* characters, tracked down outlaws and helped people in need. Among the many artists who drew the Roy Rogers comic books were Pete Alvarado (see *Gene Autry* entry for biographical information) and John Ushler. Cartoonist John Ushler specialized in drawing Western comic strips and comic books, and worked for Dell/Western Publishing from 1952 until 1962. He also drew the *Treasure Island, Davy Crockett Great Locomotive, Elfego Baca, Texas John Slaughter, The Swamp Fox, Zorro,* and *Swiss Family Robinson* comic books the Disney Company. For Dell, Ushler did the art work for the *Little Beaver, Dale Evans, Rex Allen, Buffalo Bill, Jr., Tarzan, Journey to the Center of the Earth* and *Huckleberry Finn* comic books. While he was working for the Disney Company, Ushler was also responsible for drawing the syndicated comic strips of Disney's *Treasury of Classic Tales* and *Uncle Remus,* which appeared in the daily newspapers as well as in the Sunday Funnies, and he also drew *Scamp, Bo Brummel,* and *Pier 13* daily strips, in addition to a daily comic strip panel of *Roy Rogers.*

ROY ROGERS SHOW RADIO SERIES PERFORMER

ROGERS, ROY B. 1912 – D. 1998 (ROY ROGERS)

Born Leonard Sly in Cincinnati, Ohio, cowboy actor Roy Rogers held the undisputed title of "King of the Cowboys" throughout the 1940s and 1950s and was, with Gene Autry and Tom Mix, one of the most famous cowboy/actors of all time. Before he went to Hollywood and established himself as a major motion picture star, Roy worked in a shoe factory and as a fruit picker in Cincinnati. He began his singing cowboy career performing with his guitar in various salons in Southern Ohio and eventually he was asked to sing on a popular local radio show called *Uncle Tom Murray's Hollywood Hillbillies,* in 1931. His cowboy singing on the show and his photograph, which was published in a Cincinnati newspaper and showed off his boyish good looks, attracted the attention of a Hollywood talent scout who arranged for Roy to go to Hollywood for a screen test. Roy passed the screen test with flying colors and was signed to a contract to appear in films at Republic Pictures. By 1935, he had graduated from playing small parts in films to playing leading roles in such second feature cowboys films as *Tumbling Tumbleweed* (1935), *The Arizona Kid* (1939), and *The Yellow Rose of Texas* (1944), to name just a few of the hundreds of films he made between 1935 and the late 1940s. In 1944, Roy became the star of a weekly radio series called *The Roy Rogers Show,* which remained on the air until 1955. A weekly television show followed and he also appeared in several major first feature films, including *The Paleface* with comedian Bob Hope. Throughout the 1950s and 1960s, Roy made numerous guest starring appearances on various TV variety shows and at county and state fairs. He also lent his name to s series of very popular Western fast food restaurants and, with his wife, actress Dale Evans, who also appeared on his radio and TV series, he founded a Western museum. In the late 1970s, Roy Rogers retired a very wealthy man, but he still made personal appearances in rodeos and was an occasional guest on TV talk shows. In 1979, Roy and his wife, Dale, wrote their memoirs, which they titled "Happy Trails," which was the theme song of their successful radio and TV series. Roy Rogers died in 1998 when he was eighty-six years old.

S

THE SAD SACK

During World War Two, Sgt. George Baker, who had been a cartoonist before he was drafted into the United States Army, began to draw a cartoon feature about a typical, downtrodden soldier who he called "The Sad Sack," for the U. S. Army's *Yank* magazine. The first *Sad Sack* cartoon appeared in the May, 1942 issue of *Yank* and the character, who seemed to epitomize the average soldier's experience and feeling of being a victimized pawn in a world over which he had little, if any, control. The Sad Sack cartoons became immediate favorites with servicemen who were stationed all over the world and were fighting the wicked Nazi and Nipponese forces. The *Sad Sack* character's popularity steadily grew and by 1945, Simon and Shuster decided to publish a two volume set of of *Yank's Sad Sack* cartoons, to show the people at home what was going on in the minds of their sons and husbands who were in the military. The books became best sellers and a subsequent comic strip, as well as a Sunday supplement *Sad Sack* feature, began to appear in the country's various newspapers. When World War Two ended, the *Sad Sack* character, like millions of real-life soldiers, sailors, marines and aviators, returned to civilian life and the character's post-war adjustments to civilian life continued to be chronicled in a daily comic strip, and in the Sunday Funnies. In 1949, publisher Alfred Harvey and artist George

The man who created the *Sad Sack* cartoons, which became famous during World War II, is pictured above in a sketch drawn by a fellow soldier when they were at Anzio after the invasion of Italy.

Baker met, and Harvey decided to release a series of comic books that featured the *Sad Sack* character. The comic books were published from 1949 until 1982. In the mid-1950s, a feature film starring comedian Jerry Lewis playing *Sad Sack* was released and was very popular with the general public. By that time, the Korean War had begun and in the comics, the *Sad Sack* character reenlisted in the Army and his experiences in war torn became the focus of the *Sad Sack* comic strips and comic books. It was in the mid-1950s, that artists other than George Baker began to taker over the drawing of the *Sad Sack* comics. These artists included Fred Rhodes, Jack O'Brien, Paul McCarthy (not of Beatles fame), and Joe Dennett. George Baker, however, continued to draw the *Sad Sack* comic book covers for the Harvey comic books. The *Sad Sack* comics continuously evolved and took the character through many different phases as he drifted in and out of the Army and the character continued to reflect the experiences and emotions of the young men who were drafted into military service during the troublesome 1960s and 1970s. To most Americans, *Sad Sack* was the perennial soldier of misfortune whose behavior and feelings they understood so well, because so many young men had had similar feelings regarding involuntary military service.

In the mid-1940s, it was inevitable that, because of the on-going popularity of the *Sad Sack* character, a radio program featuring the downtrodden soldier would surface. The *Sad Sack* radio series made its debut in 1946 as a summer replacement for *The Frank Sinatra Show* on the CBS network of stations. The first episode of the radio series was titled, "Sad Sack Returns from the Army." Actor Frank Vigran, and then soon after the show's debut, the vocally versatile radio actor Mel Blanc, starred as the always sad, downbeat soldier, *Sad Sack*. Also featured on the series were Jim Backus (later better known as the voice of Mr. McGoo and for playing Mr. Howell on the very popular *Gilligan's Island* TV series), played a character named Chester, Polly Moran played the Sad Sack's landlady, Mrs. Flanagan, and Ken Christy, Sandra Gould, Mary Jane Croft, Doris Singleton, and Jerry Hauser were in the supporting cast. The series' announcer was Dick Joy. Episodes of the *Sad Sack* radio series followed the same story lines as the *Sad Sack* comic cartoons and comic strip and had such titles as "Sad Sack Home for the Holidays," and "The Liberty Bell Party." The radio series did indeed remain true to the spirit of George Baker's original *Sad Sack* cartoons but, for some reason, the show did not appeal to listeners who perhaps had become somewhat weary of references to war and the military because of the country's extended involvement with those subjects long after World War Two ended. The series was aired for only a few months longer than the summer it was originally scheduled to be heard.

Sad Sack Radio Series Performer

Blanc, Mel b. 1908 – d. 1989 (Sad Sack)

There is no other voice-over actor who was more versatile and busier than Mel Blanc whose amazing vocal talents made him world famous as the voice of such celebrated animated film cartoon characters as Bugs Bunny, Daffy Duck, the Road Runner, Tweetie-Pie, Porky Pig, and many others. Mel is known to have provided the voices for over 400 characters during his long and distinguished career on radio, television, and in films. As a young man, Mel, who was born in San Francisco, California, studied music and in the mid 1930s, Mel and his wife, Estelle, won a contract to perform on radio station KEX in Portland, Oregon. Since the radio station couldn't afford to hire any other actors to play the other roles on Mel and his wife's show, Mel started to play other characters heard on the show himself. His natural talent as a mimic and his wonderful sense of comedy made Mel and his local show a much-listened-to feature on KEX and eventually network radio officials in Hollywood beckoned. In Hollywood, Mel soon became one of the most sought-after performers on the air and he was soon a regular on such popular programs as *The Jack Benny Show, Burns and Allen, The Judy Canova Show, Abott and Costello,* and, for a short time, on his own *Mel Blanc* situation comedy series. It was on *The Jack Benny Show* and the *Judy Canova Show* that Mel played some of his most unforgettable radio characters. On *Benny's* show he was: Professor LeBlanc, Jack's downtrodden, always frustrated violin teacher, the train conductor who always called out, "Anaheim, Azuza, and Cuuuuuuucamonga!" whenever Jack took a train; Jack's pet polar bear, Carmichael; Sy, Jack's Mexican gardener; and he was the sound of Jack's ancient Maxwell car that wheezed, hissed and sputtered as it was trying to start and always broke down. On the *Judy Canova Show*, Mel played: Judy's friend, Pedro, who always said, "Pardon me, Senorita, for talking in your face;" the nerdy Roscoe Wortle; and Lukey, the slow-talking country bumpkin who was always heard when Judy was recalled her hillbilly home. Mel was a natural to be cast as a cartoon or comic strip character when they found their way to radio and he played the "Sad Sack" on the *Sad Sack* situation comedy series and Mr. Twiggs on the *Major Hoople* adaptation of the *Our Boarding House* comic strip. Blanc continued to remain active as a voice-over performer for numerous animated cartoons until shortly before he died in 1989.

The Saint

Leslie Carteris' celebrated fictional character *The Saint*, in addition to being the hero of a series of successful mystery/adventure novels that were first published in the 1920s and are still being published today, also appeared in print as a comic strip and as a series of comic books that were drawn by John Belfi and Mike Roy in the 1940s. John Belfi (1924–) was an art teacher and then a commercial artist who drew newspaper and magazine ads, before he embarked upon a career as a cartoonist. Belfi's first cartooning job was with the Quality Publishing Company, where he met fellow artist Mike Roy with whom he worked on the comic strip and comic book versions of *The Saint*. In 1950, Belfi drew the *Straight Arrow* comics with artist Joe Certa. Belfi and Mike Roy continued to work in the comic art field until the early 1980s when they retired. The story lines for *The Saint* comic strip and comic books used many of the same plots that were part of the earlier Charteris' novels. As in the books, *The Saint's* real name was Simon Templar and he was a sophisticated, handsome, womanizing detective-for-hire whose questionable, often shady methods for solving a case often made the police suspicious of his motives. In the 1940s, *The Saint* novels were also adapted to films as a series of second feature productions that starred actor George Sanders in the Templar/Saint role. In the 1960s, *The Saint* also became a popular television series that starred Roger Moore, who later became one of the silver screens' James Bonds, in the title role. Several versions of *The Saint* were aired on radio between 1940 and 1951 and these various series starred film actors as Edgar Barrier, Brian Aherne, Tom Conway, and Barry Sullivan as the title character. It is actor Vincent Price, however, who played Templar/Saint character the longest on radio, from 1949 until 1951, who is best remembered in the role in that medium. When it was first aired on radio *The Saint* was a sustained program but it was subsequently broadcast on the NBC and then CBS and Mutual networks. Also featured on the series at various times were actors Larry Dobkin, who played the running role of Louie on the series when Priced was the show's star, and, at various times John Brown, Theodore von Eltz, Joe Forte, Peter Leeds, Stanley Farrar, Dan O'Herlihy, Ed Begley, Mary Shipp, and Betty Lou Gerson. Announcers for the various series included Dick Joy and Don Stanley, among others. Most often, the series was directed by Bill Rousseau, and several of the radio adaptations were produced by the original author of *The Saint* novels, Leslie Charteris.

In addition to the novels, films, radio and television series, *The Saint* was also featured in *The Saint Mystery Magazine* and the character was even seen in a series of bubble gum cards. In the 1990s, actor Val Kilmer played the Simon Templer/Saint character in a full action, big-budget feature film.

The Saint Radio Series Major Performers

Price, Vincent b. 1911 – d. 1993 (The Saint/Simon Templar)

Yale University-educated film actor, Vincent Price, is well remembered for the many villainous and macabre roles he played in such films as *House of Wax* (1953), *The Fly* (1958), *The Bat* (1959), *The House of Usher* (1960), *The Pit and the Pendulum* (1961), *Tales of Terror* (1962), *The Raven* (1963), *Twice Told Tales* (1963), and in his last filmed performance in the Johnny Depp film, *Edward Scissorhands* (1990). Price, who was born in St. Louis, Missouri, and was the son of wealthy parents, traveled around Europe extensively when he was a young man. This gave him the somewhat Continental flair he later became well known for having in films. By the time he returned to the United States, Price had decided that he wanted to be an actor and his handsome good looks and sophisticated demeanor soon landed him major roles in such classic films as *The Private Lives of Elizabeth and Essex* (1939), *The Song of Bernadette* (1943), *Laura* (1944), *The Keys to the Kingdom* (1944), *Dragonwyck* (1946), and *The Three Musketeers* (1948).

Price, who is perhaps best known for his work in films, was also very active on radio and in addition to playing The Saint/Templar on *The Saint* radio series, he was regularly heard on such radio series as *Valiant Lady* (1939), *Helpmate* (1942–1943), *Johnny Presents* (1942), and *The Sealtest Village Store* (1947). The actor was also featured on hundreds of television series throughout the 1950s through the 1990s including *The Lux Video Theater, Robert Montgomery Presents, Climax, The General Electric Theater, Crossroads, Alfred Hitchcock Presents, Playhouse 90, Have Gun, Will Travel, Adventures in Paradise, Batman* (as the villainous Egghead), *Night Gallery, Love Boat,* and many, many other programs.

Dobkin, Larry b. 1919 – d. 2002 (Louie)

New York City born actor, Larry Dobkin was one of Hollywood's busiest radio, film, and television character actors throughout the 1940s and 1950s. Dobkin was regularly featured on such popular radio programs as the *Lux Radio Theater, The First Nighter, The Eternal Light, Escape, Romance, The Adventures of Nero Wolfe, The Adventures Philip Marlowe, Ellery Queen* (as Ellery), *Gunsmoke, One Man's Family,* and many other Hollywood-based radio shows. The actor's versatility also earned him supporting roles in such diverse films as Not Wanted (1949, which was his film debut), *Twelve O'Clock High* (1949), *The Day the Earth Stood Still* (1951), *Julius Caesar* (1953), *Kiss of Fire* (1955), *The Ten Commandments* (1956), *Geronimo* (1962), *Patton* (1970), and *Rogue Spear* (1999, his last film appearances). Television viewers saw Dobkin regularly on such TV series as *You Are There, I Love Lucy, Gunsmoke, A Letter to Loretta, Have Gun, Will Travel, Wagon Train, The Rifleman, The Untouchables, Perry Mason, Hawaiian Eye, 77 Sunset Strip, Big Valley, Mission Impossible. MacGyver, L. A. Law,* and *Judging Amy.*

THE SHADOW

(Credit: Author's collection. © Street and Smith.)

After it became one of radio's most memorable programs, *The Shadow* was featured in a twice-a-month periodical.

In 1936, one of the Golden Age of Radio's legendary programs, *The Shadow,* began its long run as a series on radio. Originally the series was as a promotional device for Street and Smith, a leading publisher of pulp fiction magazines. Street and Smith had hired the Ruthrauff and Ryan Advertising Agency to adapt their popular mystery magazine, *Detective Story,* into a weekly radio series so that they could hopefully sell even more copies of the magazines than they already were. The radio series, the agency decided, would have a mysterious, creepy host who was called "The Shadow" and he would introduce each week's half hour eerie tale to the listening audience. *The Shadow,* was played by actor Frank Readick, after a few weeks' trial by actor Jimmy LaCurto who the agency didn't feel sounded as "sinister" as they wanted him to sound, and Readick instantly impressed the show' producers, and subsequently its listeners, and the series was soon one of the most popular programs on the air. The program, which was originally broadcast on the CBS network on Thursday nights, eventually evolved into an entirely different series and began to capitalize on the popularity of *The Shadow* character and made him the major focus character of each weeks' mystery adventure. The new series mad its debut on September 26, 1937. Because Readick became unavailable, due to prior commitments, to continue to play the Shadow role, the producers reluctantly hired a young actor named Orson Welles to play the part. *The Shadow* was turned into a sophisticated, super-sleuth named Lamont Cranston who was a wealthy, young man-about-town who, as the show's announcer told listeners, while in the Orient, had learned how to use "a hypnotic power to cloud men's minds so they (could) not see him." Cranston, as the invisible Shadow, used these special "powers" to track down and ultimately apprehend various criminals. In the new version of *The Shadow*, which were written by Street and Smith pulp fiction writer Walter Gibson, Lamont had a girlfriend named Margo Lane, who was the only person who knew the Shadow's true identity. Actress Agnes Moorehead played the original Margo Lane role on *The Shadow* series for two years. In 1941, Moorheard quit *The Shadow* and went to Hollywood to appear in films. Welles' career had already taken an upturn by that time. He had become the director and producer of the celebrated *Mercury Theater* stage company in New York. He then produced, hosted and directed, and sometimes starred on the *Mercury Theater of the Air* radio series and in 1939, had gone to Hollywood to pursue a career as a motion picture director. Welles had been replaced by actor William "Bill" Johnstone, who played the part of Lamont Cranston/The Shadow from 1939 until 1944. Finally, actor Bret Morrison took over the role from Johnstone in 1944, and remained with the series until it let the air in 1956. The Margo Lane role was played by Marjorie Stevenson during the summer of 1938, and then, when Moorehead left the series to pursue a career in films, the role was played by Marjorie Anderson, Gertrude Warner, Grace Matthews, and Lesley Woods. Other actors who were regularly heard on the series were Dwight Weist, Kenny Delmar, Santos Ortega, and Ted deCorsia as Commission Weston, and Kennan Wynn, Alan Reed (a.k.a. Teddy Bergman), Mandel Kramer, Everett Sloane and Bob Maxwell and many others, in the

(Credit: Photofest)

Actor Bret Morrison is seen dressed in a costume as the mysterious Shadow for a publicity photo.

supporting cast. Andre Baruch, Carl Caruso, Sandy Becker, Ken Roberts, and Ted Mallie were the series announcers over the years. *The Shadow* was directed by Dana Noyes, Harry Ingram, John Cole, Chick Vincent, Bill Sweets, and Wilson Tuttle. *The Shadow* radio program began with the announcer asking, "Who knows what evil lurks in the hearts of men?" The announcer then answered his own question, and said, "The Shadow knows!" This was followed by the Shadow's sinister laugh, which became one of the most familiar openings of Radio's Golden Age. By the 1940s, *The Shadow* was one of the United States's most celebrated fictional characters. In addition to being heard on the radio and read about in his own *Shadow* magazine, the character was seen in a 1940 fifteen-part motion picture serial that starred actor Victor Jory as Lamont/The Shadow and Veda Ann Borg as Margo Lane. He was also featured in several Big Little books as well as in a series of comic books.

Of all of the other-than-radio mediums (magazines, comic books, comic strips and movies) in which *The Shadow* was featured, *The Shadow* magazine was the most popular and was published from April, 1931 until summer, 1949. *The Shadow* made his first appearance as a comic strip character in a Ledger Syndicate newspaper feature that was first published on Monday, June 17, 1940. *The Shadow* comic strip was seen five-days-a-week (but not seen in the Sunday Funnies) and was drawn by artist Vernon Greene for the next two years. Eight of a series of comic strip panels were later reprinted as comic books. In the early 1940s, with the United States using most of its resources such as paper for the war (World War Two) effort, a paper shortage forced many newspapers to suspend their publication of many comic strips and *The Shadow* was one of the strips that were canceled. The last *Shadow* newspaper comic strip was published on Saturday, June 13, 1942. Five years later, in 1947, Street and Smith, who owned the rights to *The Shadow*, decided to enter the comic book field itself with *The Shadow* as its flagship comic book. Walter Gibson who had written many of *The Shadow* radio scripts, wrote the story lines for the comic book series and the art work was once again executed by the talented cartoonist Vernon Greene, who had previously drawn *The Shadow* comic strips in the early 1940s. Artist Vernon Greene (1908–1965) had begun his career as a staff cartoonist at The Portland Telegram, where he drew sports cartoons. Greene began drawing comic strips in 1940 and drew illustrations for *The Shadow, Perry Mason* and *Masked Lady* pulp fiction magazines, as well as *The Shadow* comic strip, and spent six years drawing the *Polly and Her Pals* comic strip. Upon the death of cartoonist George McManus, Greene took over the drawing of the popular *Bringing Up Father* comic strip for King Features Syndicate. *The Shadow* resurfaced as a comic strip in 1988, when the newly formed Eternity Comics reprinted many of the original *Shadow* strips as *The Shadow, An Historical Collection*.

The Shadow radio series performers

MOOREHEAD, AGNES (SEE *BRINGING UP FATHER* ENTRY FOR MOOREHEAD'S BIOGRAPHY)

MORRISON, BRET B. 1912 – D. 1978 (THE SHADOW/LAMONT CRANSTON)

Although several actors played the part of Lamont Cranston a.k.a. *The Shadow* on radio over the years, Bret Morrison played it longer than anyone else and is probably best remembered in the role. Born in Chicago, Illinois, Bret Morrison became a radio actor in that city shortly after he graduated from college in the early 1930s when he was in his early twenties. He was heard on such Chicago-based shows a *The First Nighter, The Chicago Theater of the Air, Best Sellers, Arnold Grimm's Daughter, Clara, Lu and Em* (one of radio's earliest successful soap opera series), and *The Guiding Light*, among others. In the late 1930s, Morrison relocated to New York City and soon became one of that city's busiest radio actors as well. He was heard on such radio

Bret Morrison, in addition to playing *The Shadow* on radio for more than nine years, was also heard on such programs as *The Romance of Helen Trent, The Story of Mary Marlin* and *Stella Dallas*.

shows as *The Listening Post, Great Gunns, The Mysterious Traveler, The Road of Life, The Romance of Helen Trent, Song of a Stranger, The Story of Mary Marlin, The Woman in White, The Carnation Contented Hour, Road to Danger, Stella Dallas*, and many other shows. In addition, he also played *The Shadow* on that long-running series from 1945 until 1954 and was frequently featured on the radio adaptation of the popular comic book series *Superman*. When radio drama eventually departed from the airwaves entirely in the late 1950s, Morrison was seen on the television series *The Edge of Night* for several seasons and appeared in the films *Guess What I Learned in School Today* and *Black Eye* in 1974. In the mid-1970s, Morrison returned to radio and was heard on Himan Brown's *CBS Mystery Theater* series. He had just finished taping a show for the new *Heartbeat Theater* radio drama program in 1978, when he died of a heart attack on the corner of Hollywood and Vine Streets in Hollywood.

READICK, FRANK (THE SHADOW. SEE *SMILIN' JACK* FOR BIOGRAPHY)

WELLES, ORSON B. 1915 – D. 1985 (THE SHADOW/LAMONT CRANSTON)
    George Orson Welles was the son of a well-to-do inventor and a mother who was a concert pianist and therefore he was born into a world of privilege and culture. George, who was always referred to by his second name, Orson, was devastated when his mother died when he was eight years old and in order to distract his son from the loss of his mother, Orson's father took the boy on a world-wide tour. When his father died three years later, Orson was made a ward of family friend Dr. Maurice Bernstein who raised the boy as if he was his own. After he graduated from the prestigious Todd School in Woodtsock, Illinois, Orson turned down college offers and went on a sketching tour of Ireland. While he was in Ireland, and then England, the precocious young man decided he wanted to become an actor in London and unsuccessfully tried to get a role in a West End London play, but failed. Disappointed, he left London and traveled in Morocco and Spain where he met playwright Thornton Wilder and celebrity columnist Alexander Woolcott, who took a liking to the would-be young actor and got him a job with actress Katherine Cornell's world wide touring company, which was performing the works of William Shakespeare in repertory. Welles made his Broadway debut in 1934 with the Cornell in the company's production of *Romeo and Juliet* playing the small-but-important role of Tybalt. That same year, Welles was married, directed his first short film, and worked on radio for the first time when he won the major role of *The Shadow* on what became one of radio's most popular mystery programs. Welles' strong, rich voice and his total lack of inhibition soon earned him roles on such radio programs as *American Home, The Cavalcade of America, Columbia Presents Corwin, Exploring the Unknown, The Adventures of Sherlock Holmes* (as Holmes' nemesis, the master villain, Dr. Moriarty). While he was working on radio, Welles founded a successful repertory stage production company of his own and rented a theater in downtown New York which he called *The Mercury Theater*. *The Mercury Theater* produced classic plays that the twenty-two year old Welles acted in and directed. A weekly, hour-long dramatic anthology series called *The Mercury Theater on the Air*, which later became *The Campbell Playhouse*, was subsequently produced on the radio for the CBS network. Welles' inventive *Mercury Theater* stage productions of such classic plays as *Julius Caesar, Dr. Faustus, Danton's Death. Ten Million Ghosts, Heartbreak House,* and *King Lear*, became the talk of the town and were acclaimed by theater critics. Over the years that followed,

Welles subsequently appeared on Broadway in such stage productions as *Native Son* (1941), *Around the World in 80 Days* (1946), *Moby Dick* (1962), which certainly made him a creditable and much admired stage presence on the Great White Way. It was, however, a documentary style radio play adaptation of H. G. Wells novel, "The War of the Worlds" which was presented on the *Mercury Theater* radio series in 1939, which had listeners actually believing the United States was being invaded by Martians, and the resulting publicity that was generated by this radio show, that had propelled Orson Welles into an overnight, much sought after celebrity and not his appearances on Broadway. Hollywood beckoned soon after the War of the Worlds broadcast and Welles directed and starred in his first big budget, feature length motion picture *Citizen Kane*. The film was called a "masterpiece" by film critics, but it did not meet with the box office success it deserved because publisher William Randolph Heart thought the film was a rather unflattering biography of his life and denied the film any publicity in his many newspapers. Welles then directed *The Magnificent Ambersons,* which also failed to attract a very sizeable audience because of poor cutting by RKO Studios and again Hearts' reluctance to accept any advertising for the film. Welles did manage, however, to play leading roles in such popular Hollywood films as *Jane Eyre* (1944), *Tomorrow Is Forever* (1946), *The Lady From Shangaii* (1947, which he also directed), *The Prince of Foxes* (1949), *The Third Man* (1949), *Othello* (1952), *A Touch of Evil* (1958, which he starred in an directed), *Compulsion* (1959) and *A Man For All Seasons* (1966). These were all excellent films and were popular with film fans, but they did not advance his career as a film director. They did, however, make him a legendary and major film celebrity. In his film acting years, Welles also continued to work on the radio and starred on such series as *Black Museum* and *The Third Man,* but he was constantly trying to raise money for other projects he felt were more worthy of his talents as a filmmaker. Unfortunately, Orson Welles' career never did reached the heights it seemed destined for when he first started out in show business. Orson Welles' last memorable roles were as the voice of Robin Masters, the wealthy writer who owns the Hawaiian estate on which *Magnum PI,* played by actor Tom Sellick, lives in the guest house on the hit TV mystery series and a TV wine commercial spokesman.

SKIPPY

Percy Crosby, the artist who created the popular *Skippy* comic strip in 1923, has been called "the Rembrandt of American cartoonists." Percy Crosby (1890–1964) was born in Richmond Hill, New York. Before his *Skippy* comic strip found favor with the American public, Crosby worked as an editorial cartoonist for the socialist newspaper the New York Call. He then went to work as a sports cartoonist at the New York Globe in 1918 and drew his first comic strip for that newspaper, *The Clancy Kids*. In 1919, with the United States heavily involved in World War One, Crosby joined the Army as a second lieutenant to fight in that so called "war to end all wars." When the war ended, Crosby went back to work as an artist and using his Army experiences as a guide, created a new comic strip he called *The Rookie from the Thirteenth Squad*, as well as a book of cartoons he titled, *Between the Shots*. Crosby decided that he wanted to have more training as an artist an enrolled at the Art Students League. Feeling more accomplished as an artist, Crosby created two several new comic strips including one he called *Always Belittlin'*, which was the prototype for the comic strip that would make him rich and famous, *Skippy*, which was first published in 1923. *Skippy* was tough, streetwise nine year old kid who lived in an unnamed American City slum. The *Skippy* comic strip had an energy and an honesty about it that centered around life among the less fortunate members of society which had never been done before in an American comic strip. The comic soon captured the attention of millions of readers. In just two years, *Skippy* was one of the most popular comic strips in the country and it seemed as if there were *Skippy*-related items everywhere people looked. There were *Skippy* dolls and figurines and games, and songs and even *Skippy* movies. The comic strip continued to gain popularity throughout the 1930s, but by 1940, Crosby's comic strip had become less about life among the poor, and more about politics. By 1945, the public lost interest in the strip and its popularity reached an all-time low just as World War Two ended in 1945. On December 8, 1945, after being in print for twenty two years, King Features Syndicate dropped *Skippy* from its roster of comic strip offerings. Crosby, who had become accustomed to the acclaim and ever-increasing income he derived from *Skippy*, was devastated by the cancellation of his comic strip and he fell into a deep state of depression. Three years after *Skippy* was canceled, Crosby had a complete nervous breakdown and attempted suicide. The artist was confined to the mental ward at the Kings Park Veterans Hospital where he spent the remainder of his life. In 1964, sixteen years after he had been confined to the mental institution, Percy Crosby died, forgotten and alone at the age of seventy four.

When *Skippy* was at the height of its popularity, the poor little slum kid was called an "All American Boy," years before radio's *Jack Armstrong* claimed that title. *Skippy*, like most boys enjoyed sports, often got into trouble, played pranks on his friends, but was always loveable and very good hearted. He was the kind of boy every kid wanted to have as a friend. Cartoonist Percy Crosby admitted that he had never grown up himself and that *Skippy's* experiences reflected his own boyhood. Typical of *Skippy's* attitude toward life in general was reflected in a poem Crosby had the character recite in one episode of the comic strip when he was going to bed one night. "Oh Lord," Skippy prayed, "give me the strength to brush my teeth every night, and if Thou canst not give me strength, give me the strength not to worry about it!" Skippy became so famous that he even had a brand of peanut butter named after him and he appeared in a series of Big Little books, in addition to his comic strip appearances, and was on the cover of *Life* and the *Saturday Evening Post* magazines in 1925 and 1934. In 1929, child film star Jackie Cooper played the Skippy role in a very popular and successful feature film. *Skippy* was also the main character on a poster for General Ice Cream that was widely distributed throughout the United States. In 1934, in addition to the *Skippy* comic strip, a series of *Skippy* comic books were published which remained in print until well into the 1940s.

It was inevitable that the *Skippy* character would eventually become the hero of a radio adventure series and in 1931, a daily radio serial surfaced that was heard five-days-a-week, late afternoons on Monday through Friday. The series was presented on the NBC network, and, after one year, the program moved to the CBS network where it remained until 1935. The show was sponsored by Wheaties breakfast cereal. On the show, many premiums were offered to listeners, such as *Skippy* badges, rings, mugs and other items which were mailed to fans of the show for one nickel and a box top from a box of Wheaties. The cast of the *Skippy* radio series included child actor Franklin Adams, Jr. as Skippy, Francis Smith as Skippy's friend, "Socky," and St. John Tyrell as Jim Lovering. The series was produced and directed by Frank and Anne Hummert and David Owen and adapted for radio by Robert Hardy Andrews and Roland Martini.

SKIPPY RADIO SERIES PERFORMER

ADAMS, FRANKLIN, JR. B. 1920 – ? (SKIPPY)

Before he played the boy/hero of the radio version of Percy Crosby's popular comic strip *Skippy* from 1931 until 1935, child actor Franklin "Frankie"Adams, Jr. was featured in the silent film *The Collegiate* in 1926. The *Skippy* radio program was only moderately successful and after it left the air, Frankie Adams worked only occasionally on radio. He had small roles in the motion pictures *Forgotten Commandments* (1932), *The Cat and the Fiddle* (1934), *Romance in the Rain* (1934), and then, except for rare performing assignments, Adams retired from acting and entered the private sector. Unfortunately, Adams had not gotten to play the role of *Skippy* in the popular film that was released in 1931, which may have made a difference to his career as an actor. That role was played by the well known child film star, Jackie Cooper.

SMILIN' JACK

Among the many popular aviation-oriented comic strips that surfaced in the late 1920s-early 1930s which included *Terry and the Pirates, Tailspin Tommy* and *Hop Harrigan*, was *Smilin' Jack*. The *Smilin' Jack* comic strip was the brainchild of a talented cartoonist named Zack Mosley. Zack Mosley (1906–1994) began

Pilot Jack Martin, affectionately known as "Smilin' Jack," was the devil-may-care hero of Zack Mosley's popular comic strip, *Smilin' Jack*, which made its first appearance as a comic strip in 1934 and remained in print until 1974. *Smilin' Jack* was also a less-than-successful radio adventure series.

his career as an artist in 1933, shortly after graduating from the Chicago Academy of Fine Arts Institute. Mosley had always been fascinated with aviation from the time he was a little boy and, when he by the time he was an adult, he had become a licensed pilot. The first comic strip Mosley drew was called *On the Wings*, which first appeared in newspapers throughout the United States in 1933. *On the Wings* did not gain the public's attention, but his second strip, which was also about aviation was called *Smilin' Jack*, and it was a runaway success, running as a daily strip in American newspapers from 1934 until 1973. Zack Mosley's *Smilin' Jack* comic strip depended heavily upon aviation and the main character in the strip was a pilot, albeit a playboy, whose real name was Jack Martin. Jack always seemed to have lots of girlfriends and people called him "Smilin' Jack" because of his cheery, good natured disposition. Because of the ever-growing success of his comic strip, Mosley was in time able to acquire five airplanes, which during World War Two he used to patrol the coast looking for enemy submarines on a volunteer basis for the United States Coast Guard. In addition to his work as a comic strip artist, Mosley also designed insignias, posters and program covers for various flying events. The cartoonist was eighty seven years old when he died in 1994.

When Mosley had first submitted his idea for a comic strip about an aviator, which he called *Smilin' Mickey*, to the Chicago Tribune Syndicate, the title did not particularly appeal to the publishers who suggested the hero's name be changed to *Smilin' Jack*. The comic strip with its new title was first seen by the public on the December 31, 1933 in the Sunday Funnies section of the Tribune and was an instant hit. A daily version of *Smilin' Jack* surfaced three years later on June 15, 1936. In the first panels of the comic strip, readers learned that Jack was a young, nervous student pilot and the early episodes of the strip were more funny than adventurous Eventually, Jack mature into a handsome, full-fledged aviation hero who fought such nasty villains The Claw, Toemain the Terrible, The Head, and the Head's evil sister, The Mongoose, and many other evil-doers. *Smilin' Jack* also had his share of romantic encounters as well, and over the years, the many pretty girls Jack romanced, who were called "de-icers, using a term that referred to keeping an airplanes equipment from frosting over. Jack eventually married one of his sweethearts and had a son, Jack. Jr., who grew up to became one of the main characters in the strip. Among the many memorable characters who appeared in the comic strip with Smilin' Jack were "Downwind Jason," a character who was even more handsome than Jack, and Fatstuff, Jack's fat Hawaiian fiend who was so stout he constantly popped the buttons off his short. The buttons were always gobbled up by a scrawny looking chicken who was always standing nearby ready to catch them. Smilin' Jack remained one of the America's favorite Sunday Funnies until Mosley decided to retire and the Chicago Tribune Syndicate ended the comic strips' long, successful run in 1973.

The popularity of the *Smilin' Jack* comic strip led to a 1943 Paramount Pictures thirteen-part film serial that starred actor Tom Brown as Jack. It was also adapted to radio as a fifteen minute a day, five day a week children's radio adventure serial that made its radio debut in 1935 and remained on the air until the mid 1940s. Veteran radio actor Frank Readick, who was radio's first *Shadow*, played Smilin' Jack on the series. Also heard on the series regularly were Jackson Beck, Ted DeCorsia and Gertrude Warner in running roles. Tom Shirley was the program's announcer and the series was directed by Alan Wallace. The story lines of the *Smilin' Jack* radio series followed many of the same adventures that had first appeared in the comic strip, and during the 1940s World War Two years, the program was usually involved with Jack's fighting the wicked German or Japanese enemies of the United States.

SMILIN' JACK RADIO SERIES PERFORMERS

BECK, JACKSON (VARIOUS CHARACTERS, SEE *THE CISCO KID* FOR BECK'S BIOGRAPHY)

READICK, FRANK B. 1896 – D. 1955 (SMILIN' JACK)

In the 1930s, actor Frank Readick played the title characters on two popular comic strips that became radio series, *Buck Rogers in the 25th Century* and *Smilin' Jack*. He was also the original *Shadow* on that radio series, which later became a comic book and comic strip series, and played Knobby Walsh on the radio adaptation of the *Joe Palooka* comic strip. Born in Seattle, Washington, after a brief time touring in various stage plays, in the early 1930s, Readick went to New York City to audition for a part in a Broadway play. Stage roles in New York, however, proved to be few and far between for the actor, and so Readick began to work on various radio programs in order to have an income. A natural radio actor whose voice always commanded attention, Readick was convincing in whatever role he had to play on radio. Before long, the actor became one of the most sought-after performers on the air. In addition to the above named radio programs, Readick was also heard on such diverse radio series as the *March of Time Quiz, America's Hour, The Adventures of Mr. Meek, Gangbusters, The Cavalcade of America, The FBI in Peace and War, The Mercury Theater on the Air, Five Minutes from Hollywood,* and practically every other show that was broadcast from New York in the 1930s and 1940s. In 1942, Readick, encouraged by his friend and director Orson Welles, appeared in the film *Journey into Fear*, but he admitted in an interview that he did particularly care for the slow pace of working in films. Readick's acting career came to an abrupt end when he died of a heart attack in the mid 1950s. Frank Readick's son, Bob Readick, was also a radio actor and was heard on such programs as *Let's Pretend, Rosemary, This is Nora Drake,* and *Your Truly, Johnny Dollar*.

STRAIGHT ARROW

Before he was a comic strip and comic book hero, *Straight Arrow* was a character in a popular Western adventure series on the radio. *Straight Arrow*, which originated on the West Coast, was first heard on the Mutual Broadcasting System's network of radio stations in 1948. The series was written for radio by Sheldon Stark and was directed by Ted Robertson. The versatile actor Howard Culver starred as a crime fighting rancher named Steve Adams, who masqueraded as a Camanche Indian and called himself "Straight Arrow." As Straight Arrow, Adams wore Native American clothes, painted his face with war paint and rode a golden palomino named Fury, as, incognito, he battled bandits, renegade Indians, con-men and other evil-doers in the outlaw ridden Old West. The program always began with the sound of a tom-tom drum beating a rhythmic beat and the announcer saying, "**N-A-B-I-S-C-O**. Nabisco is the name to know! For a breakfast you can't beat, try Nabisco Shredded Wheat!"

Then the music would swell and the announcer continued, "Keen eyes fixed on a flying target..a gleaming arrow set against a rawhide string...a strong bow bent almost to the breaking point...and then...?" The sound of a bowstring being released followed by music and the sound of an arrow reaching a target was heard, followed by the announcer saying, "Straight Arrow!" It was then explained to listeners that, "To friends and neighbors alike, Steve Adams appeared to be nothing more than the young owner of the Broken Bow cattle spread. But when danger threatened innocent people...and when evil doers plotted against justice...Steve Adams disappeared and in his place came a mysterious stalwart Indian...wearing the dress and war paint of a Camanche, riding the great golden palomino, Fury...galloping out of the darkness, to take up the cause of law and order throughout the West."

Like the *Lone Ranger* and *Red Ryder*, *Straight Arrow* was one of the most popular Western programs on the air in the late 1940s and into the 1950s. By 1950, the radio series had become so popular, a comic book series was published by Magazine Enterprises which allowed listeners to see what their radio hero, *Straight Arrow*," looked like. The comic books were immediately successful with the comic-reading public. The original *Straight Arrow* comic books were drawn by artist Fred Meagher and were published between 1950 and 1957. Although the earliest *Straight Arrow* comic books revealed that Meagher was a first-rate artist, little is known about him and there is no available information concerning his background which this author could uncover. Comic book collectors prize the few surviving issues of the original *Straight Arrow* comics that can be found. In the mid 1950s, *Straight Arrow* also surfaced as a comic strip feature in newspaper throughout the country. The comic strip was drawn by cartoonist John Belfi (See *The Saint* for Belfi's biographical information) and the text for the strip was written by Garner Fox. Most of the *Straight Arrow* comic books, as well as the comic strip, were similar to the adventures *Straight Arrow* had on his popular radio series. The simple, direct titles of some of the *Straight Arrow* radio series programs indicate the type of subjects that were usually covered in both the radio and comic book and strip versions of *Straight Arrow*; "The Wasteland," "The Leader," "Long Summer," and "Scourage" are just a few examples of episode titles.

STRAIGHT ARROW RADIO SERIES PERFORMER

CULVER, HOWARD B. 1918 – D. 1984 (STRAIGHT ARROW/STEVE ADAMS)

Howard Culver was still in high school when he was first featured on the CBS radio network as an actor. Culver, who began his professional acting career in his early teens, was heard on numerous programs that originated in Hollywood during the 1930s and 1940s. He played the title role on the

Straight Arrow radio adventure series for the entire run of the series, 1948–1957. The actor was also regularly heard on such radio series as *Ellery Queen* (playing Ellery), *Defense Attorney* (co-starring with Academy Award winning actress Mercedes Cambridge), *Mystery in the Air,* and *The Whistler,* and on many other radio series. In the mid 1950s, Culver was seen on an early episode of the *Gunsmoke* television series and he spent the next twenty years making regular appearances on such TV series as *Dragnet* (as a regular performer), *The New Adventures of Charlie Chan, Perry Mason, The Zane Grey Theater, Star Trek, Family Affair, Adam-12, CHiPs, Buck Rogers in the 25th Century,* and many others. In addition to his acting on radio and TV, Culver also played supporting roles in several films such as *The Black Whip* (1956), *Cattle Empire* (1958), *Something's Happened to Dexter* (1969), *The Bad News Bears* (1976), and *Halloween II* (1981). Howard Culver died at the age of seventy-six in Hong Kong while he was touring the Orient with his wife.

SUPERMAN

Without question, the most popular comic book/comic strip character of all time is *Superman. Superman* was created by two teenagers named Jerry Siegel and Joe Shuster in the early 1930s. The boys, with Jerry writing the stories and Joe doing the art work, began their collaborative efforts with a series of self-published "fanzines" and in 1933 they included a story called "Reign of Superman" in one of their limited edition comics that introduced the concept of a superior man who was a world-conquering villain. A year later, they re-worked their comic strip making the super villain a super hero but were unsuccessful when they tried to sell the strip to various newspapers. Jerry Siegel and Joe Shuster were both born in 1914, Jerry in Cleveland, Ohio and Joe in Toronto, Canada. When he was nine years old Joe's family moved to Cleveland, where he met Jerry Siegel in high school. The two boys became best friends when Joe drew cartoons and Jerry wrote stories for their high school newspaper, *The Glenville Torch*. In 1936, Jerry and Joe began providing comic book features such as *Dr. Occult, Federal Agents* and *Slam Bradley* to DC Comics and in 1938, they finally convinced DC to publish their "Superman" comic book idea. DC's Publisher Jack Liebowitz was looking for a feature to include in a new monthly comic book anthology that he had titled Action Comics and he decided to take a chance on Siegel's and Shuster's new comic book character. He wasn't sorry, because within a few months *Superman* was Action Comics major attraction. In 1939, *Superman* was the first character in comic books to anchor his own comic book title. Siegel continued to write the *Superman* comics until 1948, but by that time the art work for *Superman* were being done by several other artists with Siegel and Shuster remaining in firm control of all of the *Superman* spinoff comics, such as *Superboy*, as well as the subsequent *Superman* films, TV shows, and a daily and Sunday Funnies comic strip feature, which was also first published by the McClure Syndicate in 1939. The two friends remained involved with their *Superman* creation until Shuster died after suffering a heart attack in 1992.

Superman's origins and his history are well known to millions of people all over the world. Superman had been born on Krypton, a planet that was light years away from Earth and

One of the comics' most successful characters, Superman, was created by two young men not yet in their twenties, Jerry Siegel and Joe Shuster. Jerry wrote the stories for the comic strip and Joe did the original drawings (above) for the comic books.

was much further advanced than Earth as far as evolution is concerned. The citizens of Krypton were humans who had advanced to the ultimate peak of perfect development. All of the people on Krypton had the ability to run at super speed and leap an eighth of a mile. When the strip began, a character named Jor-L was racing through the streets of the capitol city on Krypton leaping to the balcony of his home as the planet is being wracked by vast earthquakes which are destroying the planet. Jon-L and his wife, Lora, faced with a catastrophe that even their super powers cannot survive, place their infant son, Kal-L (later Kal-El), into an experimental rocket and launch him into space minutes before Krypton explodes and the planet and everyone on it is destroyed. The rocket ship lands on Earth where the baby is found and adopted by a farmer and his wide, the Kents. As he grows up, Kal-L, who the Kents have named Clark, realizes that "nothing less than a bursting shell" can pierce his skin. When he is a fully grown man Clark moved to the big city, Metropolis, and gets a job as a reporter at the Daily Star newspaper. As the *Superman* comic book series and comic strip developed over the years, Clark, disguised as Superman, hides his super human strength and special flying ability from others and usually wears glasses and business suit, but he changed into specially designed costume which includes blue tights, red trunks, a form fitting blue top with a large letter "S" for "Superman" written on it, and a flowing red cape, as he battles evil-doers in Metropolis. Over the years, Superman's powers continually increased making him stronger, faster, and more invulnerable each year. Along the way, Clark Kent/Superman frequently encountered the super-villainous Luthor, often helping his girlfriend, reporter Lois Lane, and a young office boy at the newspaper named Jimmy Olsen, and others, out of some very difficult situations.

In addition to his comic book appearances and in a weekday and Sunday comic strip, by the 1940s and 1950s *Superman's* popularity led to several serialized films, an animated cartoon series, which was produced by the Max Fleischer Studios, a successful TV adventure series, that starred actor George Reeves as Clark Kent/Superman, and *Superman* was also on the air three-days-a-week as a popular radio program from 1940 until 1951. *Superman* was first heard on the radio's Mutual network on February 12, 1940. The series was developed for radio by DC Comic's press agent Allen Ducovny and pulp fiction writer Robert Joffe Maxwell, who believed that there was a large radio audience just waiting to hear the adventures of the super hero *Superman* on radio and they were right. Announcer/actor Clayton "Bud" Collyer was cast in the Clark Kent/Superman role, Joan Alexander was Lois Lane, replacing Rollie Bester in the role after the first few episodes the series aired, Julian Noa was newspaper editor Perry White, Jackie Kelk was office boy, Jimmy Olsen, and, in later adventures on the *Superman* radio series, Matt Crowley played Batman and Ronald Liss played Robin. For a short period of time, Michael Fitzmaurice took over the Superman/Clark Kent role from Bud Collyer. The stirring announcer for the series was Jackson Beck whose opening for the show became almost as famous as the show itself. "Kellogg's Pep...the super-delicious cereal presents...*The Adventures of Superman*!" Beck announced. "Faster than a speeding bullet," Beck continued, followed by the sound of a rifle bullet ricochet. "More powerful than a locomotive!" followed by sound of a train whistle and a train on tracks. "Able to leap tall buildings at a single bound!" followed by a burst of wind. "Look," Beck then said, "Look up in the sky!" which was followed by people calling out, "It's a bird....It's a Plane....It's Superman!" Two weeks after it made its on-the-air debut, *The Adventures of Superman* had achieved the very high rating of 5.6, which was the highest rating of ant thrice-weekly program on the air. The early episodes of the series were produced by Frank Chase, scripted by George Ludlum and directed by Allen Ducovny and Allen Grayson. On the first episode of the series Ned Wever and Agnes Moorehead played Kal-El's doomed parents, Jor-L and Lara. The series then followed the same story line that Siegel and Shuster had developed for the comic book and comic strip series, with, by the second episode, Clark already a grown up young man heading for Metropolis. In 1941, Bud Collyer also provided the voice for the title character in a series of animated cartoons. Although a 1948 *Superman* film serial,that starred actor Kirk Allen in the Clark Kent/Superman role, had already preceded it, a 1993 film version of Superman became a major motion picture. The film starred actor Christopher Reeve in the Superman/Clark Kent role and featured Margot Kidder as Lois Lane. The film became one of that years biggest successes at the box office. Reeve appeared in three more big-budget *Superman II, III* and *IV* films in 1980, 1983 and 1987. Reeve wrote the screenplay for the fourth film in the series. In 1993, a second weekly *Superman* television series was released called *Lois and Clark* and it starred Dean Cain as Superman/Clark and Teri Hatcher as Lois Lane. A third *Superman* TV series, which was called *Smallville* and centered around a young Clark/Kal-El as he was growing up at his adopted parents, the Kents', farm outside the town of "Smallville," and attending high school in that town, made its debut in 2001 and, as of this writing, it is still being seen on the WB network.

ADVENTURES OF SUPERMAN RADIO SERIES PERFORMERS

ALEXANDER, JOAN B. 1916 (LOIS LANE)

In addition to playing Clark Kent's girlfriend and confidante, Lois Lane, on the fifteen-minute, three day a week *Adventures of Superman* from 1941 until 1951, actress Joan Alexander also provided Lois' voice for the animated film cartoon serial that was originally released in the early 1940s. The talented American actress received her training as an actress in Europe and studied with the renowned drama coach and stage director Benno Schneider. When German dictator Adolf Hitler's dark shadow began to dominate the European landscape in the mid 1930s, Miss Alexander returned to the United States and appeared on Broadway in a revival of the play *Merrily We Roll Along*. She also worked as a fashion model before auditioning for, and being cast in a major role on the radio soap opera series *Lone Journey* in 1940. Throughout the 1940s, and well into the 1950s, the actresses distinctive voice earned her long-running roles on other popular radio series, in

(Credit: Photofest)

Joan Alexander, although not the first actress to play the role of Lois Lane on the radio series version of *Superman*, played the role for the longest period of time and also provided Lois' voice for the 1940s animated *Superman* cartoon series.

addition to *The Adventures of Superman* including *My True Story, It's Murder, Against the Storm, Bright Horizon, David Harum, Light of the World, This is Nora Drake,* and *Philo Vance* (as Ellen Deering), among others. The actress also played Della Street on the radio version of *Perry Mason,* which in the 1940s, before it became a long-running TV series, was a five-day-a-week soap opera series. In the 1950s, Miss Alexander became a familiar face, in addition to having a well recognized voice, when she appeared as a regular panelist on such TV game shows as *To Tell the Truth* and *The Name's the Same,* which was hosted by her Superman radio series co-star, Clayton "Bud" Collyer. In 1960, Miss Alexander returned to the Broadway stage in Jean Kerr's play *Poor Richard,* and then retired.

BECK, JACKSON (ANNOUNCER. SEE *CISCO KID* FOR BIOGRAPHY)

COLLYER, CLAYTON "BUD" B. 1908 – D. 1969 (SUPERMAN/CLARK KENT)

(Credit: Photofest)

Radio and television announcer, master of ceremonies, and actor Clayton "Bud" Collyer played *Superman* on radio, as well as for the animated cartoon series in the 1940s.

After attending Williams College and then transferring to and graduating from Fordham University, Clayton Collyer, who was born into a theatrical family, was determined to become a lawyer. He went to work as a law clerk and studied to prepare to take the lawyer's bar exam, but he soon found that acting and announcing jobs on radio paid him much more than he could earn as a fledgling lawyer. He decided to remain in show business. Collyer's first job on radio was as a singer on a CBS network variety show in 1936. He then became the announcer for *The Raleigh Room, Believe it or Not* and *The Shaeffer Revue* programs and was also the host of the *On Your Mark, Break the Bank* and *Winner Take All* quiz shows. As an actor, Collyer was heard on the *Terry and the Pirates* children's adventure series, playing Terry's sidekick, Pat Ryan, and on *The Story of Mary Marlin* soap opera series as the heroine Mary's love interest. He also worked as an actor on such radio programs as *The Road of Life, Life Can Be Beautiful, Abie's Irish Rose, Just Plain Bill, Pretty Kitty Kelly, Kitty Foyle, The Man I Married, Joyce Jordan, The Guiding Light, Young Widder Brown,* and *Cavalcade of America* programs and he was heard on Fletcher Markle's dramatic anthology series *Studio One* in the title role in a one-hour adaptation of the best-selling novel, "Anthony Adverse." It is certainly as Superman/Clark Kent, however, that Collyer is best remembered as a radio actor. Collyer played the Superman/Clark role for eleven years on radio, from 1940 until 1951, and he also voiced the same role for the 1940s animated film serial cartoons.

In the 1950s, Clayton "Bud" Collyer became the host of several of television's earliest and most popular quiz/panel shows including *Beat the Clock, Feather Your Nest, To Tell the Truth,* and *The Name's the Same.* Collyer died prematurely at the age of sixty-one, at the height of his career as a television host.

CROWLEY, MATT (BATMAN. SEE *JUNGLE JIM* FOR BIOGRAPHY)

FITZMAURICE, MICHAEL B. 1908 – D. 1967 (SUPERMAN/CLARK KENT)
Michael Fitzmaurice was born in Chicago, Illinois and decided he wanted to become an actor while he was still in college. His deep, resonant voice made him a natural for work on radio and as soon as he finished his schooling he began to work as an announcer on several Chicago-based radio programs. In the mid-1930s, Fitzmaurice decided to try film acting and went to Hollywood determined to break into the movies. He managed to get small supporting roles in such films as *The House of a Thousand Candles* (1936), *The Plough and the Stars* (1937), *Night Key* (1937), *Reported Missing* (1937), and *A Girl With Ideas* (1937), but he was dissatisfied with the size of the roles he was getting in films and returned to Chicago to resume working on radio. In Chicago, and then in New York, Fitzmaurice soon became one of the most sought-after actors and announcers on the air and he was heard playing leading male roles on such soap opera series as *Brenda Curtis, Her Honor, Nancy James, Joyce Jordan, Myrt and Marge, Pepper Young's Family, The Right to Happiness, Rosemary, Stella Dallas, This Life Is Mine,* and *When a Girl Marries.* He was also heard playing major roles on such prime time programs as *Highway Patrol* (as State Trooper Cpl. Steve Taylor), and *The Sparrow and the Hawk* (as Lt. Col. Spencer Mallory alias "The Hawk). In the mid 1940s, Fitzmaurice temporarily replaced Bud Collyer as Superman on *The Adventures of Superman* radio series. Like Collyer, Fitzmaurice was equally at home in front of the microphone as an announcer and Master of Ceremonies as he was as an actor and he was heard hosting the *The Land of the Lost, Nick Carter, Master Detective* and *Quiz for Two Cities* programs. In 1951, Fitzmaurice temporarily returned to film making and was seen in the

film *Fourteen Hours*. Until he retired in the early 1960s, Michael Fitzmaurice was mainly busy as a voice-over actor, dubbing and narrating foreign films and announcing various TV shows.

GRIMES, JACK (JIMMY OLSEN. SEE *ARCHIE ANDREWS* FOR BIOGRAPHY)

LISS, RONALD (ROBIN. SEE *BUCK ROGERS IN THE 25TH CENTURY* FOR BIOGRAPHY)

T

TAILSPIN TOMMY

Exactly one year after Charles Lindbergh's historic trans-Atlantic solo airplane flight from the United States to Europe, a comic strip called *Tailspin Tommy* was published in May 21, 1928. This was the first of several comic strips that capitalized on the public's ever increasing interest, after the Lindbergh flight, in everything connected with aviation. One year after *Tailspin Tommy* made his first appearance in newspapers, other aviation-oriented comic strips appeared on the scene including *Scorchy Smith, Brick Bradford, Hop Harrigan,* and then, as time went on, *Smilin' Jack* and *Terry and the Pirates,* to name just a few. It was John N. Wheeler, owner the Bell Syndicate which distributed comic strips to newspapers, who decided an aviation adventure comic strip was just what the public wanted, and he convinced writer Glenn Chaffin and artist Hal Forrest to provide one for his company to distribute. The result of Chaffin and Forrest's efforts was a strip they called *Tailspin Tommy,* which was originally seen in only four newspapers. It caught on and within a year it was being published in more than 259 newspapers throughout the country. A Sunday Funnies page was published on October 30, 1929 and by the end of the 1930s, *Tailspin Tommy* was a national sensation. There were *Tailspin Tommy* comic books, Big Little Books published by the Whitman Company, stories in pulp magazines, and feature films. In 1941, there was even a *Tailspin Tommy* children radio adventure series on the air. One of the reasons for *Tailspin Tommy's* success

Another comic strip aviator, originally drawn by Hal Forrest in 1928, *Tailspin Tommy*, was adapted to radio in 1941, thirteen years after the strip first appeared in print.

(Credit: Author's collection. © Whitman.)

was the excellent aviation art work of Hal Forrest. Forrest, who was born in 1908, and was only 21 when he began to draw *Tailspin Tommy*, was a well-trained cartoonist who began his career as an artist drawing illustrations for magazine stories. Like the comic strip character he drew, Forrest was interested in aviation from the time he was a boy and he developed a special talent for drawing airplanes. This eventually led to his being one of the most celebrated aviation artists in the country and by the mid-1930s, he was both drawing and writing the popular *Tailspin Tommy* comic strip. Forrest continued to work on *Tailspin Tommy* until 1942, when the strip was suddenly canceled, unable to compete with the many aviation-based comics that appeared on the scene by that time.

The premise of the *Tailspin Tommy* comic strip was simple. A boy who is interested in aviation eventually becomes a successful aviator and has many exciting adventures as a pilot. The boy, Tommy Tomkins, lived in a town called Littleville, Colorado. Because it was well known that he was interested in airplanes and flying, Tommy was given the nickname of "Tailspin Tommy" by his neighbors in Littleville. Tommy got his first up-close chance to see an airplane when a mail pilot named Milt Howe made an emergency landing in a field outside town. Tommy, who had witnessed the plane's troubled descent, ran to see what he could do to help the pilot. A grateful Milt Howe helped Tommy get a job working on airplanes at Three Points Airlines in Texas, and before long Tommy became a pilot himself and, with two of his friends, Betty Lou Barnes and Peter "Skeeter" Milligan, he became part owner of the Three Points Airline Company. Thus, began Tommy's exciting adventures as an aviator. Over the next several years, Tommy and his friends fought mail thieves, tracked down spies, flew dangerous missions, transported cargo to exotic ports of call, and survived many a storm and plane crash. His in-the-air adventures kept people looking forward to each and every installment of the comic strip for the next fourteen years.

Tailspin Tommy had the distinction of being the very first comic strip to appear in a pulp magazine as a featured story, and it was also the first feature to appear in a modern-day comic book, *Famous Funnies* issue #1, in the 1930s. Tommy was also the main character in several films. In 1934, Universal produced a 12-episode movie serial that featured Tommy as its main character. Actor Maurice Murphy played Tommy, Patricia Farr played Betty Lou and Noah Beery, Jr. played Skeeter. One year later, the same studio produced another serial, *Tailspin Tommy in the Great Air Mystery*, which starred Clark Williams as Tommy, Jean Rogers as Betty Lou and Noah Beery, Jr. repeating his role of Skeeter. In 1939, Monogram released four *Tailspin Tommy* second feature films with John Trent as Tommy, Marjorie Reynolds as Betty Lou and Milburn Stone as Skeeter.

It wasn't until 1941, thirteen years after *Tailspin Tommy* first appeared in print, that his adventures were finally adapted to radio as a five-day-a-week, fifteen-minute-a-day children's adventure program. Although several episodes of *Tailspin Tommy* have survived, the actors who played the roles on the radio series have never been identified. Episodes of this syndicated series had such enticing titles as "Mystery in the Sky," which was the series' first broadcast, "Movie Murder," "The Missing Comet," "Midnight Patrol," "The Hidden Mine," and "The Flying Actor Murder."

Tarzan

Edgar Rice Burroughs' *Tarzan, The Ape Man* adventure novels, the first of which was published in 1912, and its subsequent sequel novels, were adapted into a series of successful films, a daily and Sunday Funnies comic strip feature, several comic book series, and two moderately successful radio programs. The author of the *Tarzan* books, Edgar Rice Burroughs, was born in Chicago, Illinois in 1875. His father, George Tyler, was a Civil War veteran and he wanted his son to become a professional soldier. Young Edgar was enrolled at the Michigan Military Academy to prepare him for a career in the military, and when he graduated, Edgar became a member of the 7th Reserve Militia, in which he served from 1896–1897. He did not, however, become a professional soldier as his father had hoped. Edgar began working in his father's business, but following his father's wishes once again, he joined the Illinois Reserve Militia from 1918 until 1919. Unhappy doing his father's bidding, Burroughs borrowed money from friends and bought a stationary store in Pocatello, Idaho. He was, however, no more satisfied with his life as a store owner than he had been working for his father. His attitude toward his life changed when he began writing a series of pulp fiction stories when he was 35 years old. His first success as a writer was in 1912, when a series of 68 of his science fiction adventure stories, beginning with a tall tale called "Under the Moon of Mars," was published. His greatest success came later that same year with his novel *Tarzan, the Ape Man*. The novel was about a baby boy who was is raised to adulthood by apes in the African jungle when the airplane in which he is traveling with his English parents crashes, and his parents are killed. In Burroughs' novel, Tarzan grows up in a world of animals, never coming in contact with humans until he is as a grown man, and he is discovered by a group of white hunters. The novel, and the more than 24 subsequent *Tarzan* novels, was a tremendous success. Burroughs formed his own publishing company to handle the ever-increasing demand for more of his *Tarzan* books. Silent film and early sound films featuring the Tarzan character were released, the first starring strong man Elmo Lincoln, followed by numerous other actors in the role, including swimming star Buster Crabbe. In 1934, Burroughs formed his own motion picture production company, Burroughs-Tarzan Pictures, and with MGM produced a series of successful films that starred another Olympic swimming star, Johnny Weissmuller. The popular *Tarzan* films with Weissmuller as Tarzan continued throughout the 1930s and 1940s, and there were subsequent films made with other actors and a successful television series with Ron Ely from 1966 until 1968. Burroughs continued to write other works of fiction, as well as the *Tarzan* series, until his death in 1950.

Tarzan made his radio debut on September 10, 1932. The prerecorded series was unique to radio in many ways. The producers of the radio series used state-of-the-art recording techniques and elaborate sound effects to realistically portray the sounds of Tarzan's jungle habitat. When the syndicated radio series was first aired, Burroughs wrote, "They have injected all of the jungle sounds including the roaring of Numa the lion, the screaming of the panthers, the cries of the bull apes, the laughing of the hyenas, the screams and shouts of the natives. They supplied the sound…your imagination supplied the pictures!" The *Tarzan* radio show had a pretentious premiere which was broadcast before a live audience at the Fox Pantages Theater in Hollywood, with 3,000 people attending the broadcast. The show was scripted by Burroughs, and starred Burroughs' son-in-law, James Pierce, a former amateur athlete who had appeared as *Tarzan* in one film, and Burroughs' daughter, Joan, an aspiring actress, as Tarzan's mate, Jane. The recorded, syndicated programs were heard in fifteen-minute episodes, and the series was on the air over a period of two years. Fortunately, Pierce, who was not a particularly good vocal actor, rarely spoke on the radio series. For the first few weeks the series was aired, the Tarzan character merely grunted. He only began to speak in pigeon-English when Jane, an American girl who was stranded in the jungle and was saved by Tarzan from imminent danger, taught him some basic English words. In the early episodes of the series, Tarzan fell in love with Jane. He was also tempted romantically by an evil temptress, the beautiful Priestess of Opar, but he resisted and remained faithful to his first love, Jane. A second attempt to present *Tarzan* as a radio series was made in 1951, one year after Burroughs died. This series, which redid many of the original *Tarzan* radio scripts, starred radio actor Lamont Johnson in 60 consecutive half-hour episodes. The series used the same opening as the original series and began with the announcer saying, "From the heart of the jungle comes a savage cry of victory. This is Tarzan, Lord of the jungle! From the black core of dark Africa…land of enchantment, mystery and violence comes one of the most colorful figures of all time. Transcribed from the immortal pen of Edgar Rice Burroughs…*Tarzan,* the bronzed, white son of the jungle!" Even though this series was well produced and, as the surviving recordings of the series reveal, was certainly exciting, the program failed to remain on the air longer than a year. Edgar Rice Burroughs was dead, and so was his amazing ability to promote his *Tarzan* property.

It seems inevitable that *Tarzan* would eventually become a comic strip, as well as a comic book feature. The first *Tarzan* comics did not appear in print, however, until the late 1930s. Several extremely talented artists were responsible for drawing the comics, which were originally written by Gaylord DuBois, who was one of the comics' most prolific scripters. Among the many talented artists who drew the *Tarzan* comics for Dell, DC, and Gold Key Comics, and as a daily and Sunday Funnies newspaper comic feature, were Hal Foster from 1931 until 1937, who later drew the very successful *Prince Valiant,* Burne Hogarth from 1937 until 1950, who drew *Tarzan* as a comic strip, and Jesse Marsh, who drew both the comic books and comic strips from 1950 until 1965. Russ Manning then drew the *Tarzan* comics and a daily and Sunday Funnies feature until 1972 for the United Features Syndicate. Daniel Barry drew the *Tarzan* comic strip at various times from 1951 until 1972, when he left the United States and began to draw *Tarzan* comics for the European market. Hal Foster (1892–1982) was born in Canada and began his art career after studying at the Chicago Art Institute and then at the Chicago Academy of Fine Arts in the early 1920s. Foster's realistic, anatomically correct drawings made him the leading candidate to draw *Tarzan,* and he drew more than 300 illustrations for the Tarzan comic strip. Foster actually disliked what he called "the dim-witted Tarzan character," and when he was asked, went to work for William Randolph Hearst for whom he created and then drew his *Prince Valiant* comic strip until his death in 1982. Burne Hogarth (1911–1996) was, like Foster, a master of figure drawing and therefore he was a logical choice to take over the *Tarzan* comics. Hogarth began his career as an artist when he was fifteen years old and became an assistant with the Associated Editors Syndicate for whom he drew a panel strip called *Churches of the World.* His first actual comic strip was *Ivy Hemmanhaw,* which met with little success. In 1937, Hogarth began drawing the *Tarzan* comic strip and then created a new comic strip he called *Drago,* which was about the adventures of a young Argentinian who fights the Nazis in post-World War II Argentina. For a brief time in the 1970s, Hogarth resumed drawing the *Tarzan* comics, but then retired to concentrate on his art teaching career. Hogarth died in 1996 at the age of 85, after suffering a heart attack. The next artist to draw the *Tarzan* comics was Jesse Marsh (1907–1966). Marsh drew *Tarzan* when he was a staff artist for Dell comic books, and, for a time, he also drew the daily and Sunday Funnies *Tarzan* comics. Marsh was a self-taught artist who began his career as an animator at the Disney Studios in Hollywood. During World War II, Marsh worked as a radar man in the Air Force and returned to the Disney company at the end of the war in 1945. In the late 1940s, Marsh began working for Western Publishing and drew both the *Gene Autry* and 153 issues of the *Tarzan* comic book series. In 1965, one year before his death, Marsh quit drawing the *Tarzan* comics and, due to his declining health, turned *Tarzan* over to his friend, artist Russ Manning. Russell Manning (1929–1981) had studied at the Los Angeles Art Institute and soon after he ended his studies, he was drafted into the United States Army, and sent to Japan to prepare to fight in the Korean Conflict. Instead of fighting at the front in Korea, he was given the assignment to draw cartoons for the base newspaper and also took on map-making. In 1953, when he returned from Japan, Manning went to work for Dell Publishing and took over the *Tarzan* comic book series. United Features then asked Manning to draw the daily and Sunday supplement *Tarzan* comics for them, which he did until 1972. Artist Daniel Barry (1923–) was the last artist to date to draw *Tarzan* as a comic book feature. Barry had gotten his first professional job as an artist when he was a boy and had met cartoonist George Manning, who was impressed with his work and encouraged him to draw comics. Barry's first comic strip was *Airways* and he subsequently drew *The Blue Bolt* and *Doc Savage*. Barry then began to draw the *Tarzan* comic strip panels for a short time, before taking over the popular *Flash Gordon* comics. Barry abandoned *Flash Gordon* in 1990 and began to draw the Indiana Jones comic book series. He artist died in 1997 at the age of 74.

TARZAN RADIO SERIES PERFORMERS

PIERCE, JAMES B. 1900 – D. 1983 (TARZAN)

Before he played *Tarzan the Ape Man* on the radio version of Edgar Rice Burroughs' *Tarzan* series in 364 episodes aired from 1932 until 1934, James Pierce had been an all-American Indiana University center, and he had appeared in several films. Among some of the early silent films in which he was featured were *Leatherstocking* (1924), *The Return of Grey Wolf* (1926), *Tarzan and the Golden Lion* (1927), *Jesse James* (1927), *Ladies of the Mob* (1928), and the early sound films *Lightning Express* (1930), *Young As You Feel* (1931), and *Suicide Fleet* (1931). In the early 1930s, Pierce, who was married to Burroughs' daughter, Joan, was offered the role Tarzan on a radio series. Joan Burroughs Pierce, who was not a particularly experienced actress, was cast as Tarzan's love interest, Jane. *Tarzan* was the only role Pierce is known to have played on radio. After the series left the air, Pierce continued to appear in films and had featured roles in *Belle of the Nineties* (1934), *The Walking Dead* (1936), *Flash Gordon* (1936, serial), *Life Begins in College*

(1937), *Ali Baba Goes to Town* (1937), *Ambush* (1939), *Zorro's Fighting Legion* (1939, serial), *Strange Cargo* (1940), *Rainbow Over the Range* (1940), *Chad Hanna* (1940), *Love Crazy* (1941), *Roxie Hart* (1942), *Nocturne* (1946), *My Favorite Brunette* (1947), *Yes Sir, That's My Baby* (1949), *My Blue Heaven* (1950), *Right Cross* (1950), *Follow the Sun* (1951), and *Show Boat* (1951), and many others. Pierce retired from acting in the mid-1950s.

JOHNSON, LAMONT B. 1922 (TARZAN)

Actor Lamont Johnson made his acting debut on the stage and became a successful radio actor in the early 1940s. Johnson was featured on several popular radio soap opera series including *Amanda of Honeymoon Hill, Hilltop House, Wendy Warren and the News,* and *Wilderness Road.* In 1948, Johnson returned to the stage and was seen on Broadway in a revival of William Shakespeare's *Macbeth.* He was cast as *Tarzan* in 1951 on the revival of that adventure series on radio and recorded more than 60 episodes which were released in syndication. When radio drama all but disappeared from the airwaves in the late 1950s, Johnson, concentrated on directing stage plays. In addition to staging numerous regional theater and touring company productions, he directed the Broadway shows *The Perfect Setup* and *The Egg,* both in 1962.

TERRY AND THE PIRATES

The *Terry and the Pirates* comic strip made artist Milton Caniff one of very few celebrity cartoonists in America and his name became so thoroughly identified with the adventures of the handsome, young, blond pilot, Terry Lee,

Milton Caniff's *Terry and the Pirates* was as popular on the radio as it was as a comic strip. Terry Lee and his nemesis, The Dragon Lady, seen above, held forth in print from 1934 until 1973 and on the radio from 1937 until 1948.

that the two names became synonymous. Milton Caniff, who was born in Hillsboro, Ohio in 1908, had been interested in art from the time he was a small boy. When he graduated from Ohio State University in 1930 with a degree in Fine Arts, he moved to New York City and got a job as an artist with the Associated Press Syndicate, for whom he created his first comic strip *The Gay Thirties* in 1933. The strip was not a success, but his next strip, *Dickie Dare*, which was about a small boy's daily adventures, made him relatively well known to comic strip fans. In 1934, Captain Joseph Patterson of the *New York Daily News* was looking for an artist to create a new adventure strip and asked Caniff to go to work for him. Caniff came up with a comic strip feature about a young American pilot who flew airplanes in the exotic Far East, and the adventures he had while he was patrolling the China Seas tracking down thieving pirates who menaced cargo ships. Quite appropriately the strip was called *Terry and the Pirates*. The comic strip began with Terry Lee and his friend and his pal, fellow pilot Pat Ryan, arriving in China in search of a mine that had belonged to Terry's grandfather. In the second day's strip, Terry and Pat met George Webster Confucius, an Oriental gentleman whose nickname was "Connie," who became an interpreter and guide for Terry and Pat. From the moment the comic strip appeared in print, on October 22, 1934, and even more so when it became a Sunday Funnies color supplement the following December, it was a sensation. The daily and Sunday adventures of the young, handsome pilot, Terry Lee, and his dark-haired, somewhat older friend, Pat Ryan, and their female friends, Burma, Normandie Drake, and April Kane, and their many encounters with a beautiful-but-evil Eurasian woman whom Caniff called "The Dragon Lady," took America by storm. Terry actually had a rather complex relationship with the unpredictable Dragon Lady character in the comic strip, who was one of the comics' all-time great female villains. She not only frequently tried to seduce him for her own evil purposes, she even attempted to murder Terry, Pat and their friends; on one occasion, she also helped Terry overcome a case of pre-date jitters teaching him how to dance. Soon a *Terry and the Pirates* comic book series, and in 1940 a fifteen-episode serial that starred William Tracy as Terry and Sheila Darcy as the Dragon Lady, as well as several Whitman Big Little Books, and, in 1952 a television series that starred John Baer as Terry, were released. In 1946, when the *Chicago Tribune,* who retained the rights to *Terry and the Pirates,* refused to relinquish partial ownership of the strip and turn it over to its creator, artist Milton Caniff, Caniff decided to abandon *Terry and the Pirates*. Almost immediately, he came up with an idea for a new strip he called *Steve Canyon,* which became almost as popular as his *Terry and the Pirates.* Caniff continued to draw *Steve Canyon* for the next 41 years, until he died at the age of 81 in 1988. Caniff was one of the most famous cartoonists in the world at the time of his death. His name had continued to be associated with *Terry and the Pirates* and even though he had not drawn the comic strip for 41 years and the strip had been discontinued in 1973, when he died, millions of people sent letters of condolence to his family and mentioned how much they had loved his *Terry and the Pirates* comic strip.

In 1937, at the height of the *Terry and the Pirates* comic strip's popularity, a five-day-a-week, fifteen minutes a day series radio series made its debut. The show became one of the country's favorite children's radio adventure programs and remained on the air until 1948. Several actors played the Terry Lee role on radio over the years, including Jackie Kelk, Cliff Carpenter, Owen Jordan and, for a brief time, Bill Fein. Clayton "Bud" Collyer, Larry Alexander, and Bob Griffin played Pat Ryan; Agnes Moorehead, Adelaide Klein and Marion Sweet played the Dragon Lady; Frances Chaney played Burma; Cliff Norton, Peter Donald and John Gibson played Terry and Pat's Chinese interpreter and companion, Connie; and Ted DeCorsia played Flip Corkin on the series.

Actor Bill Fein only played Terry on the *Terry and the Pirates* radio series for just a few months, but he certainly looked the part.

Also frequently featured on the radio series in various supporting roles were Cameron Andrews, John Moore, Gerta Rozan, Charles Cantor, William Podmore and Mandel Kramer. The program's announcers were Douglas Browning and Chuck Leslie. Wylie Adams, Marty Andrews, and Cyril Armbruster directed the program at different times, and the series was, for most of the years it was aired, written by Al Barker. The titles of some of the series most unforgettable adventures included "The Pirate Gold Detector Ring" (which, of course, could be obtained by sending in a sponsor's label and a "thin dime"), "The Dragon Lady Strikes Back," "Fighting for Horses," "Mrs. Finch is Mother of Burma Road," "Pat Captures the Dragon Lady," "Firing Squad for Three Men," "Down the Cliffs on a Rope," "The Japs Use Pat and Terry as Bait," "The Bridge Collapses," and many others.

Terry and the Pirates Radio Series Performers

Carpenter, Cliff b. 1915 (Terry Lee)

The first actor to play the part of Terry Lee on the *Terry and the Pirates* radio program was Cliff Carpenter, who had a long and distinguished career as an actor on Broadway, radio, in films, and on television.

Actor Cliff Carpenter played the title role of Terry on the *Terry and the Pirates* radio adventure series longer than any other actor. About his work on the series Carpenter said, "I didn't half appreciate the remarkable achievement it was. All those fine artists, but some of us thought it was 'only radio,' and a kid's show at that. We had our eyes on more important venues, more public recognition as *artists* or something. I now look back on (*Terry and the Pirates*) with true affection for all those who were a part of it, those laborers in the vineyard."

Cliff Carpenter was born in San Francisco. In 1920, when he was five years old, his family moved to Southern California and Cliff attended Beverly Hills High School, where he first began to appear in school plays. When he graduated from high school, Cliff attended U.C.L.A., majoring in Fine Arts. He made his professional acting debut in Sidney Howard's play *Yellow Jack* at the Pasadena Community Playhouse in 1936. Cliff also began to work on radio in Hollywood at that time and had featured roles on such radio shows as *Burns and Allen, Big Town* (with Edward G. Robinson), *Showboat, Silver Theater,* and other programs. In 1938, Carpenter moved to New York, and was soon being heard on most of the major network radio programs that originated from that city including *Just Plain Bill, Amanda of Honeymoon Hill, We, the Abbotts, The Columbia Workshop, Prairie Folks, County Seat, Thirteen by Corwin, Grand Central Station, The Kate Smith Show, The Phillip Morris Playhouse, The Pursuit of Happiness, The Al Jolson Show,* and many, many others. In addition to his roles on radio, Carpenter appeared in several plays on Broadway including *The Eve of St. Mark, The Stars Weep, Caesar and Cleopatra,*

Borned in Texas, Inherit the Wind, Sunrise at Campobello, Nobody Loves an Albatross, and The Andersonville Trial. He also toured the country in stage productions of many other plays. In the 1960s, the actor played supporting roles on episodes of such TV series as The Defenders and The Patty Duke Show. Carpenter continued to work in show business throughout the 1970s, 1980s and into the 1990s, mainly as a voice-over performer for radio and TV commercials.

COLLYER, CLAYTON "BUD" (PAT RYAN. SEE SUPERMAN FOR BIOGRAPHY)

KELK, JACKIE (TERRY LEE. SEE THE GUMPS FOR BIOGRAPHY)

MOOREHEAD, AGNES (THE DRAGON LADY. SEE BRINGING UP FATHER FOR BIOGRAPHY)

TILLIE THE TOILER

When World War I ended and America's stodgy Victorian attitudes about women's roles in society changed, a typical working girl of the 1920s, the office secretary, who was single, independent and usually a carefree "flapper," was amusingly depicted in Russ Westover's comic strip Tillie the Toiler. Secretary Tillie Jones made her first appearance in a comic strip in 1921 and 38 years later, in 1959, the last Tiller the Toiler comic strip panel was published. During those thirty-eight years, in addition to the comic strip, there were Tillie the Toiler films, comic books, and a short-lived radio series. The artist behind the success of the comic strip, Russ Westover (1886 – 1966), got his first job as a sports cartoonist in 1904 at the San Francisco Bulletin. After this he worked at the Oakland Herald, and did freelance art work for San Francisco's Globe, Chronicle and Post newspapers. For the Post he

Russ Westover's popular working girl and flapper, who first saw the light of day as a comic strip character in the 1920s, Tillie the Toiler, became the heroine of a radio series twenty years after she made her comic strip debut, in the 1940s. The radio show was not a success.

drew his first strip, the baseball-themed *Daffy Dan*. A few years later, Westover moved to New York City and became a cartoonist for the *New York Herald*. It was for the Herald that Westover drew the comic strips *Fat Chance* and *Snapshot Bill*, which were only moderate successes. In 1921, Westover, who was impressed with the success of a comic strip called *Winnie Winkle, the Breadwinner*, published in 1920, sold an idea for a comic strip about a single working girl of his own, called *Tillie the Toiler*, to King Features Syndicate. Tillie was a pretty, somewhat scatterbrained girl who enjoyed shopping and flirting more than her work at the fashionable clothing manufacturing company owned by a mogul named Mr. J. Simpkins. At the fashion house, where she worked as a secretary and occasional model, Tillie was constantly being pursued romantically by the much shorter Clarence "Mac" MacDougall, whose attentions Tillie never really discouraged as she dated other young men. Over the years, Tillie was fired by Mr. Simpkins, rehired, and courted by every well-to-do young man who came into the office. During World War II, Tillie joined the U. S. Army and her adventures as a WAC made Tillie even more popular than she already was. The strip indeed was a huge success and soon many other comic strips about working girls, such as *Tessie the Typist, Millie the Model, Nellie the Nurse, Merely Marge, Betty, Dumb Dora* and *Sherry the Showgirl*, began to appear in newspapers throughout the country. *Tillie the Toiler* and *Winnie Winkle* remained the most popular of these strips until *Dixie Dugan, Toots and Casper, Brenda Starr* and *Fritzi Ritz* came along several years later. In 1951, after three decades of drawing *Tillie the Toiler*, Russ Westover retired and turned the comic strip over to his assistant, Bob Gustafson, who continued to draw it until the comic strip was dropped from syndication in 1959. In the very last *Tillie the Toiler* comic strip panel, Tillie finally accepted Mac's proposal of marriage, much to the relief of the strip's millions of fans.

In 1927, *Tillie the Toiler* became the main character in an MGM silent film that starred Marion Davies as Tillie, Matt Moore as Mac, and George Fawcett as Mr. Simpkins. In 1941, Columbia made a second *Tillie the Toiler* feature film that starred Kay Harris as Tillie, William Tracy as Mac, and George Watts as Mr. Simpkins. Tillie also made her debut as the main character in a radio series in 1941. The radio program, which was on the air for less than one full year, starred a young actress named Caryl Smith as Tillie and featured Billy Lynn as Mac and John Brown as Mr. Simpkins. Margaret Burlen played Tillie's mother on the series. Unfortunately, as far as this author could determine, no recordings of the radio show have survived.

Tillie the Toiler radio series performers

Brown, John (Mr. J. Simpkins. See *My Friend Irma* for Biography)

Smith, Caryl b. 1919 (Tillie Jones)

Caryl Smith's career as an actress was, apparently, as short-lived as the *Tillie the Toiler* radio series. In addition to playing Tillie, Caryl was also heard on a radio series called *Maude's Diary* in 1941, which was aired on the CBS network. It is also known that Miss Smith appeared on Broadway in *Return Engagement* in 1940, which lasted a mere eight performances, and *Liberty Jones*, for 22 performances, in 1941. After 1941, Miss Smith seems to have left show business or, at least, she kept a rather low profile as an actress after the early 1940s. There is no record of her having appeared in films or on television programs. Miss Smith seems to have disappeared into obscurity.

Tom Mix

Today, when most people hear the name Tom Mix, they think he must have been a fictional Western cowboy character like *The Lone Ranger* and *Red Ryder*, since what they hear about him makes him seem so much larger-than-life. Tom Mix was, however, a real live person and not the creation of some writer's imagination, although many of the publicity releases printed when Mix was at the height of his film career, certainly read more like fiction than fact. Although he was not a true son of the Old West, he was born in Pennsylvania, he attained enormous popularity throughout the 1920s and well into the 1940s, first as a silent, then as a sound film cowboy star. There were drawings of him as the title character in hundreds of *Tom Mix* comic books and adventure novels, and Tom Mix's name on anything guaranteed its sale, and all of the publicity these items generated made Mix the most celebrated Western cowboy star in the world. Mix, most assuredly, became the prototype for cowboy superstars of the future, such as Roy Rogers and Gene Autry, who followed. Tom, however, unlike Gene and Roy, was not a singer. He was an action hero in the truest sense of that title, and his daring escapades in films was the envy of every red-blooded boy in the United States, and then the world.

Thomas Haezekiah Mix was born in 1880 in Cameron County, Pennsylvania. An athletic boy, young Tom developed a reputation at an early age for performing daring physical stunts and it seemed only natural that as he grew into young manhood, he would pursue some sort of an occupation that would take advantage of his physical agility. Tom later claimed, in one of his many highly fictional press releases, that he was one-quarter Cherokee Indian, and that he had been born in Oklahoma, which totally ignored his

100% Irish/American roots. He also never told anyone that he had never even finished grade school. In 1898, when he was eighteen years old, Mix enlisted in the U. S. Army and he eventually reached the rank of sergeant. Unlike the publicity stories about his wartime heroism claimed, however, he never saw combat. In fact, Mix had deserted the military and joined the circus before he turned 20. Mix became an accomplished Rodeo rider, and he performed hair-raising stunts and rope tricks in the circus which, in 1909, caught the attention of a Selig Film Studios' talent scout. In a very short period of time, Mix became one of the busiest stunt men on the Selig lot. It didn't take the studio executives long to realize how talented a performer and how handsome he was, and Mix was soon being given major roles in numerous cowboy silent films. Hundreds of these films were being turned out by movie studios to fulfill the needs of the countless numbers of movie theaters that were springing up throughout the country. Between 1909 and 1917, Tom Mix appeared in 236 half-reel, one-reel and two-reel Selig films, of which 131 were Westerns, and, the remainder, adventure, drama and comedy films. Between 1917 and 1928, Tom went to work for Fox studios, where he made 85 silent films, of which 79 were five-, six-, seven- and eight-reelers, 64 of which were Westerns. In 1928, Tom made 5 Western films for FBO. The performer's sound debut was at Universal, and it was nothing short of spectacular. Because of his ever-increasing film popularity, he became one of the highest paid actors in Hollywood, making the unprecedented sum of more than $20,000 a week. In 1935, Tom made a 15-episode film serial for Mascot Pictures, putting his total motion picture appearance output at 336 films. As if that wasn't enough to keep the actor busy, Mix also produced 88 films, wrote 71 film scripts, and directed 117 films. By the time the 1940s rolled around, Tom Mix was a character of legendary status. Everything he did seem to make money. The sales of the Tom Mix comic books were most impressive and he even became the main character on a popular children's radio adventure series, although he never played the role of himself on the radio.

By the time the *Tom Mix* radio show made its on the air debut on September 25, 1933, Mix was a motion picture legend. The *Tom Mix* radio adventures, which were written by Roland Martini, were broadcast from New York City and starred radio actor Artells "Art" Dickson as Tom Mix and character actor Percy Hemus as a character named "The Old Wrangler." The series' theme music, "When It's Round-Up Time in Texas and the Bloom is on the Sage," became a rallying call telling youngsters it was time to hear *Tom Mix and His Straight Shooters'* next radio adventure. The sale of Ralston cereal, the show's sponsor, increased considerably when the radio show surfaced, since the radio adventure series was a popular success with youngsters all over the country. In 1935, the *Tom Mix* radio series moved its broadcasts to Chicago.

The show's stories were then written by Charles Tazewell, Jack Holden, and, beginning in 1938 until 1942, Russell Thorson played the role of Tom Mix. Other actors who were heard on the radio series over the years included Hal Peary, and then Willard Waterman as Sheriff Mike Shaw, Andy Donnelly, George Gobel, and Hugh Rowlands as Jimmy, Winifred Toomey, and then Jane Webb as Jane, Joe "Curley" Bradley in a variety of roles, and Sidney Ellstrom, Leo Curley, Bob Jellison, Arthur Peterson, Phil Lord, DeWitt McBride, Patricia Dunlap, and many others in the supporting cast. The *Tom Mix* program became well-known for the variety of premiums the sponsor offered its young listeners. These premiums included toy guns, airplanes, books, lariats, bandannas, badges, cowboy outfits, telegraph sets, periscopes, branding irons, and many other items. In 1943, without any fanfare, because of the introduction of daylight-saving time, Ralston cereals decided to cancel the *Tom Mix* series, convinced that children would never give up an hour of playtime to listen to a radio program. They were wrong and demands that the show be returned to the airwaves brought the series back in 1944 with actor Curley Bradley playing the role of Tom. The series remained on the air until June 1950. On the last broadcast of the show, announcer Don Gordon ended the program saying, "In the heart and imagination of the world, Tom Mix rides on, and lives on, forever." The real Tom Mix had died in an automobile accident after a night of heavy drinking in 1940.

TOM MIX RADIO SERIES PERFORMERS

DICKSON, ARTELLS B. 1895 – ? (TOM MIX)

Born into a show business family, Artells Dickson first appeared on stage as an actor and singer when he was a small boy. By 1928, he was the founding member of the Artells Dickson Concert Company, which was headquartered in Chicago and performed "songs and musical readers" throughout the Midwest. In the early 1930s, Dickson began working on radio in Chicago as a staff actor at the NBC/Red network. In 1933, he was cast in the most important role of his career, Tom Mix, on the children's radio adventure series based on the popular film star cowboy's successful films. The series made its radio debut on September 25, 1933 and Dickson remained with the show until 1935, when the series moved its broadcasts to New York City. Dickson was also heard on such popular radio programs of the 1930s and 1940s as *Maverick Jim* (also a Western adventure series), *The Mighty Show, Pretty Kitty Kelly,* and *Sunday Mornings at Aunt Susan's*. Artells Dickson's subsequent career as an actor remains a mystery, as no further record of the actor's work could be uncovered by this author.

Peary, Hal b. 1908 – d. 1985 (Sheriff Mike Shaw)

Best-known as radio's *Great Gildersleeve*, actor Hal Peary played Sheriff Mike Shaw on radio's *Tom Mix* adventure series in the late 1930s.

Actor Hal Peary is best known to radio audiences of the 1930s and 1940s as Throckmorton P. Gildersleeve, a character he originated on the *Fibber McGee and Molly* series, then carried over to a program of his own, *The Great Gildersleeve*. Hal Peary, was born in San Leandro, California, and made his debut on radio as a boy soprano on a local station in Oakland, California in 1925. By 1929, Peary had a show of his own on the air, *The Spanish Serenader*, which originated from Chicago, and he also acted on several NBC Blue network drama programs that originated from that city as well. Peary played Sheriff Mike Shaw on NBC's Western adventure series, *Tom Mix*, in the 1930s, and he was also featured on such Chicago-based shows as *Flying Time, Welcome Valley*, and on many soap opera series. In the mid-1930s, Peary returned to California and was heard on such radio programs as *Blondie*, playing Dagwood and Blondie Bumstead's next door neighbor, Herb Woodley, and in 1935 as Gildersleeve on the *Fibber McGee and Molly* show. His success as Gildersleeve led to a series of his own, *The Great Gildersleeve*, in 1941. Peary also played his Gildersleeve role in several films in the 1940s including *Comin' Round the Mountain* (1940), *Country Fair and Look Who's Laughing* (both 1941), *Seven Days Leave, Here We Go Again* (both 1942), *The Great Gildersleeve, Gildersleeve's Bad Day, Gildersleeve on Broadway* (all three 1943), and *Gildersleeve's Ghost* (1944). In 1950, Peary decided to leave the *Great Gildersleeve* radio show and he was replaced by an actor named Willard Waterman, whose voice sounded remarkably like Peary's. Waterman had previously replaced Peary as Sheriff Mike Shaw on the *Tom Mix* program, and subsequently played Gildersleeve on the 1955 television series. Hal Peary tried a new radio series, The Hal Peary Show, but he had become so identified with the Gildersleeve role that the public had trouble accepting him in any other part; the show did not remain on the air for longer than one year. Peary went on to appear in several films including *Port of Hell* (1954), *A Tiger Walks* (1964), *Clambake* (1967), and he was the voice of "Big Ben" in the Rudolph the Red-Nosed Reindeer animated television specials, *Rudolph's Shiny New Year* (1976) and *Rudolph and Frosty's Christmas in July* (1979). He also was a regular on the *Blondie* and *Fibber McGee and Molly* TV series (playing Mayor LaTrivia), and made guest starring appearances on such TV shows as *Stars Over Hollywood, The Spike Jones Show, The Bob Cummings Show, The Dick Van Dyke Show, Perry Mason, Petticoat Junction, The Addams Family* and *The Brady Bunch,* before retiring in the 1970s.

THORSON, RUSSELL B. 1906 – D. 1982 (TOM MIX)
Russell Thorson's long, distinguished career included major and supporting roles on the stage, on radio, in films, and on television over a fifty-year period. Thorson, who was born in rural Wisconsin, decided early in life that he wanted to be an actor and he auditioned for a touring stage production of a play in Wisconsin, got the part, and left that state to tour the country. Roles in other touring stage plays followed, but his wonderful, rich baritone voice led to his working on radio in Chicago, where he was heard on such radio programs as *Midstream, Mystery in the Air, The Road of Life,* and *Tom Mix* in the 1930s. When he moved to Hollywood, in the 1940s, he voiced Captain Bart Friday on the syndicated radio series *Adventures by Morse* in the 1940s, Jack Packard in a revival of Carlton E. Morse's I Love a Mystery series in the 1950s, and Paul Barbour on Morse's *One Man's Family* program (1954–1959), replacing actor Michael Raffetto, who played Paul for many years on that show. When *One Man's Family* became a TV series in the 1950s, Thorson reprised his role of Paul Barbour. Thorson's long list of film credits includes roles in *Easy Living* (1949), *Double Dynamite* (1951), *Please Murder Me* (1956), *Zero Hour* (1957), *I Want to Live!* (1958), *Gunfighters of Abilene* (1960), *Two on a Guillotine* (1965), *Hang 'Em High* (1968), *The Learning Tree* (1969), and *Walking Tall* (1973). The countless number of television series on which he appeared included *Gunsmoke, The Tales of Wells Fargo, Wagon Train, Maverick, Perry Mason, The Lawman, The Detectives* (as a regular), *Rawhide, The Rifleman, Bonanza, Dr. Kildare, Ben Casey, Gilligan's Island, Lassie, The Virginian, The Big Valley, Marcus Welby, MD, Mission: Impossible, Cannon, The Odd Couple, Emergency!, Adam-12, Barnaby Jones* and The *Rockford Files.*

BIBLIOGRAPHY

PRINT

ABRAMSON, ALBERT. *THE HISTORY OF TELEVISION, 1942-2000*. JEFFERSON, NC: MCFARLAND & CO., INC., 2003

ARCHER, GLEASON L. *THE HISTORY OF RADIO*. NEW YORK: AMERICAN HISTORICAL SOCIETY, 1938

BARNAUW, ERIK. *RADIO DRAMA IN ACTION*. NEW YORK: FARRAR AND RINEHART, 1945

BOBBITT, DAVID. G. *WORLD RADIO TV HANDBOOK*. WATSON-GUTTILL, 2000

BOEMER, MARILYN LAWRENCE. *THE CHILDREN'S HOUR: RADIO PROGRAMS FOR CHILDREN*. NEW JERSEY: SCARECROW PRESS, 1989

BROOKS, TIM & MARSH, EARLE. *THE COMPLETE DIRECTORY TO PRIME TIME NETWORK AND CABLE AND TV SHOWS*. NEW YORK: BALLENTINE BOOKS, 1999

BROWNE, GENE (ED.) *THE NEW YORK TIMES ENCYCLOPEDIA OF FILM, VOLUMES 1-13*. NEW YORK: TIMES BOOKS, 1988-PRESENT

BUXTON, FRANK & OWEN, BILL. *THE BIG BROADCAST*. LATHAM, MD. & LONDON: SCARECROW PRESS, 1997

CAMPBELL, ROBERT. *THE GOLDEN YEARS OF BROADCASTING*, NEW YORK: SCRIBNERS, 1976

CHESTER, GERARD & GARRETT, EDGAR R. *TELEVISION AND RADIO, 3RD ED*. NEW YORK: APPLETON CENTURY CROFTS, 1963

COX, JIM. *RADIO CRIME FIGHTERS*. JEFFERSON, NC: MCFARLAND & CO,. INC., 1999

DeLong, Thomas A. *Radio Stars: An Illustrated Biographical Dictionary of 953 Performers, 1920 through 1960.* Jefferson, NC & London: McFarland & Co., Inc., 1996

Donaldson, Charles E. *Radio Stars: Brief Biographical Sketches of More Than One Hundred Best-Known Actors, Musicians, Commentators, and Other Stars of Radio Programs.* Washington, D.C.: Newspaper Information Services, Inc., 1942

Douglas, George H. *The Early Days of Radio Broadcasting.* Jefferson, NC: McFarland & Co., Inc., 2001

Dunning, John. *Tune in Yesterday: The Ultimate Encyclopedia of Old-Time Radio, 1927 – 1976.* Englewood Cliffs, NJ: Prentice-Hall, 1976

Edmonson, Madeleine & Rounds, David. *The Soaps: Daytime Serials of Radio and TV.* New York: Stein and Day, 1973

French, Jack. *Private Eyelashes.* Boalsburg, PA: BearManor Media, 2004

Grams, Jr., Martin & Payton, Gordon. *The CBS Radio Mystery Theater: An Episode Guide and Handbook to Nine Years of Broadcasting, 1974-1982.* Jefferson, NC & London: McFarland & Co. Inc., 1999

Harmon, Jim. *The Great Radio Heroes.* (revised ed.) Jefferson, NC. McFarland & Co. Inc., 2001

Hickerson, Jay. *The Ultimate History of Network Radio Programming and Guide to All Circulating Shows, 3rd ed.* Hamden, CT: Hickerson, 1996

Inman, David M. *Performers' Television Credits, 1948 – 2000* (Three Volumes). Jefferson, NC, McFarland & Co., Inc., 2001

Katz, Epharim & Klein, Fred. *The Film Encyclopedia, 4th ed: The Most Comprehensive Encyclopedia of World Cinema in a Single Volume.* New York: MacMillan & Co., 2001

Lackmann, Ron. *The Encyclopedia of American Radio.* New York: Facts on File, Inc., 2000

—— *The Encyclopedia of 20th Century American Television*. New York: Facts on File, Inc., 2002

Lenberg, Jeff. *The Encyclopedia of Animated Cartoons* (2nd Ed.). New York: Facts on File, Inc., 1999

MacDonald, J. Fred. *Don't Touch That Dial: Radio Programming in American Life 1920 – 1960*. Chicago: Nelson-Hall, 1979

Maltin, Leonard. *The Great American Broadcast*. Dutton Books, 1997

—— *2003 Movie and Video Guide*. New York: Signet (New American Library), 2002

Osgood, Dick. *W.X.Y.Z.I.E. Wonderland*. Ohio: Bowling Green Univ. Press, 1981

Shulman, Arthur & Yourman, Roger. *The Golden Age of Television (How Sweet It Was)*. New York: Bonanza Books, 1979

Sies, Luther F. *The Encyclopedia of American Radio*. Jefferson, NC: McFarland & Co., Inc., 2000

Sketvedt, Randy & Young, Jordan R. *The Nostalgic Entertainment Sourcebook: The Complete Guide to Classic Movies, Vintage Music, Old Time Radio and Theater*. Beverly Hills, CA: Moonstone Press, 1991

St. John, Robert. *The Encyclopedia of Radio and Television*. Milwaukee, WI: Cathedral Square Publishing, 1967

Stumpf, Charles. *Ma Perkins, Little Orphan Annie and Heigh Ho, Silver*. New York: Carlton, 1971

Summers, Harrison B. *A Thirty-Year History of Programs Carried on National Radio in the United States*. Columbus, OH: Ohio University Press, 1958

Terrance, Vincent. *Radio Programs 1924 – 1984: A Catalog of Over 1800 Shows*. Jefferson, NC: McFarland & Co., Inc., 1999

Websites

www.Google.com
(General information)

www.biography.com
(Personalities)

www.imdb.com
(Internet Movie Date Base-Personalities, Films, and TV shows)

www.ibdb.com
(Internet Broadway Data Base-Personalities and shows)

www.comiclopedia.com
(comic strip & book artists and comics)

www.toonopedia.com
(comic strip & books, artists and comics)

Jane Kean's frank and funny memoirs of a show business life are a loving first-hand account of what it was like growing up among the Who's Who of classic Hollywood and Broadway. She tells all — and tells it like it was. Having performed extensively with her comical sister Betty, Jane is perhaps best known as Trixie in the award-winning television series, *The Honeymooners*.

The dastardly Boris Badenov from Bullwinkle. Professor Ludwig von Drake via the Wonderful World of Disney. The Pillsbury Doughboy. The Ape in George of the Jungle. 1000s of radio shows. Every old-time radio and cartoon fan in the world will want this book. Foreword by June Foray. Afterword by Jay Ward biographer, Keith Scott.

$17.95 (+$2 US p&h)   **$29.95** (+$2 US p&h)

 Bear Manor Media
PO Box 750
Boalsburg PA 16827

All orders payable by check, money order, Visa, MasterCard or online with Pay Pal or Pay Direct

www.bearmanormedia.com

Here's a small sampling of a few more books published by Bear Manor Media. Simply go online for details about these and other terrific titles.

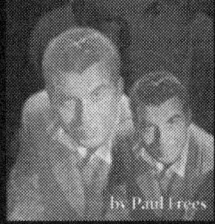

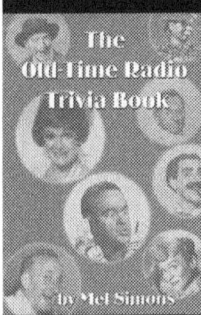

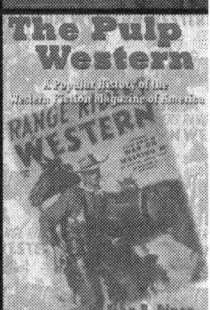

www.bearmanormedia.com

www.ingramcontent.com/pod-product-compliance
Lightning Source LLC
Chambersburg PA
CBHW020758160426
43192CB00006B/367